THE CHRISTIAN CASE FOR REINCARNATION

J. L. REYNOLDS

THE CHRISTIAN CASE FOR REINCARNATION

Published by author via Amazon KDP
ISBN 979-8-9958159-0-7

Biblical quotations are taken from the New Standard Revised Version under the gratis use policy and Young's Literal Translation which is in the public domain. See also Sources listed, page 3.

Cover art from original oil painting by the author.

Printed in the United States of America.

SOURCES

Scripture quotations are taken from the following:

New Revised Standard Version Bible (cited herein as NRSV), copyright ©1989 National Council of the Churches of Christ in the United States of America. Used by permission. All rights reserved [Gratis Use Policy up to 500 verses];

Young's Literal Translation of the Bible (1862), Robert Young: Young's Literal Translation, Oak Harbor: Logos Research Systems, 1997 (cited herein as YLT); (Public Domain)

Works also cited include:

James Strong, *The New Strong's Exhaustive Concordance of the Bible* (Nashville: T. Nelson, 1990, common edition; original 1890); and

A Greek-English Lexicon of the New Testament: Being Grimm's Wilke's Clavis Novi Testamenti, Translated, Revised, and Enlarged by Joseph Henry Thayer. New York: Harper & Brothers, 1886 (corrected editions often cited as 1889)(modern common publisher: Hendrickson Publishers (1996)).

The Antiquities of the Jews, *The Wars of the Jews*, Flavius Josephus. Translation consulted as reference: *The Works of Josephus: New Updated Edition, Complete and Unabridged in One Volume*. Peabody, Massachusetts: Hendrickson Publishers, Inc., Twenty-third printing – December 2010.

The First Seven Ecumenical Councils (325-787) Their History and Theology, (Collegeville, Minnesota: The

Liturgical Press, originally published by Michael Glazier, Inc., Wilmington, Delaware, 1983, 1990) by Leo Donald Davis.

Nicene and Post-Nicene Fathers, Second Series, Volume XIV, Edited by Philip Schaff and Rev. Henry Wallace, Cosimo Classics, New York, first published in 1900, reprinted 2007.

PROLOGUE

[10]for slaughter, ***for violence to thy brother*** Jacob, Cover thee doth shame, And ***thou hast been cut off—to the age***. (Emphasis added.)

OBADIAH, VERSE 10, YOUNG'S LITERAL TRANSLATION

[15]***For near is the day of Jehovah, on all the nations, As thou hast done, it is done to thee, Thy deed doth turn back on thine own head***. (Emphasis added.)

OBADIAH, VERSE 15, YOUNG'S LITERAL TRANSLATION

[20]And having been questioned by the Pharisees, when the reign of God doth come, he answered them, and said, 'The reign of God doth not come with observation; [21]nor shall they say, Lo, here; or lo, there; for lo, ***the reign of God is within you***.' (Emphasis added.)

LUKE 17:20, YOUNG'S LITERAL TRANSLATION

[2]'And the multitude of those sleeping in the dust of the ground do awake, some to life age-during, and some to reproaches—to abhorrence age-during. [3]And those teaching do shine as the brightness of the expanse, and those justifying the multitude as stars to the age and for ever.'

DANIEL 12:2-3, YOUNG'S LITERAL TRANSLATION

19 'Thy dead live—My dead body they rise. Awake and sing, ye dwellers in the dust, For the dew of herbs *is* thy dew, And the land of Rephaim thou causest to fall.'

ISAIAH 26:19, YOUNG'S LITERAL TRANSLATION

INDEX

INTRODUCTION

What do you believe? Why do you believe it?

What if you were dedicated to a teaching that wasn't perceived as intended, that wasn't perceived accurately? What if you have been invested in distortions and partial truths? What if the truth had been purposefully hidden from you?

What if it is possible or even demonstrable that Jesus and the very early church, during and after Jesus' lifetime, taught reincarnation as a truth, as a natural law. Disagreements as to the proper religious books for study and disagreements as to the meaning of those writings occurred even among early church leaders, following the crucifixion. Beginning in the 4th century A.D. and continuing for hundreds of years, the Holy Roman Emperor or the Roman Catholic Church held Ecumenical Councils, as well as other councils and synods, for the purpose of stamping out disagreements. These councils were held allowing a few to decide what was proper theology and official doctrine for all - and what was not. Not only were certain interpretive ideas chosen over others, the "others" were branded heretical and anathema and were forbidden. It is an unfortunate truth that any written work or message is subject to differing interpretations. That is simply fact due to the reality that reading written language is an interpretive mental act.

Ambiguities in texts create additional possibilities. Translations into other languages only heighten and magnify that truth. Many translations of the New Testament are predicated on the Latin Vulgate. The Latin Vulgate translation was commissioned by the early church hundreds of years after the crucifixion - *after* church and secular authority began to exert power and influence over interpretational and doctrinal disputes.

To add to the difficulty, the books of the Bible were

written at different times by different authors. What did Jesus teach during his lifetime? What did Jesus introduce that was distinctive or even revelatory?

You may think you already know what the Bible says and the existence of any "new" ideas on the meaning or interpretation of scripture is preposterous, but isn't it a worthwhile line of inquiry and consideration? What did Jesus teach and how did he teach it?

Why would the early church fear attempts to understand Jesus' meaning? Why fear disagreement? Why fear individual thought and contemplation on these matters? Doesn't keeping everyone on the same page, especially if that page is dictated, solidify power and influence? God does not force any of us to follow any dictate. We are given unfettered free will by the Creator. In seeking God, a higher power, or spiritual truth, why should the church or any secular power employ means that God himself refuses to employ? Does that sound authentic? Does the manipulation of free will violate universal law and trigger consequences of responsibility? Is a policy and doctrine that requires an intermediary between each of us and God, or a truth that is sought, authentic to the teachings of Jesus?

The Catholic Church has, and has historically had, great wealth and power. Is it at all possible that down through history any of the powerful figures that controlled the Church, including emperors, would use the power and the influence of religious beliefs to attempt to garner more power, influence, wealth, and control for themselves?

Religion is still being used to garner power and money. What is the truth? Beliefs are more rigid than ideas. Beliefs are much more resistant to question and change than ideas are. Beliefs are frequently accepted and not questioned and people typically act in conformity with them. Beliefs are powerful. Beliefs have the ability to deny facts, to reject knowledge. *It was believed for many years that the Earth was the center of the Universe,* but the Earth is not the center of the Universe. Never was. Beliefs such as this were endorsed and enforced by the Church, even when verifiable discoveries were made to the contrary. If a set of people could tap into a belief or set of beliefs, or better yet, shape them, and use them for their own purposes, what would that mean?

What if it is simply not true that you only live once, die, and are judged before existing for eternity in a heaven or hell? What do you believe about an afterlife? Do you believe that each of us lives, as the individual case may be, moments, years, decades, or even a century to spend *eternity* as determined in that short span? What is it about those fleeting moments during a lifetime, however short it may be, that seems an appropriate counterbalance to all of eternity?

What if people were also instructed, indoctrinated, that you must live the way you are instructed, and do what you are instructed, or else you'll burn in hell? Forever. If this were an untruth, or at the very least, a distortion of Jesus' message, it would be one monumental error.

Does it seem correct to you that the Creator created this vast space and time and everything in it for you to live as little as two seconds or as much as 100 years and to then spend eternity with the consequences of those few moments alone?

NASA posits that the universe is 13.7 billion years old. www.imagine.gsfc.nasa.gov. Doesn't that seem like a huge waste of creation, of time and space, and energy, in light of the brevity of one, single lifetime? Does it feel somewhat unfair for each of us to be judged and rewarded or punished for only one lifetime under the wildly variant lengths and circumstances each of us experience? What if Jesus actually taught that our time here is a learning process, effectuated through successive lifetimes? What if we learn by receiving and experiencing exactly what we ourselves generate, send out, or embody?

What if the basic principle of the universe is energetic,

frequency, vibration, instead of the limitations of the physical world we see, hear, and touch all around us? What if your thoughts, intentions, words, and acts carried specific energetic frequencies that you send out into an energetic field that both recognizes and responds in a regular, predictable fashion? What if those thoughts, intentions, words, and deeds, that each of us chooses, voluntarily, are sent out to the energetic field of the universe and *determine* what returns back to us, determine the external circumstances of our lives, what our life becomes, be it a heaven or a hell.

CHAPTER ONE

REINCARNATION IN SCRIPTURE

Many believe the Bible is understood, but do we really know what it says?

The books in the Bible were written a very long time ago by authors we have difficulty identifying, if they can be identified at all. Because of their age, the books are in languages that are ancient, archaic, and foreign.

In this text, Biblical citations are taken from *The Holy Bible: New Revised Standard Version. Nashville: Thomas Nelson Publishers, 1989*, "NRSV," and more generally, from *Young's Literal Translation*. Young, Robert: *Young's Literal Translation*. Oak Harbor: Logos Research Systems, 1997, "YLT." Comparisons of translations are also further noted herein.

Jesus himself is represented to have made assertions in the Biblical texts. However, readers will note that different books often have the same or similar content with slight variations.

For example, see Mark 8:27-30, *New Revised Standard Version*, or NRSV.

> 27 Jesus went on with his disciples to the villages of
> Caesarea Philippi; and on the way he asked his
> disciples, "***Who do people say that I am***?" 28 And
> they answered him, "***John the Baptist; and others,
> Elijah; and still others, one of the prophets***." 29 He
> asked them, "But who do you say that I am?" Peter
> answered him, "You are the Messiah." 30 And he

> sternly ordered them not to tell anyone about him. (Emphasis added.)

Compare the above text to Luke 9:18–20, NRSV.

> 18 Once when Jesus[d] was praying alone, with only
> the disciples near him, he asked them, "***Who do the***
> ***crowds say that I am***?" 19 They answered, "***John the***
> ***Baptist; but others, Elijah; and still others, that one***
> ***of the ancient prophets has arisen***." 20 He said to
> them, "But who do you say that I am?" Peter
> answered, "The Messiah[e] of God." (Emphasis
> added.)

Notice the use of the word *arisen*. What could be meant by the word *arisen*? Why is this word used here, when it is so often used in reference to Jesus having *arisen* following his crucifixion? This seems matter-of-fact and is clearly used in relating an event *before* the crucifixion.

Compare the literal translation of the same scripture from *Young's Literal Translation* (Luke 9:18-20, YLT).

> 18 And it came to pass, as he is praying alone, the
> disciples were with him, and he questioned them,
> saying, 'Who do the multitudes say me to be?' 19 And
> they answering said, 'John the Baptist; and others,
> Elijah; and others, *that a prophet, one of the*
> *ancients,* ***was risen***;' 20 and he said to them, 'And
> ye—who do ye say me to be?' and Peter answering
> said, 'The Christ of God.' (Emphasis added.)

---

[d] Gk *he*

[e] Or *The Christ*

Notice that both the literal and non-literal translations use a form of the word "arisen" in the answer to the question posed by Jesus.

This is an interesting question for Jesus to ask of his disciples. Most of us go through life with one name, or at least a limited number of possible references to ourselves. This is even more interesting since Elijah is *known* to Jesus, the apostles, and at least some of the Jewish population *to have long been dead.* The ancient prophets are *known* to Jesus, the apostles, and at least some of the Jewish population *to have long been dead.* John the Baptist himself dies in the course of events recounted in the New Testament.

Why would Jesus ask the disciples who “the multitudes” and “the crowds” say he is?

Why would the disciples, the people, or “the crowds” answer that question with people *known to be* other, different individuals, not currently living? *How does this discourse make any sense unless they are speaking of entities that they believed had lived, physically died, and could return to physically live again?*

Similarly, consider the passage following the transfiguration.

See Matthew 17:9-13, NRSV.

> [9] As they were coming down the mountain, Jesus
> ordered them, “Tell no one about the vision until
> after the Son of Man has been raised from the dead.”
> [10] And the disciples asked him, “Why, then, do the
> scribes say that Elijah must come first?” [11] He
> replied, “Elijah is indeed coming and will restore all
> things; [12] but I tell you that Elijah ***has already come***,

> and they ***did not recognize him***, but they did to him whatever they pleased. So also the Son of Man is about to suffer at their hands." 13 ***Then the disciples understood that he was speaking to them about John the Baptist***. (Emphasis added.)

Compare the literal translation of the same scripture from *Young's Literal Translation*, "YLT," which is different:
See Matthew 17:9–13, YLT.

> 9And as they are coming down from the mount, Jesus charged them, saying, 'Say to no one the vision, ***till the Son of Man out of the dead may rise***.' 10And his disciples questioned him, saying, 'Why then do the scribes say that Elijah it behoveth to come first?' 11And Jesus answering said to them, 'Elijah doth indeed come first, and shall restore all things, 12and I say to you—***Elijah did already come, and they did not know him***, but did with him whatever they would, so also the Son of Man is about to suffer by them.' 13***Then understood the disciples that concerning John the Baptist he spake to them***. (Emphasis added.)

See also Mark 9:9-13, NRSV.

> 9 As they were coming down the mountain, he ordered them to tell no one about what they had seen, until after the Son of Man had risen *from the dead.* 10 So they kept the matter to themselves, ***questioning what this rising from the dead could mean***. 11 Then they asked him, "Why do the scribes say that Elijah must come first?" 12 He said to them,

> “Elijah is indeed coming first to restore all things. How then is it written about the Son of Man, that he is to go through many sufferings and be treated with contempt? [13] But I tell you that ***Elijah has come***, and they did to him whatever they pleased, as it is written about him.” (Emphasis added.)

Young's Literal Translation of the same passage has verse 9 and 10 of the foregoing passage translated differently.

> [9]And as they are coming down from the mount, he charged them that they may declare to no one the things that they saw, except when the Son of Man may rise ***out of the dead***; [10]and the thing they kept to themselves, *questioning together* what the rising ***out of the dead is***. (Emphasis added.)

This distinction of “out” of the dead present in the literal translation of the older Greek text that has been lost or suppressed in most translations is highly relevant. This conversation is stranger still. The small difference here - "out" - between the literal translation and the non-literal translation is important. It is fairly clear that the disciples did not question or ponder what Jesus meant when he asked who the crowds say he is. They answered with known individuals, some of whom *had long been dead,* and they understood the concept that the people may believe that Jesus is one of those *who had been dead* returned to live again or reincarnated. Jesus himself expects people to be speculating as to who he was prior to this lifetime, as his question asks. The concept of a person being dead, even long dead, but *risen from* the dead, the disciples, as well as some other people, seem to be familiar with and understand. However, the disciples do *not* understand what Jesus says about the Son of Man rising "out" from the dead, as shown in the *literal* translation, and they question the meaning of that phrase among themselves. It is worth noting that the non-literal translation is the more confusing of the two. Because it lacks the word "**out,**" there is *no difference* in the (NRSV) nonliteral translation between the question and answer which causes the disciples no confusion, which they readily understand (The people say that you are [various people] *arisen* (Luke 9:18-20)) and the phrase which we are told they do *not* understand (Tell no one until after the Son of Man *had risen* (Mark 9:9-10)).

Both translations use a form of the word "rise" with both phrases. It is completely unclear in the nonliteral translation why one phrase is understood by the disciples but the other is not.

However, in the written text of the literal translation the two phrases have a *difference* that is not present or reflected in the nonliteral translation. In the literal translation, the phrase which the disciples understand is different from the phrase which they do not understand. The first situation and phrase is given in an answer to Jesus' question and is an answer understood by everyone to the conversation regarding persons who have *arisen* and live again as new identities. But the second situation has a different term given, which we are clearly told is not understood by the disciples, that term being "*raised* ***out*** *of the dead.*"

In the literal translation, Jesus uses this phrase "*out* of the dead" in reference to a future consequence regarding "the Son of Man." (The "Son of Man" appears to refer to man, mankind, the human race, and Jesus may also use it to refer to himself.) The understood phrase regarding people who were dead being "risen" or "arisen" living new lifetimes is referring to *a completely different concept* than that which is referred to by the phrase Jesus gives regarding being raised "out" of the dead. *This is why the disciples understand one of them and do not understand the other. These phrases and situations refer to two separate and distinct concepts that are blurred and discussed without distinction in the nonliteral translation.* One, reincarnation, is understood and accepted by Jesus, the disciples, and at least some of the people. Individuals may *rise* and return as someone else, someone new, later. The second phrase, *rising <u>out</u> from the dead,* is used by Jesus to refer to a future event in reference to himself (as the "Son of Man," a term also used to reference mankind in general) as opposed to the rebirth of reincarnation, and is *not* understood by the disciples. There is substantial difference between the two concepts.

The difficulty in trying to appreciate and understand the difference in what is being stated is increased by the fact that both concepts are frequently translated as simply "rise/raise/arisen," or, as we shall see, both terms are frequently translated as simply "resurrection." Most translations make no attempt to preserve the differences present in the Greek text. ***The larger point which is discernible in the foregoing literal translation of the scripture is that two different concepts are set forth, and cannot be understood to refer to the same thing.*** The disciples and others are familiar with and understand one concept and are unfamiliar with and do not understand the second. *"Rising of the dead" and "rising* ***out*** *of/from the dead" are differences present in the Greek text and reflected in a literal translation of the Greek text that are not meant or understood to be the same thing.* In fairness to the non-literal translators, while they appear to completely ignore the "out," they sometimes use the word "from," as in "rising from the dead," although it does not appear to be reliably done where the literal translation has the phrase "*out* of/from the dead."

This is not the only place where Jesus clearly discusses two different ideas but modern translations take no account of these differences. The Greek texts are older than later translations and would be expected to be closer to the original message than later translations.

Try as you might to contort it, in the above biblical passage, Jesus is clearly telling his disciples that John the Baptist was the reincarnation of Elijah and *they did not recognize him.* Many have contorted this to avoid the obvious. Jesus does *not* say one "like" Elijah returned, but Elijah, or the one known as Elijah, himself, returned. What is the significance of Jesus telling this to his closest followers, the pupils who received his *advanced* teachings, as opposed to what he spoke to the masses?

There are scriptures employed to support opposition to what is so obviously stated (purportedly) by Jesus himself.

To begin, John the Baptist denies that he is Elijah.

See John 1:19-28, NSRV.

> 19 This is the testimony given by John when the
> Jews sent priests and Levites from Jerusalem to ask
> him, "Who are you?" 20 He confessed and did not
> deny it, but confessed, "I am not the Messiah."[g] 21
> And they asked him, "What then? *Are you Elijah*?"
> He said, "I am not." "*Are you the prophet*?" He
> answered, "No." 22 Then they said to him, "Who are
> you? Let us have an answer for those who sent us.

[g] Or *the Christ*

> What do you say about yourself?" [23] He said,
> "I am the voice of one crying out in the wilderness,
> 'Make straight the way of the Lord,' "
> as the prophet Isaiah said.
> [24] Now they had been sent *from the Pharisees*. [25]
> They asked him, "Why then are you baptizing if you are neither the Messiah,[h] nor Elijah, nor the prophet?" [26] John answered them, "I baptize with water. Among you stands one whom you do not know, [27] the one who is coming after me; I am not worthy to untie the thong of his sandal." [28] This took place in Bethany across the Jordan where John was baptizing. (Emphasis added.)

See the same scripture translated literally, in John 1:19–31, YLT.

> [19] And this is the testimony of John, when *the Jews* sent out of Jerusalem priests and Levites, that they might question him, 'Who art thou?' [20]and he confessed and did not deny, and confessed—'I am not the Christ.' [21]And they questioned him, 'What then? Elijah art thou?' and he saith, 'I am not.'—'The prophet art thou?' and he answered, 'No.' [22]They said then to him, 'Who art thou, that we may give an answer to those sending us? what dost thou say concerning thyself?' [23]He said, 'I *am* a voice of one crying in the wilderness: Make straight the way of the Lord, as said Isaiah the prophet.' [24]*And those sent were of the Pharisees*, [25]and they questioned him and said to him, 'Why, then, dost thou baptize,

---

[h] Or *the Christ*

> if thou art not the Christ, nor Elijah, nor the
> prophet?' [26]John answered them, saying, 'I baptize
> with water, but in midst of you he hath stood whom
> ye have not known, this one it is who is coming after
> me, who hath been before me, [27]of whom I am not
> worthy that I may loose the cord of his sandal.'
> [28]These things came to pass in Bethabara, beyond
> the Jordan, where John was baptizing.
>
> [29] On the morrow John seeth Jesus coming unto
> him, and saith, 'Lo, the Lamb of God, who is taking
> away the sin of the world; [30]this is he concerning
> whom I said, After me doth come a man, who hath
> come before me, because he was before me: [31]and I
> knew him not, but, that he might be manifested to
> Israel, because of this I came with the water
> baptizing. (Emphasis added.)

Why would the author make specific note that "the Jews" sent out his questioners and that his questioners were "of the Pharisees"? Is John the Baptist not a Jew?

If you consider the foregoing passage, those who are questioning John clearly believe and accept that Elijah or some prophet *could* return as John and they believe that John *could* have an identity as something other than just "John." The questioners are noted to come from "the Pharisees." Per this scripture, Pharisees appear to know and accept the concept of reincarnation. John, too, appears to have full understanding of what they are asking him, which would mean he has some concept, at the very least, of the idea that entities can return through reincarnation. John answers their question of "who thou art" that he is not Elijah *now*. Jesus said that he had *been* Elijah but returned. Who is more authoritative? Could it be that John does not know himself to have been Elijah? Might John have a reason to believe any claims he might make of being Elijah may not be well received? Does John answer no because they asked "who thou art" rather than who he had been? If reincarnation is a truth, then most of humanity does not recall their past identities, or it would be accepted as a truth around the globe. In fact, it appears common to not know your past. Even if John knew he was or may have been Elijah, one can't be expected to rest on what you might have done previously. We are all here for a purpose and his purpose this lifetime is as John the Baptist. So who do we believe, John or Jesus? Who is more authoritative, John or Jesus? Who does John believe is more authoritative between himself and Jesus? Doesn't John say, "I am not worthy to untie the thong of his sandal"? Is it plausible that they are both truthful? Might John not know he had been Elijah previously, or be truthfully answering who he is *now* as is posed by the question actually asked?

John does appear to understand the question asked of his identity and he makes no quarrel or inquiry of the question. John understands the question to ask about his prior identity but he asserts his current identity. Does this show a better understanding of the functions of reincarnation than the Pharisees have if they attempt to refer to him currently as someone past?

Further, John affirms that Jesus has gone before and *has been* before John. John states that Jesus had lived prior to John this lifetime. Why doesn't John acknowledge his prior identity if he was Elijah as Jesus states? *If Jewish faith, practice and custom does not allow or accommodate one to declare himself to be a prophet, can this explain why John does not declare himself, but must be declared to be Elijah, or a prophet, by another? Isn't this why John declares Jesus to be "he who comes to baptize with the Holy Spirit" or "testifies" to Jesus' authority? Might this be why Jesus informs the disciples of John's prior identity rather than John doing so?*

Consider John 1:15, YLT.

> [15] John doth testify concerning him, and hath cried, saying, 'This was he of whom I said, He who after me is coming, hath come *before me*, for *he was before me*;'
> (Emphasis added.)

According to scripture, before John is born his parents are told of him.

See Luke 1:11–17, YLT.

> [11]And there appeared to him a messenger of the Lord standing on the right side of the altar of the
> perfume, [12]and Zacharias, having seen, was troubled,
> and fear fell on him; [13]and the messenger said unto
> him, 'Fear not, Zacharias, for thy supplication was heard, and thy wife Elisabeth shall bear a son to
> thee, and thou shalt call his name John, [14]and there
> shall be joy to thee, and gladness, and many at his
> birth shall joy, [15]for he shall be great before the Lord,
> and wine and strong drink he may not drink, and of the Holy Spirit he shall be full, even from his
> mother's womb; [16]and many of the sons of Israel he
> shall turn to the Lord their God, [17]and he shall go
> before Him, ***in the spirit and power of Elijah, to turn hearts of fathers unto children***, and disobedient ones to the wisdom of righteous ones, to make ready for the Lord, a people prepared.'

(Emphasis added.)

The angel tells Zecharia that John will come “in the spirit and power of Elijah.” Those opposed to the plain meaning of Jesus’ words claim that this indicates that John is not Elijah reborn, but is “like” Elijah or “similar” to Elijah. However, that is not what is stated.

Consider that rather than noting only similarity, the quote of being “in the spirit...of Elijah” directly supports Jesus’ clear assertion that John the Baptist is Elijah come again. What part of Elijah has come again? His spirit. What part would be here again if he were reincarnated? Clearly not his old flesh, long decayed; it would be his spirit, the part of Elijah that was not physical, in a new body. This phrase, far from denouncing John the Baptist as Elijah, reinforces that it is your spiritual self that “comes again.”

Furthermore, note also that the Old Testament admonishment that Elijah will come again makes no bones about it being Elijah and *not* one like or similar to Elijah. ***Jesus said “they did not recognize him.”*** You can’t recognize someone to be someone he isn’t. You can’t fail to recognize someone who is in fact another, even if similar. It makes no sense to say you fail to recognize someone as another. You can only fail to recognize someone as himself. Jesus’ own statements do not make sense in an interpretation that denies reincarnation.

There are other indications in scripture that Elijah and John the Baptist are the same, not just similar.

See Malachi 4:5–6, YLT.

5Lo, ***I am sending to you Elijah*** the prophet, Before the coming of the day of Jehovah, The great

> and the fearful. [6]***And he hath turned back the heart of fathers to sons, And the heart of sons to their fathers***, (Emphasis added.)

The phrase, "***he hath turned back the heart of fathers to sons, and the heart of sons to their fathers,***" emphasized above was also alluded to in the messenger's announcement to John's parents. They are told that John's purpose is "***to turn hearts of fathers unto children.***" Note as well the physical description of John the Baptist given in the gospels. See Mark 1:6-8, YLT.

> [6]And John was clothed with camel's hair, and a girdle of skin around his loins, and eating locusts and honey of the field, [7]and he proclaimed, saying, 'He doth come—who is mightier than I—after me, of whom I am not worthy—having stooped down—to loose the latchet of his sandals; [8]I indeed did baptize you with water, but he shall baptize you with the Holy Spirit.'

See Matthew 3:4-6, YLT.

> [4]And this John had his clothing of camel's hair, and a girdle of skin round his loins, and his nourishment was locusts and honey of the field. [5]Then were going forth unto him Jerusalem, and all Judea, and all the region round about the Jordan, [6]and they were baptized in the Jordan by him, confessing their sins.

Compare how Elijah is described in the Old Testament. See 2 Kings 1:7-8, YLT.

> [7]And he saith unto them, 'What *is* the fashion of the man who hath come up to meet you, and speaketh unto you these words?' [8]And they say unto him, 'A man—hairy, and a girdle of skin girt about his loins;' and he saith, 'He *is* Elijah the Tishbite.'

Not only does Jesus tell us that John the Baptist is Elijah reincarnated, but descriptions of John are like descriptions of Elijah. This sort of descriptive detail is not commonly given, even for Jesus and his disciples. Inclusion of these details is no accident but is offered as further proof of John's prior identity as Elijah. If a spirit returns to live physically, in body, wouldn't he bring some influence of his previous experiences? Otherwise, what is the purpose of the continuation of experience, the accumulation of experience? Doesn't it seem like individuals have likes and dislikes, predilections and tendencies which are evidenced from a very young age, from birth, which could not be attributable to experience thus far in that one life?

The text further states that John the Baptist disapproved of Herod's relationship with his brother's wife, Herodias, and had been a critic of them both. Herodias, the brother's wife, conspires to gain John's head - and succeeds.

See also Luke 3:18-20, YLT.

> [18]And, therefore, indeed with many other things, exhorting, he was proclaiming good news to the people, [19]and Herod the tetrarch, being reproved by him concerning Herodias the wife of Philip his brother, and concerning all the evils that Herod did, [20]added also this to all, that he shut up John in the prison.

Even King Herod had commentary about John the Baptist that reflected certain beliefs.

See Matthew 14:1–12, NSRV.

> [1] At that time did Herod the tetrarch hear the fame of Jesus, [2]and said to his servants, ***'This is John the Baptist, he did rise from the dead, and because of this the mighty energies are working in him.'*** [3]For Herod having laid hold on John, did bind him, and did put him in prison, because of Herodias his brother Philip's wife, [4]for John was saying to him, 'It is not lawful to thee to have her,' [5]and, willing to kill him, he feared the multitude, because as a prophet they were holding him. [6]But the birthday of Herod being kept, the daughter of Herodias danced in the midst, and did please Herod, [7]whereupon with an oath he professed to give her whatever she might ask. [8]And she having been instigated by her mother—'Give me (says she) here upon a plate the head of John the Baptist; [9]and the king was grieved, but because of the oaths and of those reclining with him, he commanded *it* to be given; [10]and having sent, he beheaded John in the prison, [11]and his head was brought upon a plate, and was given to the damsel, and she brought *it* nigh to her mother. [12]And his disciples having come, took up the body, and buried it, and having come, they told Jesus. (Emphasis added.)

Herod hears of Jesus, his good news and his healings.

See Luke 9:7-9, YLT.

> 7And Herod the tetrarch heard of all the things being done by him, and was perplexed, because ***it was said by certain, that John hath been raised out of the dead; 8and by certain, that Elijah did appear, and by others, that a prophet, one of the ancients, was risen***; 9and Herod said, 'John I did behead, but who is this concerning whom I hear such things?' and he was seeking to see him. (Emphasis added.)

See Mark 6:14–29, YLT.

> 14 And the king Herod heard, (for his name became public,) and he said—***'John the Baptist out of the dead was raised, and because of this the mighty powers are working in him.' 15Others said—'It is Elijah,' and others said—'It is a prophet, or as one of the prophets.' 16And Herod having heard, said—'He whom I did behead—John—this is he; he was raised out of the dead.'*** 17For Herod himself, having sent forth, did lay hold on John, and bound him in the prison, because of Herodias the wife of Philip his brother, because he married her, 18for John said to Herod—'It is not lawful to thee to have the wife of thy brother;' 19and Herodias was having a quarrel with him, and was willing to kill him, and was not able, 20for ***Herod was fearing John, knowing him a man righteous and holy, and was keeping watch over him, and having heard him, was doing many things, and hearing him gladly.*** 21And a seasonable day having come, when Herod on his birthday was making a supper to his great men, and to the chiefs of thousands, and to the first men of Galilee, 22and the daughter of that Herodias

> having come in, and having danced, and having
> pleased Herod and those reclining (at meat) with
> him, the king said to the damsel, 'Ask of me
> whatever thou wilt, and I will give to thee,' [23]and he
> sware to her—'Whatever thou mayest ask me, I will
> give to thee—unto the half of my kingdom.' [24]And
> she, having gone forth, said to her mother, 'What
> shall I ask for myself?' and she said, 'The head of
> John the Baptist;' [25]and having come in immediately
> with haste unto the king, she asked, saying, 'I will
> that thou mayest give me presently, upon a plate, the
> head of John the Baptist.' [26]And the king—made
> very sorrowful—because of the oaths and of those
> reclining (at meat) with him, would not put her
> away, [27]and immediately the king having sent a
> guardsman, did command his head to be brought,
> [28]and he having gone, beheaded him in the prison,
> and brought his head upon a plate, and did give it to
> the damsel, and the damsel did give it to her mother;
> [29]and having heard, his disciples came and took up
> his corpse, and laid it in the tomb. (Emphasis added.)

Consider that the above passages show that Herod feared John and knew him to be righteous, and he sought to protect him from Herodias's revenge but was tricked into delivering John's head to her. Consider also that in the above passages, some people around Herod and even Herod himself believe that Jesus may be John *arisen out of the dead*, and he attributed Jesus' power to other, additional, previous experience. Others have stated that Jesus could also be Elijah or one of the prophets *arisen from the dead.* What is all this talk in the scripture of *arising from the dead to live again physically* ***before*** the crucifixion? Clearly more than a few people seem to believe that it is entirely possible and likely that dead people arise in some manner. What manner could be meant? What makes sense in the context of these scriptural writings?

See Matthew 11:7–19, YLT.

> [7]And as they are going, Jesus began to say to the multitudes concerning John, 'What went ye out to the wilderness to view?—a reed shaken by the wind?
>
> [8]'But what went ye out to see?—a man clothed in soft garments? lo, those wearing the soft things are in the kings' houses.
>
> [9]'But what went ye out to see?—a prophet? yes, I say to you, and more than a prophet, [10]***for this is he of whom it hath been written, Lo, I do send My messenger before thy face, who shall prepare thy way before thee***. [11]Verily I say to you, there hath not risen, among those born of women, a greater than John the Baptist, but he who is least in the reign of the heavens is greater than he.
>
> [12]'And, from the days of John the Baptist till now, the reign of the heavens doth suffer violence, and violent men do take it by force, [13]for all the prophets and the law till John did prophesy, [14]***and if ye are willing to receive it, he is Elijah who was about to come; [15]he who is having ears to hear—let him hear***.
>
> [16]'And to what shall I liken this generation? it is like little children in market-places, sitting and calling to their comrades, [17]and saying, We piped unto you, and ye did not dance, we lamented to you, and ye did not smite the breast.
>
> [18]'For John came neither eating nor drinking, and

> they say, He hath a demon; [19]the Son of Man came eating and drinking, and they say, Lo, a man, a glutton, and a wine-drinker, a friend of tax-gatherers and sinners, and wisdom was justified of her children.' (Emphasis added.)

Jesus certainly seems to understand that there may be no way to objectively prove John is Elijah, and that some people will, and do, find it hard to believe. Nevertheless Jesus plainly asserts it to be the case and says ***if you have ears*** he has stated it plainly and directly enough for you to know the truth if you but want to hear it.

The text above stating, "***I do send My messenger before thy face***" is also interesting given that Christians readily accept that it is referring to John even if they refuse the plain language of Jesus declaring John to be the reincarnation of Elijah. This states that John (as well as Elijah) is a messenger. "Messenger" is frequently translated as angel in nonliteral translations. The literal translation does not use angel, but messenger. This means that messengers (and for that matter what is frequently translated as angels, i.e. higher beings) can not only take human form but can be born as human. Think about what this means for every visitation or pronouncement made by a messenger in the texts. It could very well be understood to be a human and a particular human who may be understood to be an advanced or higher being born into humanity. Consider also that Jesus said "Verily I say to you, there hath not risen, among those born of women, a greater than John the Baptist, but he who is least in the reign of the heavens is greater than he." As a messenger (angel) born unto a woman, John is highest among men, but the least in the reign of heavens is greater than he is.

[Note also that whatever the "reign of heavens" refers to, it is *already* in existence and not empty, as *the least in the kingdom of heaven are compared to John.*]

Jesus himself asserted that John the Baptist was Elijah and John the Baptist declared Jesus to be the Messiah. If John the Baptist was not Elijah then Jesus could not be the Messiah; Elijah's return would still be awaited prior to the Messiah if that were the case. What is the significance of both John and Jesus not declaring themselves but having their status declared by another, in this case, by each other?

See John 5:31-36, YLT.

> [31] 'If I testify concerning myself, my testimony is not true; [32]***another there is who is testifying concerning me***, and I have known that the testimony that he doth testify concerning me is true; [33]***ye have sent unto John, and he hath testified to the truth.***
>
> [34] 'But I do not receive testimony from man, but these things I say that ye may be saved; [35]he was the burning and shining lamp, and ye did will to be glad, for an hour, in his light.
>
> [36] '***But I have the testimony greater than John's, for the works that the Father gave me, that I might finish them, the works themselves that I do, they testify concerning me***, that the Father hath sent me. (Emphasis added.)

Jesus himself acknowledges that he does not declare himself. He states he is declared by another, John, and by his works.

As we have seen, numerous Biblical passages prior to the crucifixion affirm an understood concept of reincarnation, or "raising of the dead," that is translated as resurrection.

Jesus speaks of reincarnation (dead people being raised) and his apostles understand his references. The passages where Jesus discusses this with the apostles ("who do people say that I am?"; John "is Elijah") do not prompt a question or discussion of reincarnation (or "raising of the dead") by his apostles. The apostles already understand and accept the concept of reincarnation as is plain from the text. In this passage the new information revealed to the apostles by Jesus is that John the Baptist is in fact the reincarnation of the same entity that also lived as Elijah, *and the prophecy of the Old Testament has been fulfilled.* Elijah returned ***and they knew him not***. John, himself, it would appear from the text, did not confirm it. But Jesus revealed it to the disciples and they understood. (If it is the case that a prophet has greater authority if he is recognized by others rather than self-declared, then John affirmed Jesus' status, and Jesus later affirmed John's. Such a practice would be useful in dissuading self-declared authority from God.)

While it is clear from biblical passages cited in the foregoing discussion that some people during Jesus' time, and within his community, believed in reincarnation or at least consider it a possibility, all do not seem to share that belief. We see the tone of Jesus' words in the texts again and again *urging* the belief to those who may not yet have accepted it. His own disciples have accepted it and do not question it as is clear from their discourse with him in passages already shown.

See Acts 23:8, NRSV.

> 8 (The Sadducees say that there is no resurrection, or angel, or spirit; but the Pharisees acknowledge all three.)

Young's Literal Translation also translates the same verse (Acts 23:8, YLT).

> [8]for Sadducees, indeed, ***say there is no rising again***, nor ***messenger***, nor spirit, but Pharisees confess both. (Emphasis added.)

Matthew 22:23 also states clearly that the Sadducees did not believe in reincarnation (i.e. "rising again" that is reincarnation); this is stated in Matthew *before* the crucifixion).

See Matthew 22:23-24, YLT.

> [23] ***In that day there came near to him Sadducees, who are saying there is not a rising again***, and they questioned him, saying, [24]'Teacher, Moses said, If any one may die not having children, his brother shall marry his wife, and shall raise up seed to his brother. (Emphasis added.)

Acts 23:8 reiterates what we are told in Matthew 22:3, specifically, that the Sadducees do not believe in a rising again (reincarnation), but that the Pharisees do. This also explains the point of the scriptural author noting that John's questioners in the earlier cited passage were of *the Pharisees*. The biblical texts evidence that Pharisees believed in the concept of reincarnation and so asked John who it was that had reincarnated as him in this life (or rather who he had been in previous lives). This demonstrates that they expected him to have been someone they would recognize as noteworthy from history – someone with spiritual clout.

The Pharisees belief is in "the rising again" but the text

does not reference the rising again that is "out" from the dead mentioned by Jesus and not understood by the disciples. Jesus references both a "rising again" and "a rising "out" of the dead." The disciples understand the first but do not understand the second.

The Pharisees and the disciples understand the concept of reincarnation, a general "rising again" that is the mechanism for making all people subject to the law of reaping what they sow (unfortunately and confusedly translated as simply "resurrection"). The resurrection Christians understand to be new with Jesus, "*out* of the dead" where one does not "die anymore" is the concept of the coming "harvest" at "the next age," the "harvest" where the separation of the wheat and chaff shall come. The scripture clearly contains reference to two different kinds of "resurrections," a contrast and difference that is *harder to detect* in translations without reference to a literal translation and the literal meaning of the older Greek texts.

There is yet further evidence that Jesus spoke of two different concepts unfortunately and erroneously both translated the same, as "resurrection," and that Jesus relates one of these concepts to a "harvest."

See the nonliteral translation of Matthew 22:23-33, NRSV.

> 23 The same day some *Saddducees came to him, saying there is no resurrection*;[a] and they asked him
> a question, saying, 24 "*Teacher*, Moses said, 'If a
> man dies childless, his brother shall marry the
> widow, and raise up children for his brother.' 25 Now

---

[a] Other ancient authorities read *who say that there is no resurrection*

> there were seven brothers among us; the first
> married, and died childless, leaving the widow to his
> brother. 26 The second did the same, so also the third,
> down to the seventh. 27 Last of all, the woman
> herself died. 28 In the resurrection, then, whose wife
> of the seven will she be? For all of them had married
> her."
>
> 29 Jesus answered them, "You are wrong, because
> you know neither the scriptures nor the power of
> God. 30 ***For in the resurrection they neither marry***
> ***nor are given in marriage, but are like angels***[b] ***in***
> ***heaven. 31 And as for the resurrection of the dead***,
> have you not read what was said to you by God, 32 'I
> am the God of Abraham, the God of Isaac, and the
> God of Jacob'? He is God not of the dead, but of the
> living." 33 And when the crowd heard it, they were
> astounded at his teaching. (Emphasis added.)

This appears confusing. Upon careful examination, we can at least tell Jesus is recognizing two different concepts which are both translated as "resurrection" (shown as "the resurrection" and "the resurrection of the dead").

It becomes somewhat clearer if we examine the *Young's Literal Translation* of this passage in Matthew 22:23-33.

> 23 In that day there came near to him ***Saddducees,***
> ***who are saying there is not a rising again***, and they
> questioned him, saying, 24'Teacher, Moses said, If
> any one may die not having children, his brother
> shall marry his wife, and shall raise up seed to his
> brother.

---

[b] Other ancient authorities add *of God*

> 25 'And there were with us seven brothers, and the
> first having married did die, and not having seed, he
> left his wife to his brother; 26in like manner also the
> second, and the third, unto the seventh, 27and last of
> all died also the woman; 28***therefore in the rising***
> ***again***, of which of the seven shall she be wife—for
> all had her?' 29And Jesus answering said to them,
> 'Ye go astray, not knowing the Writings, nor the
> power of God; 30***for in the rising again they do not***
> ***marry, nor are they given in marriage, but are as***
> ***messengers of God in heaven***.
>
> 31 '***And concerning the rising again of the dead***,
> did ye not read that which was spoken to you by
> God, saying, 32I am the God of Abraham, and the
> God of Isaac, and the God of Jacob? God is not a
> God of dead men, but of living.' 33And having heard,
> the multitudes were astonished at his teaching.
> (Emphasis added.)

The Sadducees do not believe in reincarnation ("rising again"). Jesus tells them the resurrection ("out" of the dead) yields messengers (angels, spiritual beings – which they also do not believe in). Jesus also tells them the rising of the dead (reincarnation) means none are dead to God, they are all living. Being dead is not a permanent, or final state. Of importance is the "And" at the beginning of verse 31. It denotes in addition to; the first concept is *in addition to* the second, each with differing meanings.

This is illustrated even more clearly if we examine the parallel passage, in Mark, first in one translation, the NRSV, then in the literal translation, YLT.

See Mark 12:18–27, NRSV.

18 ***Some Sadducees, who say there is no resurrection***, came to him and asked him a question, saying, 19 "Teacher, Moses wrote for us that if a man's brother dies, leaving a wife but no child, the man[b] shall marry the widow and raise up children for his brother. 20 There were seven brothers; the first married and, when he died, left no children; 21 and the second married the widow[c] and died, leaving no children; and the third likewise; 22 none of the seven left children. Last of all the woman herself died. 23 In the resurrection[d] whose wife will she be? For the seven had married her."

24 Jesus said to them, "Is not this the reason you are wrong, that you know neither the scriptures nor the power of God? ***25 For when they rise from the dead, they neither marry nor are given in marriage, but are like angels in heaven.*** 26 ***And as for the dead being raised***, have you not read in the book of Moses, in the story about the bush, how God said to him, 'I am the God of Abraham, the God of Isaac, and the God of Jacob'? ***27 He is God not of the dead, but of the living; you are quite wrong."*** (Emphasis added.)

If you examine verses 25 and 26, Jesus refers to two different kinds of "rising." Here when Jesus says, "when they rise from the dead" they "are like angels," he is speaking of a resurrection *out* of death altogether, out of the need to be reincarnated to live successive lives to learn

---

[b] Gk *his brother*

[c] GK *her*

[d] Other ancient authorities add *when they rise*

lessons. This is the resurrection Christians think of when they hear the word resurrection. It is a different "resurrection" than the rising again that is the cycle of reincarnation. It is the harvest of men who are spiritual beings, to become something higher, Sons of God rather than men, and to enter the "kingdom of heaven." But when Jesus says, "and as for the dead being raised," or, as we shall see in the literal translation, "***And concerning the dead*, *that they rise,***" Jesus is talking about another, different kind of resurrection from the first. Everyone experiences the reincarnation cycle, by rising and being born again, *until* they are raised "out" of it. This is why the first mentioned rising - to messenger/angel status –is given as *when* they rise. Reincarnation may be an automatic process, but people don't automatically rise *out* from the dead, *out* of the reincarnation cycle; they will only make that cut if they have adequately prepared for it, or grown to it, but the rising of the dead that is reincarnation is more generally applicable and is applied in cyclical fashion. In verse 26, the "and" references "another" resurrection where "and" means *in addition to.* This refers to reincarnation and Jesus has an expectation that his listeners would be familiar with this known concept. Many great thinkers and philosophers and cultures of previous times believed in reincarnation, including Pythagoras, Plato, and Socrates.

In fact, the question quite rightly addresses the concern of the Sadducees who we are told do not believe in rising again (reincarnation). Their question to Jesus itself appears to confirm that Jesus taught and affirmed reincarnation. *Whose wife is she if she has married all the brothers?* Jesus tells them they have no understanding. If she is "out" of the reincarnation cycle (raised "out" of the dead) she is a heavenly being. If she incarnates again, she lives a new life.

Reincarnation (rising again) is different from rising "out" of the dead (out of the cycle of death and rebirth). Reincarnation is not the new or "different" resurrection Jesus introduces, although he does affirm it. Reincarnation is a teaching that is known to some, the Pharisees, at least, but not accepted by all, as shown by the Sadducees' rejection of it. Nevertheless, Jesus, his disciples, and the Pharisees know and accept reincarnation as truth, fact, a law. This is why Abraham, Isaac, and Jacob are not dead men, but living men, through reincarnation, and why he can tell the Sadducees, "you are quite wrong." The Pharisees at least are more correct than the Sadducees in their acceptance of the rising again of the dead, reincarnation.

The truth of this passage is better revealed when a literal translation of the older Greek is examined.

Consider the same passage in Mark 12:18–27, YLT.

> 18 And the ***Sadducees*** come unto him, ***who say there is not a rising again***, and they questioned him, saying, 19 'Teacher, Moses wrote to us, that if any one's brother may die, and may leave a wife, and may leave no children, that his brother may take his wife, and raise up seed to his brother.
>
> 20 'There were then seven brothers, and the first took a wife, and dying, he left no seed; 21 and the second took her, and died, neither left he seed, and the third in like manner, 22 and the seven took her, and left no seed, last of all died also the woman; 23 ***in the rising again, then, whenever they may rise***, of which of them shall she be wife—for the seven had her as wife?' 24 And Jesus answering said to them, 'Do ye not because of this go astray, not knowing the Writings, nor the power of God? 25 for ***when they***

***may rise <u>out</u> of the dead, they neither marry nor are they given in marriage, but are as messengers who are in the heavens*.

[26] '***And concerning the dead, that they rise***: have ye not read in the Book of Moses (at The Bush), how God spake to him, saying, I *am* the God of Abraham, and the God of Isaac, and the God of Jacob; [27]***he is not the God of dead men, but a God of living men; ye then go greatly astray***.' (Emphasis added.)

Consulting a literal translation of the Greek more closely not only avoids the redundancy of the word "resurrection" it also more clearly establishes the difference between the two different manners of arising. The dead do rise again through reincarnation, but rising ***out of*** the dead yields messengers (angels) who are in heaven, who neither give nor are given in marriage. Those in this age (not yet having risen ***out*** of the dead) still live the kind of lives envisioned by the circumstances of the question. Those in the next age become heavenly beings, are "harvested" to the "kingdom of God" or the "kingdom of heaven."

To make clear that Jesus refers to two different concepts note that the rising **out** *of the dead yields messengers/angels. But with the second concept, the literal translation makes very clear that God is a God of living* **men.** *The second "resurrection" must be different than the first "resurrection" or concept of "arising" because the first one mentioned yields heavenly beings,* ***not living men.***

The death and rebirth cycle of reincarnation is what happens to every individual when they die and lose their temple, their temporal vessel, or physical body. We currently occupy a material plane and experience that materiality in our physical bodies. Between incarnations there is a spiritual being, not a spiritual being housed in a physical vessel. "...***When they may rise out of the dead***" refers to the overcoming of and graduation from the cycle of successive lives and deaths and the need to reincarnate physically. When that occurs there is no more need to be reborn physically. It won't happen to long dead bodies that have already decayed. None of us really dies, we have periods between incarnations, and we live physically again, until we achieve the second manner of resurrection, the conquering of the need to be reborn into this physical existence, at least in the sense we know of currently. To do this we must perfect ourselves (in accordance with our example) or else your real being (your spiritual self) will not be able to harmonize with a higher state of being.

Would you let a bunch of rebellious children who did not know how to control themselves and behave for the greater good of all into any advanced locales you administrated over? You don't miraculously get "good" because you died, or because you say you "believed." You "believed" what? If you truly understood the message, as it really is, and "believed," you'd understand that belief alone is the seed, the germ. A true belief (and not a mere profession of one) is one you cannot help but act in conformity with. And many of us are not in conformity with Jesus' actual message *and do not believe we are expected to be*. We align with God, or improve, through the application of will and intention toward an ideal. Jesus came to provide the ideal, the example, the *way*. In trying to explain the rising *out* of the dead, the resurrection *out* of the cycle of reincarnation, Jesus tells of a harvest, of separating wheat and chaff, and of many not making the harvest.

See Matthew 9:37–38, NRSV.

> [37] Then he said to his disciples, "*The harvest is plentiful, but the laborers are few*; [38] therefore ask the Lord of the harvest to send out laborers into his harvest." (Emphasis added.)

See John 4:35–38, NRSV.

> [35] Do you not say, 'Four months more, then comes the harvest'? But I tell you, look around you, and see how *the fields are ripe for harvesting*. [36] The reaper is already receiving[f] wages and is gathering fruit for eternal life, so that sower and reaper may rejoice together. [37] For here the saying holds true, 'One sows and another reaps.' [38] I sent you to reap that for which you did not labor. Others have labored, and you have entered into their labor." (Emphasis added.)

How do you reap what others have sown? All of your circumstances, your experiences and your previous choices have culminated in the you that exists at the time of harvest. The person that is harvested reaps not only what he has done in this life but in previous lives as well. You never die a permanent death as you are a spiritual being, but you will not depart the cycle of physical incarnations until you master yourself, your ego, your will, and conform/align it to the example, the way. "You have entered into their labor" may also refer to all those who have gone before who diligently tried to teach and lead people to truth.

Consider again the Sadducees' question now presented in

---

[f] Or [35]... *the fields are already ripe for harvesting.* [36]*The reaper is receiving*

a another different gospel. See first, a nonliteral translation of Luke.

See Luke 20:27-40, NRSV.

> [27] Some Sadducees, *those who say there is no resurrection,* came to him [28] and asked him a question, "Teacher, Moses wrote for us that if a man's brother dies, leaving a wife but no children, the man[b] shall marry the widow and raise up children for his brother. [29] Now there were seven brothers; the first married, and died childless; [30] then the second [31] and the third married her, and so in the same way all seven died childless. [32] Finally the woman also died. [33] In the resurrection, therefore, whose wife will the woman be? For the seven had married her."
>
> [34] Jesus said to them, "*Those who belong to this age marry and are given in marriage;* [35] *but those* ***who are considered worthy of a place in that age and in the resurrection from the dead*** *neither marry nor are given in marriage.* [36] *Indeed* ***they cannot die anymore****, because they are* ***like angels*** *and* ***are children of God, being children of the resurrection***. [37] ***And the fact that the dead are raised*** Moses himself showed, in the story about the bush, where he speaks of the Lord as the God of Abraham, the God of Isaac, and the God of Jacob. [38] Now he is God not of the dead, but of the living; for ***to him*** all of them are alive." [39] Then some of the scribes answered, "Teacher, you have spoken well." [40] For they no longer dared to ask him another question.

---

[b] Gk *his brother*

(Emphasis added.)

See the same passage from a literal translation of the Greek in Luke 20:27-38, YLT.

> 27 ***And certain of the Sadducees, who are***
> ***denying that there is a rising again***, having come
> near, questioned him, 28 saying, 'Teacher, Moses
> wrote to us, If any one's brother may die, having a
> wife, and he may die childless—that his brother may
> take the wife, and may raise up seed to his brother.
> 29 'There were, then, seven brothers, and the first
> having taken a wife, died childless, 30 and the second
> took the wife, and he died childless, 31 and the third
> took her, and in like manner also the seven—they
> left not children, and they died; 32 and last of all died
> also the woman: 33 in the rising again, then, of which
> of them doth she become wife?—for the seven had
> her as wife.' 34 And Jesus answering said to them,
> ***'The sons of this age do marry and are given in***
> ***marriage, 35 but those accounted worthy to obtain***
> ***that age, and the rising again that is out of the***
> ***dead, neither marry, nor are they given in***
> ***marriage; 36 for neither are they able to die any***
> ***more—for they are like messengers—and they are***
> ***sons of God, being sons of the rising again.***
> 37 ***'And that the dead are raised, even Moses***
> ***shewed at the Bush, since he doth call the Lord, the***
> ***God of Abraham, and the God of Isaac, and the***
> ***God of Jacob; 38 and He is not a God of dead men,***
> ***but of living, for all live to Him.***' (Emphasis added.)

"Those who belong ***to this age***" are living through

successive incarnations *in order to learn and grow.* "Those who are *considered worthy* of place ***in that age***" are those who will no longer be mere men; the worthy will be *harvested* and *become children of God*. *This is a response by Jesus explaining that resurrection out of the dead, to that age (out of the cycle) yields children of God, heavenly beings, and affirming reincarnation to the Sadducees who argued with Jesus that "there is no resurrection," or reincarnation.*

The Sadducees are defined in the scripture as those who do not believe in the resurrection that is reincarnation and this separates them from Pharisees. This is why the earlier scripture (John 1:24) specifically notes that it is 'the Pharisees' who ask John who he is. The Pharisees believe in the concept of 'rising again.' The Sadducees are distinctly stated to not believe in 'rising again.' From what is stated in scripture, very few, if any, understand Jesus' discussion of the second kind of rising again, *out* of the dead, overcoming the cycle of death and rebirth, the harvest and becoming children of God. Even the disciples, Jesus' closest associates, who do understand the resurrection or rising from the dead that refers to reincarnation, did not understand his teaching on the second type of resurrection, the rising "out" of the dead which transforms one into a messenger, angel, heavenly being, child of God.

The literal translation of the Greek in this passage is far less confusing without the English translator's redundancy of "resurrection." Translators have made no distinction because, at best, they do not know or understand the need for the distinction that is made in the Greek. At worst, earlier translators, or the powers that employed them, may have *deliberately* attempted to suppress this teaching.

"The sons of this age do marry and are given in

marriage...." We are in this age. We know a life where many (even most) are married and given in marriage, as the context of the question poses.

"...But those accounted *worthy* to obtain that age, and the rising again that is OUT of the dead...." This is a resurrection separate and apart from reincarnation. This is the resurrection that the disciples, Jesus' closest confidants, did not understand when Jesus mentioned it at the transfiguration (Mark 9:9). This is a graduation/shift from "this age" to "that age." In that age they do not marry and *neither are they able to die* ***any more***. How does it make sense to say 'neither are they able to die *any more,*' if they only die once? It only makes sense to say someone doesn't do something anymore if it is a repetitive occurrence. That they cannot die *anymore* does *not* suggest an event that happens only once. If you believe you only die once there isn't "any" "more." It does not suggest living once and being forever in a hereafter. "Neither are they able to die any more" refers to a repeated occurrence or process involving death that will cease.

The shift in rising "out" of the dead yields messengers (angels), *sons of God*, like Jesus. Examine again the end of verse 36. They are "sons of god" *because* they are "sons of the rising again" "out" from among the dead.

"*And that the dead are raised....*" is in addition to the foregoing discussion, meaning, that the dead rise through reincarnation. There is no qualification to rising again through reincarnation: all the dead rise, but only the "*worthy*" rise "*out*" of the dead, out of the reincarnation cycle.

What resurrection, what ideas are referenced here by the Sadducees? They deny reincarnation. *Their question asks whose wife the woman will be in the rising again.* Jesus clarifies that *in the next age* (the rising *out* of the dead, *out* of the cycle) she will be a child of God and not dwell in an age that marries. *But Jesus also affirms reincarnation*, in an effort to correct the Sadducees' error. To God, all *men* are living – past and present (and those sleeping in between incarnations). God knows their prior identities even if they do not. Men (belonging to this age) reincarnate; heavenly beings, children of God (belonging to the next age) do not incarnate and do not die "any" "more." Jesus confirms that the Sadducees' denial of the rising again that is reincarnation shows that they *lack understanding*. Jesus says that ***those who are considered worthy*** will be raised ***out from the dead***, out from the cycle, and ***cannot die anymore.***

Jesus' closest students and followers understood reincarnation as evidenced by their discussions in scripture. But they did not appear to at first understand what Jesus meant by rising *out* of the cycle of death and rebirth prior to his crucifixion. As proof, consider the following, first in a non-literal translation and then in a literal translation.

See John 20:1–10, NRSV.

> [1]Early on the first day of the week, while it was still dark, Mary Magdalene came to the tomb and saw that the stone had been removed from the tomb. [2] So she ran and went to Simon Peter and the other disciple, the one whom Jesus loved, and said to them, "They have taken the Lord out of the tomb, and we do not know where they have laid him." [3] Then Peter and the other disciple set out and went toward the tomb. [4] The two were running together, but the other disciple outran Peter and reached the tomb first. [5] He bent down to look in and saw the

> linen wrappings lying there, but he did not go in. [6] Then Simon Peter came, following him, and went into the tomb. He saw the linen wrappings lying there, [7] and the cloth that had been on Jesus' head, not lying with the linen wrappings but rolled up in a place by itself. [8] Then the other disciple, who reached the tomb first, also went in, and he saw and believed; [9] ***for as yet they did not understand the scripture, that he must rise from the dead***. [10] Then the disciples returned to their homes. (Emphasis added.)

See also the literal interpretation from the Greek in *Young's Literal Translation.*

> [1]And on the first of the sabbaths, Mary the Magdalene doth come early (there being yet darkness) to the tomb, and she seeth the stone having been taken away out of the tomb, [2]she runneth, therefore, and cometh unto Simon Peter, and unto the other disciple whom Jesus was loving, and saith to them, 'They took away the Lord out of the tomb, and we have not known where they laid him.' [3]Peter, therefore, went forth, and the other disciple, and they were coming to the tomb, [4]and the two were running together, and the other disciple did run forward more quickly than Peter, and came first to the tomb, [5]and having stooped down, seeth the linen clothes lying, yet, indeed, he entered not. [6]Simon Peter, therefore, cometh, following him, and he entered into the tomb, and beholdeth the linen clothes lying, [7]and the napkin that was upon his head, not lying with the linen clothes, but apart, having been folded up, in

> one place; [8]then, therefore, entered also the other disciple who came first unto the tomb, and he saw, and did believe; [9]***for not yet did they know the Writing, that it behoveth him <u>out</u> of the dead to rise again.*** (Emphasis added.)

Even the disciples didn't understand the rising '*out* of the dead,' *out* from the reincarnation cycle, spoken of by Jesus. It is clear from scripture that they did understand the rising again that refers to reincarnation, so what has all the scripture referencing "resurrection" in the non-literal translation before Jesus' death by people *other than Jesus*, been about, if not reincarnation? Why did Jesus speak of two different 'risings,' unfortunately identically translated as 'resurrection' – the rising of the dead and the rising *out* of the dead, as reflected in the literal translation?

If you 'rise again' *in this age* you may live another physical life – and reincarnate. But if you are worthy at *the next age* you are worthy of a different kind of resurrection - out of the reincarnation cycle.

Why do the Sadducees want to say ***to*** Jesus that there is no resurrection or 'rising again'? *Because Jesus has been teaching and affirming reincarnation. The law is you reap what you sow.* And because they already deny the 'rising again' that is reincarnation. Jesus has not yet been crucified. The Sadducees are not taking issue with Jesus about something that even the disciples don't understand – the *other* rising – *out* of the cycle. *The Sadducees question him because he is teaching the principal of reincarnation as the mechanism of the law, the way in which we all reap what we sow*, as a foundation for teaching the 'rising *out* of the dead,' the good news of how to be reaped in the harvest at the next age *as a child of God*. Jesus is aligned with the frequency to exist at that level. He is trying to teach others how to align with a new kind of existence in "the next age." He is trying to show them "the Way."

Jesus also drew other distinctions between 'this age' and 'the next age' that implicated a teaching of reincarnation. Jesus promised rewards to those who had lost in this lifetime for his sake. Note the following from a non-literal translation.

See Mark 10:28–31, NRSV.

> [28] Peter began to say to him, "Look, we have left everything and followed you." [29] Jesus said, "Truly I tell you, there is no one who has left house or brothers or sisters or mother or father or children or fields, for my sake and for the sake of the good news,[f] [30] ***who will not receive a hundredfold now in this age—houses, brothers and sisters, mothers and children, and fields, with persecutions—and in the age to come eternal life***. [31] But many who are first will be last, and the last will be first." (Emphasis added.)

Compare the same scripture from *Young's Literal Translation*.

> [28]And Peter began to say to him, 'Lo, we left all, and we followed thee.' [29]And Jesus answering said, 'Verily I say to you, there is no one who left house, or brothers, or sisters, or father, or mother, or wife, or children, or fields, for my sake, and for the good news', ***[30]who may not receive an hundredfold now***

---

[f] Or *gospel*

> ***in this time*, houses, and brothers, and sisters, and mothers, and children, and fields, with persecutions, *and in the age that is coming, life age-during*;** [31]and many first shall be last, and the last first.' (Emphasis added.)

Jesus is promising the reward of life (without death) as a heavenly being in the "age that is coming," but in addition to that, he promises receipt "now in *this* time" or "in *this* age" of a hundredfold of houses, brothers and sisters, mothers and children, and fields. How are these individuals to receive Jesus' promise in *this* age if not in their successive lives when they reincarnate? We know a number of disciples who are reported to have died martyrs without the receipt of these promises in their life-time. How else will Jesus' promise to them be fulfilled?

Jesus' closest followers, with whom he shared *secret* teachings and *explanations* understood and agreed amongst themselves about Jesus' teaching of reincarnation. Their shared and accepted understanding and belief in the concept and reality of reincarnation is demonstrated by the disciples and by Jesus in the following scripture.

See John 9:1–3, NRSV.

> [1]As he walked along, he saw a man blind *from birth*. [2] His disciples asked him, "Rabbi, *who sinned, this man or his parents*, that he was *born blind*?" [3] Jesus answered, "Neither this man nor his parents sinned; he was born blind so that God's works might be revealed in him. (Emphasis added.)

It is clear from the scripture that it is known and accepted that the man was blind *from birth*. Yet the disciples ask

Jesus if it was this man's sin or his parents' sin that *caused* him to be born blind. How does one sin *before* birth? Why do the disciples *already believe* a person can sin before birth? Why do they *already* believe it is possible to cause oneself *future consequences* by doing so? Jesus answers that it is neither the man's sin nor his parents' sin *in this case*; it was the man's choice or purpose to be blind so that God's works might be revealed in him. The question posed by the disciples makes it a necessary possibility that the man ***could sin before his birth*** and that possibility, inherent in the question, is accepted by Jesus.

Contrast Jesus' acceptance of the question posed by the disciples about the blind man, and the response he gave the Sadducees' question about the seven brothers' widow. Jesus told the Sadducees in response to their question that they lacked understanding. He does not state anything of the kind to the disciples' question about the blind man. He understands full well why they would ask such a question. He is teaching them about the law and mechanism of reaping what you sow through reincarnation.

Both Jesus and his followers believe not only that the man *could have* sinned before his birth, but that sin from a previous life may be answered in the next. The principle and truth of reincarnation is a fact accepted by Jesus and his disciples. Furthermore, it is clear that a malady, disease, or disfigurement may be caused by sin in a prior life, but isn't necessarily. Stop and consider that. Have you ever wondered how it is fair or equitable that some of us are born into healthy bodies and some into frail bodies? The concept of reincarnation can yield purpose and cause to every disparity of our circumstances, and beyond that, our circumstances are largely within our own control and of our own making even if we do not remember the making. What more accurate reflection of reaping what you sow could there be? And lest we are tempted to think those of us with less adversity are running ahead, it seems rather obvious that many focused on progressing spiritually might choose adversity as a catalyst for growth in a positive direction and as a means of identifying with the downtrodden, or providing assistance or example, as Jesus did. Some of the more advanced souls may not appear so from their circumstances. Some of the hardest workers spiritually may well come from modest and challenging circumstances willingly undertaken for the purposes of growth and assistance to others. Free will means that each of us may cause damage or affliction to others for which we may be required to answer (if we utilize our will in that manner). Our free will may also mean that much of our adversity is for the purpose of progress whether to answer for our own previous actions and learn understanding or whether voluntarily undertaken.

The disciples all understand the rising of the dead that is reincarnation, but do not yet appear to understand the rising *out* of the dead that Jesus is attempting to teach them, the way to become worthy of the next age and to become a son or child of God.

Jesus states *in the text* that all those who achieve this type of rising "*out* from the dead" are *sons of God*: "[36]***For neither are they able to die any more—for they are like messengers—and they are <u>sons of God</u>, being sons of the rising again***." (YLT, Luke 20:36-38).

Jesus isn't the only "son" of God. He is called the 'first born' and other scripture supports this. It is a dramatic shift in existence from the one known by men, in the cycle of death and rebirth, to become aligned with a graduation/harvest at the next age, to become a child of

God. The process to become aligned is experience gained by reincarnation and the opportunity to learn from our mistakes. There is even Old Testament scripture affirming reincarnation.

See Obadiah, Verse 15, YLT (predating Jesus).

> [15]For near *is* the day of Jehovah, on all the nations, As thou hast done, it is done to thee, Thy deed doth turn back on thine own head.

There is also Old Testament scripture affirming the harvest at an unknown appointed time.

See Daniel, 12:7, YLT.

> [2] 'And the multitude of those sleeping in the dust of the ground do awake, some to life age-during, and some to reproaches—to abhorrence age-during....'

This has been understood to be an end-times judgment. But in truth, it is the harvest that comes at the end of an age, which offers the opportunity of a graduation, a shift in existence if one has sufficiently learned his lessons and is ready for life without death. If not, one remains in the reincarnation cycle for another age ("age-during") until the next harvest, until reaping what one has sown allows one the same opportunity once again. We are each determining our own judgment and our own consequences. We reap what we sow, no more, no less.

CHAPTER TWO

PROBLEMS OF TRANSLATION AND THE OUT-FROM-RESURRECTION

Translations which render the differing Greek terms all as "resurrection" and ignore the differences that exist in the older Greek text make gleaning meaning difficult. As additional proof that Jesus' teachings contained two different concepts which are both frequently translated as "resurrection," with the first being the rising again that is reincarnation, and the second being the rising *out* of the cycle of reincarnation, there are additional passages and wording that can be examined.

The Greek word most often translated as "resurrection" is "*anastasis,*" Strong's Greek Concordance number 386. This word is composed of "*ana*" meaning "up" and "*stasis*" meaning "to rise" or "to stand." This is the Greek word frequently used in the New Testament texts which is translated as "resurrection." [Similar Greek words are also *anisthmi (aninstemi)* for "to stand/raise up," and *eigeirw (egeiro)* for "to raise up."]

However, there is one place in the New Testament where English translations have "resurrection," but a different word is used in Greek and no notice is taken of this in the English translations. In Phillipians 3:11, the Greek word translated as 'resurrection' is not 'anastasis' as would be expected but '*ex*anastasis.' The prefix *ex*, which is Strong's Greek Concordance number 1537, means "out."

See Philippians 3:10-21, NRSV, shown in the non-literal translation as follows.

10 I want to know Christ[f] and the power of his
resurrection and the sharing of his sufferings by
becoming like him in his death, 11 **if somehow I may
attain the resurrection [EXANASTASIS (Greek)]
from the dead**.

*12 Not that I have already obtained this or have
already reached the goal;[g] but I press on to make it
my own*, because Christ Jesus has made me his own.
13 Beloved,[h] I do not consider that I have made it my
own;[i] but this one thing I do: forgetting what lies
behind and straining forward to what lies ahead, 14 *I
press on toward the goal for the prize of the
heavenly[j] call of God in Christ Jesus*. 15 Let those of
us then who are mature be of the same mind; and if
you think differently about anything, this too God
will reveal to you. 16 Only let us hold fast to what we
have attained.

17 Brothers and sisters,[k] join in imitating me, and
observe those who live according to the example you
have in us. 18 For many live as enemies of the cross
of Christ; I have often told you of them, and now I
tell you even with tears. 19 Their end is destruction;
their god is the belly; and their glory is in their
shame; their minds are set on earthly things. 20 But

---

[f] Gk *him*

[g] Or *have already been made perfect*

[h] Gk *Brothers*

[i] Other ancient authorities read *my own yet*

[j] Gk *upward*

[k] Gk *Brothers*

> our citizenship[l] is in heaven, and it is from there that we are expecting a Savior, the Lord Jesus Christ. [21] He will transform the body of our humiliation[m] that it may be conformed to the body of his glory,[n] by the power that also enables him to make all things subject to himself. (Emphasis and bracketed EXANASTASIS reference added.)

Even the literal translation ignores the "ex" in *exanastasis*. See the passage in *Young's Literal Translation* (Php 3:9-21, YLT).

> [9] Not having my righteousness, which *is* of law, but that which *is* through faith of Christ—the righteousness that is of God by the faith,] [10]to know him, and the power of his rising again, and the fellowship of his sufferings, being conformed to his death, [11]**if anyhow I may attain to <u>the rising again of the dead</u>. [EXANASTASIS (Greek)]** [12]*Not that I did already obtain, or have been already perfected; but I pursue,* if also I may lay hold of that for which also I was laid hold of by the Christ Jesus; [13]brethren, I do not reckon myself to have laid hold; and one thing—the things behind indeed forgetting, and to the things before stretching forth— [14]*to the mark I pursue for the prize* of the high calling of God in Christ Jesus.
>
> [15] As many, therefore, as *are* perfect—let us think this, and if *in* anything ye think otherwise, this also

[l] Or *commonwealth*
[m] Or *our humble bodies*
[n] Or *his glorious body*

shall God reveal to you, [16]but to what we have come—by the same rule walk, the same thing think.

[17] Become followers together of me, brethren, and observe those thus walking, according as ye have us—a pattern; [18]for many walk of whom many times I told you—and now also weeping tell—the enemies of the cross of the Christ! [19]whose end *is* destruction, whose god *is* the belly, and whose glory *is* in their shame, who the things on earth are minding. [20]For our citizenship is in the heavens, whence also a Saviour we await—the Lord Jesus Christ— [21]who shall transform the body of our humiliation to its becoming conformed to the body of his glory, according to the working of his power, even to subject to himself the all things. (Emphasis and bracketed EXANASTASIS added.)

Despite the similarity in the translations, the word translated from Greek in Philippians 3:11 as "resurrection" in the *New Standard Revised Version*, and as "rising again" in *Young's Literal Translation* (both shown above with underlining) is *not* the usual Greek word for resurrection, which would be "*anastasis.*" Even the literal translation suffers here by not reflecting the "ex" in the older Greek text, presumably due to tradition.

"*Anastasis,*" Strong's concordance number 386, has a definition given as "a rising again, resurrection" and "a standing up." However, the Greek word used in the text here is "***ex**anastasis.*" *Exanastasis*, Strong's number 1815, has a definition that Strong's gives as "a rising up *and out*, resurrection" and "a rising again," the prefix *ex*, or *ek*, Strong's number 1537, has a definition given as "from out, out from among, from, suggesting from the interior outwards" and "from, from out of."

A literal and more accurate translation of "***exanastasis***" would be "**the out-from-rising again.**" This would mean "**out from among those rising again.**" Why is this *different* word used here? And why do the English translations ignore this marked difference in the wording? This would mean the author is really talking about hoping to attain a resurrection or rising again *out* of the cycle: **"[11] if somehow I may attain to" the OUT-FROM-AMONG "the rising again of the dead."** Do translators have a need to avoid the term the "out-from-resurrection" or the "out from among the rising again?" They have ignored or suppressed the differences in wording used with the terms 'rising of the dead' and 'rising *out* of the dead?' (The "out" in the oft used phrase "out of the dead" is *ek/ex*, Strong's Greek Concordance number 1537, the same word placed as prefix in front of *anastasis*). Are translators trying to avoid something they don't understand, can't explain, or don't wish to explain? Is it at all significant that this term 'out-from-resurrection' mirrors Jesus' language in the following scripture from *Young's Literal Translation*, Luke 20:35-36?

> [35]but those accounted worthy to obtain that age, and the rising again that is ***out*** of the dead, neither marry, nor are they given in marriage; [36]for ***neither are they able to die any more—for they are like messengers—and they are sons of God, being sons of the rising again***. (Emphasis added.)

In *Young's Literal Translation*, with the exception of Phillipians 3:11, the text generally appears to include the translation of this Greek word meaning "out" or "out from" when it is given in the Greek. See John 2:18–22, YLT.

> [18]the Jews then answered and said to him, 'What sign dost thou shew to us—that thou dost these things?' [19]Jesus answered and said to them, 'Destroy this sanctuary, and in three days I will raise it up.' [20]The Jews, therefore, said, 'Forty and six years was this sanctuary building, and wilt thou in three days raise it up?' [21]but he spake concerning the sanctuary of his body; [22]when, then, ***he was raised <u>out</u> of the dead***, his disciples remembered that he said this to them, and they believed the Writing, and the word that Jesus said. (Emphasis added.)

See also Luke 24:46, YLT.

> "Thus it hath been written, and thus it was behoving the Christ to suffer, ***and to rise <u>out</u> of the dead*** the third day...." (Emphasis added.)

In the above examples the literal translation shows the complete expression of the Greek "***out*** of the dead." Why is the 'out' dropped from many other translations?

In the context of the passage from Philippians Chapter Three it is clear that the "out-from-the rising again" is not certain, it is something other than the kind of rising again which is certain, reincarnation. The author is *uncertain* whether or not he will attain it – "[11]**if *<u>anyhow</u>* I *<u>may</u>* attain to the" [out from among those] "rising again of the dead**." The author further notes that it is attained *upon perfection of self* – "[12]*Not that I did already obtain, or have been already perfected.*"

This phrase "rising <u>out</u> from" the dead is also used by Jesus in Mark 9:9–10, YLT.

> [9]And as they are coming down from the mount, he charged them that they may declare to no one the things that they saw, except when the Son of Man may rise out of the dead; [10]and the thing they kept to themselves, *questioning together what the rising out of the dead is*. (Emphasis added.)

From what we can tell from the texts, the disciples did not question *how* Elijah could return as John. They did not question *how* the blind man could sin before birth. They did not question reincarnation as a natural law. But this rising "***out*** from" the dead (as opposed to the rising of the dead, or reincarnation) appears unknown to them. This second kind of rising again is referred to by the author of Philippians 3:11 as the "out-from-resurrection" in the Greek texts. It is, literally, an *"out-from-among those rising-again."*

The Philippians' author is stating that some may achieve a rising that is out from among the general rising (or rather, reincarnation), a resurrection out of the birth and death cycle. The law is that you reap what you sow through the death and rebirth cycle. *But if you are **worthy** you **may attain*** the second kind of resurrection/rising out from that cycle and become a son or child of God.

And how do we endeavor to make it out of the cycle? See Romans 8:14, from *Young's Literal Translation.*

> [14]for as many as are led by the Spirit of God, these are the sons of God….

Look again at Philippians 3:11, YLT.

> "…if anyhow I may ***attain*** to the" [out from

> among those] "rising again of the dead..." (Emphasis and bracketed text added.)

The Greek word used here in Philippians 3:11 for "attain" is '*katantēsō*', Strong's Greek Concordance Number 2658, from the verb '*katantaó,*' and is defined as "I come down, either from high land to lower (or actually to the sea-coast), or from the high seas to the coast; hence met: I arrive at, reach (my destination)." In other words, the word signifies "to arrive at" my destination. See also I Corinthians 15:20-28 from *Young's Literal Translation.*

> 20 And now, ***Christ hath risen out of the dead—***
> ***the first-fruits of those sleeping he became***, 21for
> since through man *is* the death, also through man *is* a
> rising again of the dead, 22for even as *in Adam all*
> *die*, so also *in the Christ* **all shall be made alive,**
> ***23and each in his proper order, a first-fruit Christ,***
> *afterwards those who are the Christ's*, in his
> presence, 24then—the end, when he may deliver up
> the reign to God, even the Father, when he may have
> made useless all rule, and all authority and power—
> 25for it behoveth him to reign till he may have put all
> the enemies under his feet— 26*the last enemy is done*
> *away—death*; 27for all things He did put under his
> feet, and, when one may say that all things have
> been subjected, *it is* evident that He is excepted who
> did subject the all things to him, 28and when the all
> things may be subjected to him, then the Son also
> himself shall be subject to Him, who did subject to
> him the all things, that God may be the all in all.
> (Emphasis added).

Jesus is the *first fruit* of those *sleeping*. There is only a first if others follow. What does sleep refer to? Sleep refers to the impermanent death, the death that is temporary, from which you wake, born anew. Jesus is the example, the way, to achieve triumph over that temporary death, to sleep no more.

How shall "all" "be made alive" in the Christ? "And each in his proper order?" To "be made alive" is to live without death, the graduation into a more harmonious existence as a child of God. If all are to be "made alive" "each in his proper order," then God intends no one to be perpetually punished. Each is to make the harvest and graduation in his proper order according to his own actions, according to what he has sown. The only punishment we receive is the punishment we make for ourselves in meeting the circumstances we have created or imposed on others.

See I Corinthians 15:29-34, YLT.

> [29]Seeing what shall they do who are baptized for the dead, ***if the dead do not rise at all***? why also are they baptized for the dead? [30]why also do we stand in peril every hour? [31]***Every day do I die***, by the glorying of you that I have in Christ Jesus our Lord: [32]if after the manner of a man with wild beasts I fought in Ephesus, ***what the advantage to me if the dead do not rise? let us eat and drink, for to-morrow we die***! [33]Be not led astray; evil communications corrupt good manners; [34]awake up, as is right, and sin not; for certain have an ignorance of God; for shame to you I say *it*. (Emphasis added.)

Jesus is the first fruits out of the dead, of those sleeping, still sleeping in between incarnations, and "asleep" because they are unaware of the truth of their existence. Sleep is a fitting metaphor because *there is little or no recollection of sleep by the conscious mind.* "Every day do I die…." The author is very clearly stating death is but sleep. The original Greek says sleep, *not* death, but most English translations do not stay true to the text. Most translations take the liberty of substituting "death" for "sleep" even though that is not what the Greek text states. Why? See I Corinthians 15:6, from *Young's Literal Translation.*

> 6afterwards he appeared to above five hundred brethren at once, of whom the greater part remain till now, ***and certain also did fall asleep***; (Emphasis added.)

The Greek text does not state some "have died," but rather that some have "*fallen asleep.*" It is a state that goes unremembered by the conscious mind. See I Corinthians 15:12–20 from *Young's Literal Translation.*

> 12 And if Christ is preached, that ***out of the dead he hath risen, how say certain among you, that there is no rising again of dead persons***? 13and ***if there be no rising again of dead persons, neither hath Christ risen***; 14and if Christ hath not risen, then void *is* our preaching, and void also your faith, 15and we also are found false witnesses of God, because we did testify of God that He raised up the Christ, **whom He did not raise if then dead persons do not rise**; ***16for if dead persons do not rise, neither hath Christ risen, 17and if Christ hath not risen, vain is your faith, ye are yet in your sins***; ***18then, also, those having fallen asleep in Christ did***

perish; [19]if in this life we have hope in Christ only, of all men we are most to be pitied.

[20] **And now, Christ hath risen out of the dead—the first-fruits of those sleeping he became….** (Emphasis added.)

Here again the Greek text actually says at verse 18 that if the dead do not rise then those who died believing in Christ did perish (rather than sleep). "…***then, also, those having fallen asleep in Christ did perish,"*** - because they are hard pressed to become worthy, aligned with higher existence, in only *one* lifetime. If this statement is true then faith alone can *never* achieve the out-resurrection. Those who have died/fallen asleep in Christ have perished. What hope do we have? The scripture is a ringing affirmation that the dead are raised, a ringing affirmation of reincarnation. The author is clearly stating that for Jesus to rise *out* of the cycle of death and rebirth, there must *be* a cycle of death and rebirth. "If for this life only we have hoped in Christ, we are of all people most to be pitied." *We are to be pitied because it's impossible to do in only one lifetime.* Anyone hoping to teach the resurrection *out* of the cycle of death and rebirth, *the out-from-resurrection*, must teach that the cycle is what happens to us in the first place. Death is but sleep, and fortunately, we get more than one opportunity to learn, grow, and align ourselves. We have more than one lifetime to reap what we sow.

The sleep of death is a temporary condition that you wake from repeatedly. But you don't get out of the sleeping and waking cycle (death and rebirth) until you attain the out-from-resurrection. Let us examine the foregoing more closely.

"And if Christ is preached, that out of the dead he hath risen, how say certain among you, that there is no rising again of dead persons?"

If it is preached that Christ has risen "out" of the cycle of death and rebirth, how say certain among you that there is no cycle of death and rebirth (reincarnation)?

[13]and if there be no rising again of dead persons, neither hath Christ risen; [14]and if Christ hath not risen, then void is our preaching, and void also your faith,

And if there is no reincarnation, then neither can Christ be risen *out* of that cycle of death and rebirth, and void is our preaching and your faith in achieving the "out-from" resurrection.

[15]and we also are found false witnesses of God, because we did testify of God that He raised up the Christ, ***whom He did not raise if then dead persons do not rise; [16]for if dead persons do not rise, neither hath Christ risen, [17]and if Christ hath not risen, vain is your faith, ye are yet in your sins***;

God did not raise Jesus *out* of the reincarnation cycle if there is no reincarnation cycle.

[18]then, also, ***those having fallen asleep in Christ did perish; [19]if in this life we have hope in Christ only, of all men we are most to be pitied***.

If the dead do not rise through reincarnation, then those who died (having fallen asleep), though believing in Christ, *did perish*; for if we have hope in Christ *only in this life* (if we must become aligned with a higher existence in only one lifetime), we must be most pitied of all men. *That would be a virtual impossibility*.

The New Testament is replete with translations of the term 'sleep,' or 'fallen asleep' as death. Why not translate it literally? Why would the older Greek text so prevalently use the term "fallen asleep" rather than death? It is used because it is a more accurate term. The author knows and understands that death is only a period in between lives, just as sleep is only a period in between waking days as stated – "I die every day." That statement does not shore up the frequency and regularity with which one sleeps – everyone knows that – but the frequency and regularity with which one dies and the nature of death as a recurring cyclical process.

Jesus himself speaks of death specifically as sleep when referring to Lazarus. See John 11:11-15, YLT.

> 'Lazarus our friend ***hath fallen asleep***, but I go on that I may awake him;' [12]therefore said his disciples, 'Sir, if he hath fallen asleep, he will be saved;' [13]but Jesus had spoken about his death, but they thought that about the repose of sleep he speaketh. [14]Then, therefore, Jesus said to them freely, 'Lazarus hath died; [15]and I rejoice, for your sake, (that ye may believe,) that I was not there; but we may go to him;' (Emphasis added.)

Speaking of Lazarus' ailment, Jesus had already said the following (John 11:4, YLT).

> 'This ailment is not unto death, but for the glory

of God, that the Son of God may be glorified through it.'

Think about what it could mean to bring back someone from the dead if people live successive lives through reincarnation. It could mean disruption of their course of learning to tamper with the exits and entries. But Jesus explicitly states that he knows that he will cause no such disruption, that this ailment and death are to serve the purpose of helping him to bring belief. There would be little purpose to Jesus making this distinction if Lazarus were only going to die once. Whenever that might occur (in lasting fashion), he would still have the rest of time to be dead. But Jesus knows and calls the period between lives "sleep" and specifically states it is "for the glory of God" that he bring Lazarus back from this particular slumber.

In between lives, where are we? Jesus says we go a way we have known before.

See John 14:4, YLT.

[4] And whither I go away ye have known, and the way ye have known.'

The author's repeated reference to death as sleep is not accidental. I die *every day*. You don't wake just once, or even only twice. You wake many, many times. The author's metaphor is telling. You fall asleep many times. You wake many times. Sleep would *not* be an apt or appropriate metaphor for something that only happened once. Paul was a Pharisee and presumably already believed in reincarnation before he became a proponent of Christianity. After becoming a follower of "the Way," according to the text, he believes in the *ex-anastasis*, the *out-from-resurrection*, the resurrection *out* from among the cycle of death and rebirth. He wishes to arrive at a prize that is won by the worthy, or those that are aligned.

Isn't this why the good news is so important to be spread and taught? People need to know how the process works, the mechanism to which their lives and circumstances are subject. People need to know "the way" to the out-from-resurrection or else you remain in the cycle of death and rebirth, repeating lessons. It is difficult to understand our circumstances and purpose when we are born again, with memories erased. But if there is an example, if the feat of the out-from-resurrection were achieved and witnessed, then a testimonial could be made for others to understand and learn the teaching early in each and every lifetime, for each and every person to understand the purpose of their lives, their circumstances, and their challenges, and to make the most of their time and opportunities. If that is not the case, then why is Christ called the 'first-fruits of those sleeping?' See again 1 Corinthians 15:20, YLT.

> [20] And now, ***Christ hath risen out of the dead—the first-fruits of those sleeping he became***, (Emphasis added.)

Void is our teaching of rising out of the cycle of death and rebirth if there is not a cycle of death and rebirth to begin with. How can you grasp the 'out-from-among-those rising again' (graduation/harvest) that Jesus taught if you do not understand rising again (reincarnation)? The whole tone of the passage is that it is a truth that dead persons rise again, are reincarnated. It is not a tone of only Jesus has risen, but *all* dead rise again. It is given factually. They just do. In contrast, Jesus has risen *out from* among the rest of the sleeping – out from those subject to physical deaths.

The tone of the paragraph affirms again and again that all the dead rise again, even if only the worthy achieve the out-from-resurrection, the rising out from the cycle.

What you do, not just what you believe, is important in achieving the out-from-resurrection, which is achieved through having learned how to live harmoniously with yourself and others, having learned to recognize the divinity and kinship in all, having become aligned with a higher existence.

Consider the parable of the talents. See Matthew 25:14-45, YLT.

> 14 'For—as a man going abroad did call his own
> servants, and did deliver to them his substance, 15 and
> to one he gave five talents, and to another two, and
> to another one, to each according to his several
> ability, went abroad immediately.
> 16 'And he who did receive the five talents,
> having gone, wrought with them, and made other
> five talents; 17 in like manner also he who *received*
> the two, he gained, also he, other two; 18 and he who
> did receive the one, having gone away, digged in the
> earth, and hid his lord's money.
> 19 'And after a long time cometh the lord of those
> servants, and taketh reckoning with them; 20 and he
> who did receive the five talents having come,
> brought other five talents, saying, 'Sir, five talents
> thou didst deliver to me; lo, other five talents did I
> gain besides them.
> 21 'And his lord said to him, Well done, servant,
> good and faithful, over a few things thou wast
> faithful, over many things I will set thee; enter into

the joy of thy lord.

22‘And he who also did receive the two talents having come, said, Sir, two talents thou didst deliver to me; lo, other two talents I did gain besides them.

23‘His lord said to him, Well done, servant, good and faithful, over a few things thou wast faithful, over many things I will set thee; enter into the joy of thy lord.

24‘And he also who hath received the one talent having come, said, Sir, I knew thee, that thou art a hard man, reaping where thou didst not sow, and gathering from whence thou didst not scatter; 25and having been afraid, having gone away, I hid thy talent in the earth; lo, thou hast thine own!

26 ‘And his lord answering said to him, Evil servant, and slothful, thou hadst known that I reap where I did not sow, and I gather whence I did not scatter! 27it behoved thee then to put my money to the money-lenders, and having come I had received mine own with increase.

28‘Take therefore from him the talent, and give to him having the ten talents, 29for to every one having shall be given, and he shall have overabundance, and from him who is not having, even that which he hath shall be taken from him; 30and the unprofitable servant cast ye forth to the outer darkness; there shall be the weeping and the gnashing of the teeth.

31‘And whenever the Son of Man may come in his glory, and all the holy messengers with him, then he shall sit upon a throne of his glory; 32and gathered together before him shall be all the nations, and he shall separate them from one another, as the shepherd doth separate the sheep from the goats,

[33]and he shall set the sheep indeed on his right hand,
and the goats on the left.
[34]‘Then shall the king say to those on his right
hand, Come ye, the blessed of my Father, inherit the
reign that hath been prepared for you from the
foundation of the world; [35]for I did hunger, and ye
gave me to eat; I did thirst, and ye gave me to drink;
I was a stranger, and ye received me; [36]naked, and ye
put around me; I was infirm, and ye looked after me;
in prison I was, and ye came unto me.
[37]‘Then shall the righteous answer him, saying,
Lord, when did we see thee hungering, and we
nourished? or thirsting, and we gave to drink? [38]and
when did we see thee a stranger, and we received? or
naked, and we put around? [39]and when did we see
thee infirm, or in prison, and we came unto thee?
[40]‘And the king answering, shall say to them,
Verily I say to you, Inasmuch as ye did *it* to one of
these my brethren—the least—to me ye did *it*.
[41]Then shall he say also to those on the left hand, Go
ye from me, the cursed, to the fire, the age-during,
that hath been prepared for the Devil and his
messengers; [42]for I did hunger, and ye gave me not
to eat; I did thirst, and ye gave me not to drink; [43]a
stranger I was, and ye did not receive me; naked, and
ye put not around me; infirm, and in prison, and ye
did not look after me.
[44]‘Then shall they answer, they also, saying,
Lord, when did we see thee hungering, or thirsting,
or a stranger, or naked, or infirm, or in prison, and
we did not minister to thee?
[45]‘Then shall he answer them, saying, Verily I say
to you, Inasmuch as ye did *it* not to one of these, the

> least, ye did *it* not to me. [46]And these shall go away to punishment age-during, but the righteous to life age-during.'

For all that Jesus and the books of the New Testament continually advocate kindness and assistance to the poor, the servant with the least is punished the harshest. It cannot be because he *had* the least. The servants are given their talents "to each according to his several ability." It is because he *did* the least with what he had.

None of us are here to stagnate without learning and growth. If you do not use what you have productively, yield an increase, in awareness, in compassion, in applying knowledge to gain wisdom, then you are not doing what you are supposed to be doing. All of us are currently reaping what we have sown in *previous* lives. If you do little, you have little to reap. It is your purpose here to grow an awareness of your actions and intentions – and their consequences - toward others as well as yourself. The reaping is the consequence, the effect of, what is sown. What are we reaping? *"And these shall go away to punishment age-during, but the righteous to life age-during."* You will 'suffer punishment,' or rather, make efforts at correction, for an age through the meeting again of what you meted out to others through reincarnation. You can only achieve life age-during (without physical death) through your actions (thoughts, intentions, words, and deeds).

See James 2:14–26, YLT.

> [14]***What is the profit, my brethren, if faith, any one may speak of having, and works he may not have? is that faith able to save him?*** [15]and if a brother or

sister may be naked, and may be destitute of the daily food, [16]and any one of you may say to them, ‘Depart ye in peace, be warmed, and be filled,’ and may not give to them the things needful for the body, what *is* the profit? [17]***so also the faith, if it may not have works, is dead by itself***. [18]But say may some one, Thou hast faith, and I have works, shew me thy faith out of thy works, and I will shew thee out of my works my faith: [19]thou—thou dost believe that God is one; thou dost well, and the demons believe, and they shudder! [20]***And dost thou wish to know, O vain man, that the faith apart from the works is dead***? [21]Abraham our father—was not he declared righteous out of works, having brought up Isaac his son upon the altar? [22]dost thou see that the faith was working with his works, and out of the works the faith was perfected? [23]and fulfilled was the Writing that is saying, ‘And Abraham did believe God, and it was reckoned to him—to righteousness;’ and, ‘Friend of God’ he was called. [24]***Ye see, then, that out of works is man declared righteous, and not out of faith only***; [25]and in like manner also Rahab the harlot—was she not out of works declared righteous, having received the messengers, and by another way having sent forth? [26]***for as the body apart from the spirit is dead, so also the faith apart from the works is dead***.
(Emphasis added.)

Even Jesus admonishes that we must strive to be perfect. See Matthew 5:43-48, YLT:

[43] ‘Ye heard that it was said: Thou shalt love thy

> neighbour, and shalt hate thine enemy; [44]but I—I say to you, Love your enemies, bless those cursing you, do good to those hating you, and pray for those accusing you falsely, and persecuting you, [45]***that ye may be sons of your Father in the heavens***, because His sun He doth cause to rise on evil and good, and He doth send rain on righteous and unrighteous.
>
> [46] '***For, if ye may love those loving you, what reward have ye***? do not also the tax-gatherers the same? [47]and if ye may salute your brethren only, what do ye abundant? do not also the tax-gatherers so? [48]***ye shall therefore be perfect, as your Father who is in the heavens is perfect.***
> (Emphasis added.)

See *Young's Literal Translation* of Romans 3:9–18.

> [9]What, then? are we better? not at all! for we did before charge *both Jews and Greeks with being all under sin*, [10]according as it hath been written—'*There is none righteous, not even one*; [11]There is none who is understanding, there is none who is seeking after God. [12]All did go out of the way, together they became unprofitable, there is none doing good, there is not even one. *[13]A* ***sepulchre opened is their throat****; with their tongues they used deceit; poison of asps is under their lips*. [14]Whose mouth is full of cursing and bitterness. [15]Swift *are* their feet to shed blood. [16]Ruin and misery *are* in their ways. [17]And a way of peace they did not know. [18]There is no fear of God before their eyes.' (Emphasis added.)

"Both Jews and Greeks" are under sin. "A sepulchre opened is their throat," tongues of deceit, lips of poison. "Ruin and misery are their ways." What is this saying but that deceitful words and actions lead you again to a sepulcher, to death? And that your mouth may be as destructive as bad deeds. What comes out of your mouth *is* a deed, with effects to yourself and others. See Romans 3:19–20, YLT.

> [19]And we have known that as many things as the law saith, to those in the law it doth speak, that every mouth may be stopped, and all the world may come under judgment to God; [20]wherefore by works of law shall no flesh be declared righteous before Him, ***for through law is a knowledge of sin.*** (Emphasis added.)

The law is you reap what you sow. The law is learning through reincarnation: "…by works of law shall no flesh be declared righteous before Him, ***for through law is a knowledge of sin."*** "The law speaks to those under the law" so that "the whole world may be accountable to God." Who isn't under the law of reincarnation? Those who achieve the out-from-resurrection. The law exists so that all may be accountable, those who are aligned with the out-from-resurrection already hold themselves accountable and act accordingly.

Consider the following passage from *Young's Literal Translation,* Romans 3:21-31.

> [21]And now apart from law hath the righteousness of God been manifested, testified to by the law and the prophets, [22]and the righteousness of God *is*

> through the faith of Jesus Christ to all, and upon all
> those believing,—for there is no difference, 23for all
> did sin, and are come short of the glory of God—
> 24being declared righteous freely by His grace
> through the ***redemption*** that *is* in Christ Jesus,
> 25whom God did set forth a mercy seat, through the
> faith in his blood, for the shewing forth of His
> righteousness, ***because of the passing over of the***
> ***bygone sins*** in the ***forbearance*** of God— 26for the
> shewing forth of His righteousness in the present
> time, for His being righteous, and declaring him
> righteous who *is* of the faith of Jesus. 27Where then
> *is* the boasting? it was excluded; by what law? of
> works? no, but by a law of faith: 28therefore do we
> reckon a man to be declared righteous by faith, apart
> from works of law. 29The God of Jews only *is He*,
> and not also of nations? 30yes, also of nations; since
> one *is* God who shall declare righteous the
> circumcision by faith, and the uncircumcision
> through the faith. ***31Law then do we make useless***
> ***through the faith? let it not be! yea, we do establish***
> ***law***. (Emphasis added.)

The Greek word for "law" is a form of "nomos" (Strong's Greek Concordance number 3551) whose word origin is from "nemo" – "to parcel out." If the law is a reincarnation cycle where we "reap" what we "sow," that matches very well the word, "law," derived from a word meaning "to parcel out." The irony is the "law" has us "parceling out" our own results and consequences to ourselves. What greater justice could there be?

Furthermore, the Greek word translated as "redemption" in verse twenty-four is "apolutrósis," Strong's Greek

Concordance number 629, which translates as "release effected by payment of ransom; redemption, deliverance" and is clearly applied only to our ***bygone, previous*** sins in verse twenty-five. The Greek word translated as a "mercy seat" is Strong's Greek Concordance number 2435, "hilastérion," translated as "a sin offering, by which the wrath of the deity shall be appeased; a means of propitiation." The Greek word translated as "bygone" is a form of Strong's Greek Concordance number 4266, "progegonotōn" which definition is given as "to happen before."

The verse tells us the "redemption" of our past, previous sins is possible because of the "forbearance" of God. The Greek word translated as "forbearance" is Strong's Greek Concordance number 3929, "paresis" which is translated as "overlooking, suspension, remission of punishment for."

If, as Romans 9:25 states, the redemption is *only of our past,* ***bygone*** *sins*, which happened before the crucifixion, what does that say about our current actions, deeds, and intentions? There does not appear to be authority for the redemption to apply to future sins, but only to *past* sins.

See also 2 Peter 1:9, YLT.

> "[9]…for he with whom these things are not present is blind, dim-sighted, having become forgetful of the cleansing of his ***old*** sins; (Emphasis added.)

The passage in Romans goes on to clearly affirm that the law is not made useless but is established and affirmed. Despite the crucifixion and redemption from past sins the law of reincarnation still applies to our actions going forward and we will answer for them by reaping what we sow. If Jesus believed the harvest to be near (as he states in several scriptures), then this absolution from past sins and the confirmation of the presence and reason for the reincarnation cycle is intended to help as many as possible have a greater chance to make the graduation at the harvest to become children of God. Jesus is teaching "the Way" to do so. But we must still learn the lesson and find "the way."

Meeting the circumstances you are compelled to under the law of reincarnation may teach you what your sin has been, what it feels like to be receive certain treatment, energy, or vibration. You will reap what you sow. In order to achieve the out-resurrection and no longer be subject to the law (of reincarnation), you must, of your own free will and accord align with God/Christ consciousness in your treatment of others, yourself, and your world.

All have sinned and fallen short. The author asks, in other words, do we overthrow the law by this faith? On the contrary we uphold the law. No need to boast of good works. All have only to go back far enough to find their errors which warrant no boasting, for we all have them.

Faith in Jesus is faith in the out-from-resurrection, faith that the out-from-resurrection is a truth and a reality and can be achieved. The reincarnation lessons are automatic for everyone based on what they have sown. To be worthy, we must choose the appropriate route and conduct of our own accord, believing in the eventual fulfillment. The new converts, Greeks and Gentiles have not lived under the requirements of Mosaic Law and the Jewish religion as the Jews have. All have lived with the law of reincarnation. But the fact that the converts, "the nations" have not shared the same history and religion as the Jews does not mean they cannot be justified. Neither does it exempt anyone from the law of reaping what you sow (of reincarnation). "***Law then do we make useless through the faith? let it not***

be! yea, we do establish law. Only the achievement of the out-from-resurrection, the becoming of a spiritual being without need for the lessons learned in the flesh, releases us from the law of reincarnation.

We saw in Philippians Chapter Three that the author seems to express no doubt regarding the "rising again" that is reincarnation.

Remember also 1 Corinthians 15:12-19, YLT.

> [12] And if Christ is preached, that out of the dead he hath risen, ***how say certain among you, that there is no rising again of dead persons***? [13]and if there be no rising again of dead persons, neither hath Christ risen; [14]and if Christ hath not risen, then void *is* our preaching, and void also your faith, [15]and we also are found false witnesses of God, because we did testify of God that He raised up the Christ, whom He did not raise if then dead persons do not rise; [16]***for if dead persons do not rise, neither hath Christ risen***, [17]and if Christ hath not risen, vain is your faith, ye are yet in your sins; [18]then, also, those having fallen asleep in Christ did perish; [19]if in this life we have hope in Christ only, of all men we are most to be pitied.

The author urges everyone to accept and understand the cycle of reincarnation to teach the graduation from the cycle. It is an accepted precept that the dead *do* rise, worthy or not. But the discussion of the out-from-resurrection is different. It is something to be striven for, a prize, whose achievement is uncertain.

See again Philippians 3:11-12, YLT.

> [11]if anyhow I may attain to the rising again [*out from*] of the dead. [12]Not that I did already obtain, or have been already perfected; but I pursue, if also I may lay hold of that for which also I was laid hold of by the Christ Jesus; (Bracketed "out from" added per prior discussion re translation of the Greek word <u>*ex*</u>*anastasis*.)

Perseverance is required if one hopes to gain this "prize" of the 'out-from-resurrection.' The word used for "prize" in the "out-from-resurrection" scripture, Philippians Chapter Three, is "*brabeion.*" This word is Strong's Greek Concordance Number 1017, which definition is given as "a prize."

This "out-from-resurrection" is a prize to be won, achieved. Brabeion appears to only be used twice in the New Testament - here and in 1 Corinthians 9:24, YLT, shown below.

> [24] Have ye not known that those running in a race—all indeed run, but one doth receive the prize? so run ye, that ye may obtain; ....

This word, meaning "prize" is also used following the verse regarding the "out-from-resurrection."

See Philippians 3:13-16, YLT.

> [13]brethren, I do not reckon myself to have laid hold; and one thing—*the things behind indeed forgetting*, and to the things before stretching forth—
> [14]to the mark I pursue for the ***prize*** of the high calling of God in Christ Jesus.
> [15] As many, therefore, as *are* perfect—let us think

> this, and if *in* anything ye think otherwise, this also shall God reveal to you, [16]but to what we have come—by the same rule walk, the same thing think. (Emphasis added.)

Note that we are told "if *in* anything ye think otherwise, this also shall God reveal to you." None of us is here to force beliefs on another. We have many lives to learn our lessons and we are all at different points on the journey. If any are not yet of a "mature" mind, God will reveal truth to each as they seek it, as they grow mature enough to seek it. But encouragement is found here to stay the course toward eventual fulfillment. The race is not short.

"By the same rule walk, the same thing think." If you know it, or think it, then walk it, or do it.

See again, "If, by any means, I may attain to the resurrection" [out] "from the dead." Belief alone does not achieve the out-from-the dead resurrection, but how you run the race.

In current Christian theology, much is made of belief alone achieving salvation through Christ. This cannot be entirely accurate if reincarnation is a law, a teaching, a mechanism to which we are all subject. If you claim a belief that is not reflected in your actions you will still reap what you sow.

Consider again James 2:24–26, YLT.

> [24]Ye see, then, that out ***of works is man declared righteous, and not out of faith only***; [25]and in like manner also Rahab the harlot—was she not out of works declared righteous, having received the messengers, and by another way having sent forth? [26]for as the body apart from the spirit is dead, so also

the faith apart from the works is dead. (Emphasis added.)

If faith alone were enough, then there would be no prize or goal that must be *achieved* in order to *attain* the out-from-resurrection. It is why the author of Philippians is himself unsure of his achieving the out-from-resurrection, even though he acknowledges himself to have faith.

It is unfortunate that mainstream Christianity and the church as a power construct chose to press belief as the only teaching and only requirement. (While "faith" in colloquial practice is used interchangeably with "belief," biblically, the texts appear to make a distinction between the two, with "faith" being given from God. In other words, we may claim our "beliefs" as our own, and our own doing, but "faith" is persuasion and assurance given from God that no one can credit to himself.) Faith, in many people's minds, does not necessarily require or necessitate good works (although sincere faith should be expected to have them). *Spiritual infancy is insured to endure with this distortion of Jesus' teachings.*

The scripture also speaks of the unbending result of the law, of reaping what you sow, of not erasing one jot or tittle from (the requirements of) the law (the "parceling out"). That does not square with belief alone is required. It does square with you receive back what you have done, said, thought, and intended.

Reincarnation itself is not a result of faithfulness or good works, but your circumstances can be.

[It may be noted that in Young's Literal Translation a rising/raising "***out*** of the dead" refers to Jesus' resurrection virtually exclusively, or the "out-from-resurrection" occurring generally, in conjunction with the harvest as opposed to reincarnation. The only two exceptions noted appear to be when Herod states Jesus may be John the Baptist raised *out* of the dead (Mark 6:16, YLT) and when Lazarus is said to be raised *out* of the dead (John 12:1,YLT) . Both of these refer to very unusual, not customary situations or references to death. In the case of Herod's reference to John the Baptist he is stating the possibility that Jesus, a contemporary of John, may be John the Baptist risen out of the dead. If this were to be considered a possibility, then John could not have died and been reborn as Jesus as Jesus would be far too old for that to have occurred (but of course would not be for the suggestion that Jesus – or John - could be Elijah or one of the prophets). Additionally, there is reference in the scripture to Herod having listened to John, having believed John to be holy and righteous, and Herod might have heard of Jesus' teaching about the coming harvest, the out-from-resurrection.

Lazarus was brought back from the dead without rebirth and, presumably, without having achieved the out-from-resurrection.

It is worth nothing that while Jesus leaves no doubt that John the Baptist is the reincarnation of Elijah from birth (as also suggested by the messenger who appeared to John's parents), the above passages of the discussion around Herod note the question of whether Jesus could be John the Baptist arisen out from the dead. Since John the Baptist lived and was killed in Jesus' lifetime this would suppose the possibility that John's spiritual self could become associated with Jesus' body (or another's body) then existing. Jesus' words do not address this possibility but they clearly and unequivocally address reincarnation. In any case, scriptures, as well as Jesus' several exorcisms, show disembodied spirits, good and bad, can be associated with flesh and Herod may be expected to believe such a possibility exists. At any rate, John's abilities, and Jesus' for that matter, are *not* considered by Herod (and others) to have sprang up in one lifetime alone, but to be attributable to practice and experience accumulated previous to their current lives.]

CHAPTER THREE

SON OF GOD AND JESUS AS MAN

What does it mean for Jesus and his disciples to refer to him as the Messiah? Jesus is referred to in scripture as rabbi, teacher, and master. Jesus' audience is generally described as Jewish. The Jews believed a Messiah to be foretold. But the Messiah was expected to be a man, not God. Jesus called himself "the Way," "the Messiah," the "Son of Man," and "the Son of God." Jesus did not call himself God. He called himself the "Son of God." But what did he mean by that?

The phrase "Son of God" is used a number of times in the Old Testament.

See Genesis 6:1-4, NRSV.

> [1]When people began to multiply on the face of the ground, and daughters were born to them, [2] the ***sons of God*** saw that they were fair; and they took wives for themselves of all that they chose. [3] Then the Lord said, "My spirit shall not abide[a] in mortals forever, for they are flesh; their days shall be one hundred twenty years." [4] The Nephilim were on the earth in those days—and also afterward—when the ***sons of God*** went in to the daughters of humans, who bore children to them. These were the heroes that were of old, warriors of renown. (Emphasis

---

[a] Meaning of Heb uncertain

added).

It can be argued that the plural phrase "sons of God" refers to something here other than just "people." It appears from the text that these "sons of God" are present long before the birth of Jesus. It is also interesting to note that the scripture states, "My spirit shall not abide in mortals forever...."

See the same passage from *Young's Literal Translation*.

> 1 And it cometh to pass that mankind have begun
> to multiply on the face of the ground, and daughters
> have been born to them, 2 and ***sons of God*** see the
> daughters of men that they *are* fair, and they take to
> themselves women of all whom they have chosen.
> 3 And Jehovah saith, ***'My Spirit doth not strive in***
> ***man—to the age; in their erring they are flesh***:'
> and his days have been an hundred and twenty years.
> 4 ***The fallen ones were in the earth in those days,***
> ***and even afterwards when sons of God come in***
> ***unto daughters of men, and they have borne to***
> ***them—they are the heroes, who, from of old, are***
> ***the men of name.*** (Emphasis added.)

In the literal translation, this passage sounds even stranger. "My spirit doth not strive in man – to the age." "To the age" is of limited duration and what shall happen at the end of the age, at the coming of the next age? "My spirit doth not strive in man – to the age" because "*in their erring they are flesh*." It is because of their erring that men are flesh. It is because of erring, sin, that our spiritual selves are held temporarily in fleshly bodies. (We have not yet become worthy of the rising out of the cycle of death and rebirth.) And it is because of our erring, sinning, in repeated fashion that we return to flesh. Our years are then limited, due to erring.

The fallen ones were in the earth in those days. What can that mean? It appears to refer back to whoever the sons of God are. These appear to be higher beings. "***And even afterwards when sons of God come in unto daughters of men, and they have borne to them"*** – to what can this refer? "After" what? After the time when the fallen ones were on the earth. This certainly seems to indicate that while fallen sons of God came to earth on their own, that later sons of God came in "unto daughters of men" and were "borne to them." This appears to say that spiritually advanced entities are not only sons of God, and have been on the earth before, having fallen, or come "from above," but they have also incarnated here, having been born to women.

Might this add any context or meaning to Jesus' response to the question by Nicodemus about being born from above – or perhaps, more accurately, *from the top*? In John, Chapter 3, Nicodemus had wondered how Jesus could perform such miracles, knowing his powers to come from God. And Jesus asked him did he know about being born from above, or from the top. Jesus could well have been telling Nicodemus he was an advanced spiritual entity incarnating here and now (or there and then) by choice rather than as a requisite. He came to help others and his advanced wisdom and knowledge were manifest. He was a son of God and he came to teach others how to become sons, or children of God.

Other biblical references to "sons of God" are also found. See Job 1:6, NRSV.

> [6] One day *the heavenly beings*[a] came to present themselves before the Lord, and Satan[b] also came among them. (Emphasis added).

The editors to this translation of the Bible note that what they have translated as "heavenly beings," in Hebrew actually states, "Sons of God."

The literal translation (from *Young's Literal Translation*) reads as follows.

> [6] And the day is, that ***sons of God*** come in to station themselves by Jehovah, and there doth come also *the Adversary* in their midst. (Emphasis added.)

It is worth noting that not only does the literal translation of the text state "sons of God" but what has been translated as Satan is originally written as "the Adversary."

Here again "sons of God" are noted in the biblical narrative prior to the birth, baptism, and death of Jesus. How can Jesus be the "only" one?

See also Job 2:1, NRSV.

> **[1]** One day the *heavenly beings*[a] came to present themselves before the Lord, and Satan[b] also came among them to present himself before the Lord. (Emphasis added.)

See *Young's Literal Translation* of the same verse.

---

[a] Heb *sons of God*
[b] Or *the Accuser*; Heb *ha-satan*
[a] Heb *sons of God*
[b] Or *the Accuser*; Heb *ha-satan*

> [6] And the day is, that ***sons of God*** come in to station themselves by Jehovah, and there doth come also the Adversary in their midst. (Emphasis added.)

Here again, the editor's note that what is translated as "heavenly beings" in the nonliteral translation actually reads "sons of God" in Hebrew. (Additionally what has been translated as "Satan" actually reads "the Accuser" in Hebrew, or, as stated in the literal translation, "the Adversary").

Is it beginning to seem like there is a translator's bias to shield you from what the text really says? Why would anyone not want you to read or know of other "sons of God?"

Consider Job 38:4-7, NRSV.

> [4] "Where were you when I laid the foundation of the earth?
> Tell me, if you have understanding.
> [5] Who determined its measurements—surely you know!
> Or who stretched the line upon it?
> [6] On what were its bases sunk,
> or who laid its cornerstone
> [7] when the morning stars sang together
> and all the ***heavenly beings***[a] shouted for joy? (Emphasis added.)

See also the same passage from the *Young's Literal Translation*.

---

[a] Heb *sons of God*

> [4] Where wast thou when I founded earth? Declare, if thou hast known understanding. [5]Who placed its measures—if thou knowest? Or who hath stretched out upon it a line? [6]On what have its sockets been sunk? Or who hath cast its corner-stone? [7]In the singing together of stars of morning, ***And all sons of God*** shout for joy…. (Emphasis added.)

Again, what is literally "sons of God" in the texts is translated as something else in the nonliteral translation. Why?

The New Testament also has many references to "Son of God." As we might expect, many are a reference to Jesus, himself. [For example, from *Young's Literal Translation* - See 1 John 5:5, Luke 3:38, 1 John 3:8, Luke 4:41, John 9:35, Hebrews 4:14, Galatians 3:26, Matthew 27:43, 2 Corinthians 1:19, John 10:36, Ephesians 4:13, Mark 3:11, Matthew 8:29, Mark 1:1, Galatians 2:20, John 11:4, and Acts 8:37.]

But a number of these references talk about others being and becoming sons, or children of God, like Jesus.

See Romans 8:10–25, NRSV.

> [10] But if Christ is in you, though the body is dead because of sin, the Spirit[i] is life because of righteousness. [11] ***If the Spirit of him who raised Jesus from the dead dwells in you, he who raised Christ[j] from the dead will give life to your mortal***

---

[i] Or *spirit*

[j] Other ancient authorities read *the Christ* or *Christ Jesus* or *Jesus Christ*

bodies also through[k] his Spirit that dwells in you.
12 So then, brothers and sisters,[l] we are debtors, not
to the flesh, to live according to the flesh— 13 ***for if
you live according to the flesh, you will die; but if
by the Spirit you put to death the deeds of the body,
you will live***. 14 ***For all who are led by the Spirit of
God are children of God***. 15 For you did not receive
a spirit of slavery to fall back into fear, but you have
received a spirit of adoption. When we cry,
"Abba![m] Father!" 16 it is that very Spirit bearing
witness[n] with our spirit ***that we are children of God,
17 and if children, then heirs, heirs of God and joint
heirs with Christ***—if, in fact, we suffer with him so
that we may also be glorified with him. 18 I consider
that the sufferings of this present time are not worth
comparing with the glory about to be revealed to us.
19 ***For the creation waits with eager longing for the
revealing of the children of God***; 20 for the creation
was subjected to futility, not of its own will but by
the will of the one who subjected it, ***in hope 21 that
the creation itself will be set free from its bondage
to decay and will obtain the freedom of the glory of
the children of God***. 22 We know that the whole
creation has been groaning in labor pains until now;
23 and not only the creation, but we ourselves, ***who
have the first fruits of the Spirit***, groan inwardly
while we wait for adoption, the redemption of our

---

[k] Other ancient authorities read *on account of*

[l] Gk *brothers*

[m] Aramaic for *Father*

[n] Or 15*a spirit of adoption, by which we cry, "Abba! Father!"* 16*The Spirit itself bears witness*

> bodies. 24 For in[o] hope we were saved. Now hope
> that is seen is not hope. For who hopes[p] for what is
> seen? 25 But if we hope for what we do not see, we
> wait for it with patience. (Emphasis added.)

But even more telling is the same scripture from *Young's Literal Translation,* Romans 8:10-25.

> 10 And if Christ *is* in you, the body, indeed, *is*
> dead because of sin, and the Spirit *is* life because of
> righteousness, 11and if the ***Spirit of Him who did***
> ***raise up Jesus out of the dead doth dwell in you, He***
> ***who did raise up the Christ out of the dead*** shall
> ***quicken also your dying bodies, through His Spirit***
> ***dwelling in you***. 12So, then, brethren, we are debtors,
> not to the flesh, to live according to the flesh; 13***for if***
> ***according to the flesh ye do live, ye are about to***
> ***die; and if, by the Spirit, the deeds of the body ye***
> ***put to death, ye shall live***; 14for ***as many as are led***
> ***by the Spirit of God, these are the sons of God***; 15for
> ye did not receive a spirit of bondage again for fear,
> but ye did receive a spirit of adoption in which we
> cry, 'Abba—Father.' 16***The Spirit himself*** doth
> testify with our spirit, that ***we are children of God***.
>
> 17 ***And if children, also heirs, heirs, indeed, of***
> ***God, and heirs together of Christ***—if, indeed, we
> suffer together, that we may also be glorified
> together. 18For I reckon that the sufferings of the
> present time *are* not worthy *to be compared* with the
> glory about to be revealed in us; 19for the earnest

---

[o] Or *by*

[p] Other ancient authorities read *awaits*

looking out of the creation doth expect ***the revelation of the sons of God***; [20]for to vanity was the creation made subject—not of its will, but because of Him who did subject *it*—in hope, [21]that also the creation itself shall be set free from ***the servitude of the corruption to the liberty of the glory of the children of God***; [22]for we have known that all the creation doth groan together, and doth travail in pain together till now. [23]And not only *so*, but also we ourselves, ***having the first-fruit of the Spirit***, we also ourselves in ourselves do groan, adoption expecting—the redemption of our body; [24]for in hope we were saved, and hope beheld is not hope; for what any one doth behold, why also doth he hope for *it*? [25]and if what we do not behold we hope for, through continuance we expect *it*. (Emphasis added.)

Why should the translators avoid the "sons of God" used in the older text, as shown in the literal translation, where the status of "sons of God" is promised to *all* who meet the criteria?

At this point it should be obvious that a literal translation is infinitely more helpful in discerning what the meaning of the text might be. In avoiding the literal translation and utilizing other interpretive translations, substitutions are made and opinions are imposed on what the meaning of the text is, or can be. The translations foreclose and close off possibilities of meanings and limit the text to readers. Even with a literal translation there may still be long-standing translational biases reflected and examination of the Greek (or Hebrew) is helpful.

What can be meant by "***for if according to the flesh ye do live, ye are about to die; and if, by the Spirit, the deeds***

of the body ye put to death, ye shall live; [14]for ***as many as are led by the Spirit of God, these are the sons of God"***? If "according to the flesh ye do live, ye are about to die," then you are unaware that you are here to learn and you live without regard or awareness, you are stuck in your flesh, due to sin, and must come back again to learn better and gain greater awareness. But if "the deeds of the body ye put to death, ye shall live." "…For as many as are led by the Spirit of God, these are the sons of God." If your deeds reflect no morality, (you do not do unto others as you would have done unto you) you are living of the flesh and are destined to continue repeating the cycle of death and rebirth. But if your deeds are moral, (you recognize your kinship to others and treat all the way you wish to be treated) you are living of the spirit, and have hope of graduating the cycle. Verse 11 above states, God can "***quicken also your dying bodies***, ***through His Spirit dwelling in you."***

There is nothing in the above cited passages using the phrase "son of God" to suggest that Jesus was ever an *only* son of God, or was anticipated to be an only son of God. Sons of God are entities who have graduated from their earthly existence, who have been harvested to an existence that no longer have any need to take flesh and reincarnate for lessons or payments of debt, although they may do so to aid humanity. Jesus drew criticism for claiming to be the Son of God.

See John 10:31–38, NRSV.

> [31] The Jews took up stones again to stone him. [32] Jesus replied, "I have shown you many good works from the Father. For which of these are you going to stone me?" [33] The Jews answered, "It is not for a good work that we are going to stone you, but for

> blasphemy, ***because you, though only a human being, are making yourself God.***" [34] Jesus answered, ***"Is it not written in your law,[d] 'I said, you are gods'***? [35] If those to whom the word of God came were called 'gods'—and the scripture cannot be annulled— [36] can you say that the one whom the Father has sanctified and sent into the world is blaspheming because I said, '***I am God's Son***'? [37] If I am not doing the works of my Father, then do not believe me. [38] But if I do them, even though you do not believe me, believe the works, so that you may know and understand[e] that the Father is in me and I am in the Father." (Emphasis added.)

See also the same scripture from *Young's Literal Translation.*

> [31]Therefore, again, did the Jews take up stones that they may stone him; [32]Jesus answered them, 'Many good works did I shew you from my Father; because of which work of them do ye stone me?' [33]The Jews answered him, saying, 'For a good work we do not stone thee, but for evil speaking, and because thou, being a man, ***dost make thyself God***.' [34]Jesus answered them, '***Is it not having been written in your law: I said, ye are gods***? [35]if them he did call gods unto whom the word of God came, (and the Writing is not able to be broken,) [36]of him whom the Father did sanctify, and send to the world, do ye

---

[d] Other ancient authorities read *in the law*

[e] Other ancient authorities lack *and understand*; others read *and believe*

> say—Thou speakest evil, because I said, ***Son of God I am***? [37]if I do not the works of my Father, do not believe me; [38]and if I do, even if me ye may not believe, the works believe, that ye may know and may believe that in me *is* the Father, and I in Him.' (Emphasis added.)

If, as stated in Romans 8:11, YLT, "His Spirit" dwells in all of us then, as Jesus says above, isn't the Father "in" all of us, as well?

The law that Jesus refers to that states "ye are Gods" can be found in Isaiah 41:23, shown below from *Young's Literal Translation.*

> [23]Declare the things that are coming hereafter, And we know that ***ye are gods***, Yea, ye may do good or do evil, And we look around and see *it* together. (Emphasis added.)

See also Psalm 82, YLT.

> Psalm 82 1.—A Psalm of Asaph. God hath stood in the company of God, In the midst God doth judge.
>
> [2] Till when do ye judge perversely? And the face of the wicked lift up? Selah.
>
> [3] Judge ye the weak and fatherless, The afflicted and the poor declare righteous.
>
> [4] Let the weak and needy escape, From the hand of the wicked deliver them.
>
> [5] They knew not, nor do they understand, In darkness they walk habitually, Moved are all the foundations of earth.
>
> **[6] I—I have said, 'Gods ye *are*, And sons of the**

Most High—all of you,

[7] **But as man ye die, and as one of the heads ye fall,**

[8] **Rise, O God, judge the earth, For Thou hast inheritance among all the nations!** (Emphasis added.)

It is worth noting that Jesus never referred to himself as God, but only as "Son of God." Jesus was familiar with the Jewish written Mosaic "law" and texts of Jewish "law" even to the point of being called Rabbi in the scripture and teaching openly and publicly in the synagogues and temples. It is more than plausible to expect Jesus to be familiar with the usage of the phrase "sons of God" in Old Testament texts.

Even within the New Testament texts, Jesus himself acknowledges *other* "sons of God."

See Matthew 5:9, YLT.

> [9] 'Happy the peacemakers—because they shall be called **Sons of God**. (Emphasis added.)

And yet the nonliteral versions, as usual, avoid the usage of the phrase "Sons of God" in an attempt to keep it reserved for Jesus only, even though it is repeatedly used in the text to refer to others, even by Jesus himself as shown above.

Consider again Jesus' words in Luke 20:34–36, YLT.

> [34]And Jesus answering said to them, 'The sons of this age do marry and are given in marriage, [35]***but those accounted worthy to obtain that age, and the rising again that is <u>out</u> of the dead,*** neither marry,

> nor are they given in marriage; [36]***for neither are they able to die <u>any more</u>***—for they are like messengers—***and they are <u>sons of God</u>***, being sons of the rising again. (Emphasis added.)

Jesus seems to know or expect that he will be raised out of the reincarnation cycle. He predicted his body (temple) would rise in three days (John 2:19). Jesus himself tells us that those who achieve the rising again "out of the dead" (the cycle of death and rebirth) become "sons of God."

Jesus believes and affirms that he is a "Son of God" and that others will be as well. There is a harvest. There is a time when the sons of men, in the cycle of death and rebirth, if they are worthy, will graduate out of the dead (cycle of death and rebirth) into a different existence. Jesus likens their new existence to messengers, angels, spiritual beings. Jesus calls these graduates, like himself, "sons of God."

Consider Matthew 17:9–13, YLT.

> [9]And as they are coming down from the mount, Jesus charged them, saying, 'Say to no one the vision, till the ***Son of Man <u>out</u> of the dead may rise***.'

Why does Jesus use "son of man" here? Isn't it significant that sons of men become sons of god *when* they rise "out" of the dead?

See Matthew 5:43–48, YLT.

> [43]'Ye heard that it was said: Thou shalt love thy neighbour, and shalt hate thine enemy; [44]but I—I say to you, Love your enemies, bless those cursing you, do good to those hating you, and pray for those

accusing you falsely, and persecuting you, [45]***that ye may be <u>sons of your Father in the heavens</u>***, because His sun He doth cause to rise on evil and good, and He doth send rain on righteous and unrighteous.

[46]'For, if ye may love those loving you, what reward have ye? do not also the tax-gatherers the same? [47]and if ye may salute your brethren only, what do ye abundant? do not also the tax-gatherers so? [48]***ye shall therefore be perfect, as your Father who is in the heavens is perfect***.
(Emphasis added.)

Jesus is explaining the law. You reap what you sow. Men are under the law of reincarnation. If you understand the law, you can understand your circumstances are not the product of whim or inexplicable randomness - you are reaping what you have previously sown. Even more importantly, what you do currently, your actions and choices, can and will determine your circumstances of tomorrow. If you understand the law, you can understand how to improve, learn and grow, by having the awareness to do unto others what you would have done unto you. Why? Because you *will* have it done unto you. Your actions will be revisited upon you and will create a need to return in the flesh until you learn better. That is the law. Who are 'others'? They are all, like you, derivative of God. You must be able to think and do in harmony with others, with love and acceptance of others and yourself before you are able to, or allowed to, graduate to a more advanced, harmonious sphere of existence.

The question of who are the "others" encompassed here is a valid question. The argument can easily be made that Jesus may have encompassed more than just other *people* within our responsibility of treatment. He cast out the money changers in the temple at Jerusalem who were selling animals for sacrifice. His teachings are close enough to Essene teachings and principals as explored in Chapter Twelve to invite comparisons and questions regarding his exposure to and association with their group who were known to be vegetarians who did not participate in animal sacrifices. Likewise, the Essenes were known to be great horticulturists. *Responsibility to all other living things and creation, including animals and plants, may well be encompassed within the directive of the law that has us reaping what we sow*. If all of creation is energetic and derivative of the God/Source energy, then it is all united as universal and part of the one whole. Treatment of others matters because others are, like ourselves, also part of the whole, part of the God/Source. Our treatment of others *is* treatment toward ourselves and, in mirrored fashion, our treatment of ourselves *is* treatment of others, as we are united in our energetic source and essence.

A discussion of Jesus *not* being the *only* son of God would be obviously incomplete without a discussion of John 3:16.

See below a nonliteral translation, John 3:16, NRSV.

> [16] "For God so loved the world that he gave his only Son, so that everyone who believes in him may not perish but may have eternal life…."

See the same scripture as shown in the literal translation, YLT.

> [16]for God did so love the world, that His Son- the only begotten-He gave, that every one who is

> believing in him may not perish, but may have life age-during.

It is obvious that these translations of John 3:16 conflict with all of the previously cited scriptures given as the words of Jesus himself regarding other sons of God. In fact, as they are translated above, they are in direct opposition to the previous scriptures of Jesus not only discussing other sons of God, but telling how to become sons of God. How is this the translation? What does the older Greek text state?

The Greek word translated as "only-begotten is The Greek is *monogenē,* Strong's Greek Concordance number 3439. What is the meaning given for *monogenē*? Strong's definition for this word is "*only, only-begotten; unique.*" It appears fair that the word be translated as only or only-begotten. But it appears equally fair to translate the word as *unique* rather than only. In fact, *monogenē* literally means *one (mono) of a class (genē), one of a particular group*. If so, *where is the rest of the class or group*? Which translation or meaning fits the other numerous scriptures and contexts better? Which scriptures are purported to be the words of Jesus? According to the Gospels of the New Testament, Jesus *never* said he was the only, or only begotten, son of God. Scriptures previously quoted demonstrate that Jesus stated there was a way to become a son of God and attempted to teach it.

See John 5:4-5, YLT.

> [4]because ***__every one__ who is begotten of God*** doth *overcome the world*, and this is the victory that did overcome the world—our faith; [5]who is he who is overcoming the world, if not he who is believing that Jesus is the Son of God? (Emphasis added.)

This scripture, *which is also from the Gospel of John*, unequivocally denotes others expected to be (become) "begotten of God." It also asks the question how one can overcome the world and become a son of God if one doesn't believe that Jesus is the son of God. It is not restricting the status, removing it from others, it is extending it to others through the knowledge of an example, and the meeting of the stated criteria (overcoming the world).

See John 1:9–14, YLT, (speaking of the Logos, or the Word).

> 9He was the true Light, which doth enlighten
> every man, coming to the world; 10in the world he
> was, and the world through him was made, and the
> world did not know him: 11to his own things he came,
> and his own people did not receive him; 12***but as many***
> ***as did receive him to them he gave authority to***
> ***become sons of God***—to those believing in his name,
> 13who—not of blood nor of a will of flesh, nor of a
> will of man but—***of God were begotten***. 14And the
> Word became flesh, and did tabernacle among us, and
> we beheld his glory, glory as of an only begotten of a
> father, full of grace and truth. (Emphasis added.)

What if the above read "unique" or "one of a class" rather than "only begotten"? Even though we are accustomed to "only begotten" being used in relation to Jesus, '"begotten" of God' is here used with "as *many* as did receive him" and "to *those* believing in his name," both containing clearly plural terms. "Begotten of God" is not limited in scripture to Jesus alone and shouldn't be understood to mean that no one else will ever be or can be a "son of God."

See 1 John 3:7-10, YLT.

> [7]Little children, let no one lead you astray; he who is ***doing*** the righteousness is righteous, even as he is righteous, [8]he who is doing the sin, of the devil he is, because from the beginning the devil doth sin; for this was the Son of God manifested, that he may break up the works of the devil; [9]***<u>every one who hath been begotten of God</u>***, sin he doth not, because his seed in him doth remain, and he is not able to sin, because ***<u>of God he hath been begotten</u>***. [10]***In this manifest are the children of God***, and the children of the devil; every one who is not doing righteousness, is not of God, and he who is not loving his brother (Emphasis added.)

Again others, aside from Jesus, are clearly discussed as being "begotten" of God and "children" of God. This is in direct conflict with the customary translation and meaning attributed to John 3:16.

See Hebrews 5:1-9, YLT.

> [1]*For every chief priest—out of men taken—in behalf of men* is set in things *pertaining* to God, that he may offer both gifts and sacrifices for sins, [2]*able to be gentle to those ignorant and going astray, since himself also is compassed with infirmity*; [3]and *because of this infirmity* he ought, as for the people, so *also **for himself** to offer for sins*; [4]and no one to himself doth take the honour, but he who is called by God, as also Aaron: [5]so also the Christ did not glorify himself to become chief

> priest, but He who spake unto him: '***My Son thou art, I to-day have begotten thee***;' [6]as also in another *place* He saith, 'Thou *art* a priest—to the age, according to the order of Melchisedek;' [7]who in the days of his flesh both prayers and supplications unto Him who was able to save him from death—with strong crying and tears—having offered up, and having been heard in respect to that which he feared, [8]through being a Son, did learn by the things which he suffered—the obedience, [9]and having been made perfect, he did become to all those obeying him a cause of salvation age-during. (Emphasis added.)

Doesn't this state that chief priests like Jesus are also part of humanity so that they can empathize with the trials and weaknesses of humanity? Doesn't it also say that the chief priests, like Melchizedek and Jesus, must also offer for others *and themselves because of their own infirmity*? Look again.

> "*For every chief priest—out of men taken—in behalf of men* is set in things *pertaining* to God, that he may offer both gifts and sacrifices for sins, [2]*able to be gentle to those ignorant and going astray, since* ***himself also is compassed with infirmity***; [3]and ***because of this infirmity*** he ought, as for the people, ***so also for himself to offer for sins….***" (Emphasis added.)

Jesus had had infirmity just like the rest of humanity. What does it mean to say "I *today* have begotten thee?" Doesn't that suggest Jesus *became* a son rather than always was a son? Isn't Jesus repeatedly trying to tell us how to become a son and graduate out from the need to physically reincarnate? "He did become *a cause of* salvation age-during" - not salvation itself (verse 90). See Acts 13:32-37, YLT.

> 32 'And we to you do proclaim good news—that the promise made unto the fathers, 33 God hath in full completed this to us their children, having raised up Jesus, as also in the second Psalm it hath been written, ***My Son thou art—I <u>to-day</u> have begotten thee.***
>
> 34 'And that He did raise him up ***out*** of the dead, ***<u>no more</u> to return to corruption***, he hath said thus—I will give to you the faithful kindnesses of David; 35 wherefore also in another *place* he saith, Thou shalt not give Thy kind One to see corruption, 36 for David, indeed, his own generation having served by the will of God, *did fall asleep*, and was added unto his fathers, *and saw corruption,* 37 *but he whom God did raise up, did not see corruption.* (Emphasis added).

Today Jesus was begotten; raised out of the dead (out of the cycle of reincarnation); no more to return to corruption. Why "no more to return to corruption"? What happens to us still present in the reincarnation cycle? Our bodies die and decay, become corrupted. When raised out of the cycle we no longer die anymore, we no longer decay, or have our bodies corrupted anymore. It makes little sense to say that any of us "no more" return to corruption if it only happens once, if we only die once. David fell asleep, or died, but saw corruption, his body decayed. Only those who God raises, who are worthy to be raised *out* of the dead, out of the reincarnation cycle, do not see corruption anymore.

Jesus was proclaimed and acknowledged himself to be the son of God and the Messiah. He never claimed to be God himself, nor did the Jewish people believe the Messiah they expected would be God himself. Jesus spoke of other sons and children of God and attempted to teach the way to that status. The translation of *monogenē* as "only begotten" rather than "unique" or "one of a class" runs counter to the context of many other scriptures and references. Even if one took the position that "only begotten" is the only acceptable translation, one would still have to reconcile the numerous other references of many people being referred to as "begotten of God," which necessarily renders Jesus not the "only" one "begotten of God" and essentially robs the phrase "only begotten" of the meaning foisted upon the original word in the first place.

See John 12:35-36, YLT.

> [35]Jesus, therefore, said to them, 'Yet a little time is the light with you; walk while ye have the light, that darkness may not overtake you; and he who is walking in the darkness hath not known where he goeth; [36]while ye have the light, believe in the light, ***that sons of light ye may become.*** ' (Emphasis added.)

Jesus attempts to teach us the way and offers himself as the example.

JESUS AS MAN

Although Jesus did acknowledge himself to be the Messiah, the foretold prophet, the Messiah was expected by the Jewish people to be a man, a great prophet, but still, a man.

Jesus did not separate himself from other men, rather his reference to the Father puts his relationship to the Father the same as all of ours.

See John 20:15-17, YLT, where Mary Magdalene encounters Jesus after his crucifixion.

> [15]Jesus saith to her, 'Woman, why dost thou weep? whom dost thou seek;' she, supposing that he is the gardener, saith to him, 'Sir, if thou didst carry him away, tell me where thou didst lay him, and I will take him away;' [16]Jesus saith to her, 'Mary!' having turned, she saith to him, 'Rabbouni;' that is to say, 'Teacher.' [17]Jesus saith to her, 'Be not touching me, for I have not yet ascended unto my Father; ***and be going on to my brethren, and say to them, I ascend unto my Father, and your Father, and to my God, and to your God***.'

The above citation is from John, the *same book* that "only-begotten" is used in translation. Here it is clear that Jesus believes and states that he has *brethren*. Jesus says *my Father is your Father, my God is your God.* He gives himself no relation to God that he does not also confer on Mary Magdalene and others.

Jesus does not make himself a God. See, again, John 14:28, YLT.

> I go on to the Father, ***because my Father is greater than I***

How can Jesus be God when Jesus himself states the

Father is greater than I? Jesus only refers to himself as a god in a similar fashion that all of us are referred to as gods.

See John 10:34–38, NRSV.

> [34] Jesus answered, ***"Is it not written in your law,[d] 'I said, you are gods***'? [35] If those to whom the word of God came were called 'gods'—and the scripture cannot be annulled— [36] can you say that the one whom the Father has sanctified and sent into the world is blaspheming because I said, 'I am God's Son'?
>
> [37] If I am not doing the works of my Father, then do not
> believe me. [38] But if I do them, even though you do not believe me, believe the works, so that you may know and understand[e] that the Father is in me and I am in the Father." (Emphasis added.)

Jesus echoes Psalm 82:6-8, YLT, in the following passage.

> [6] I—I have said, '***Gods ye are, And sons of the Most High—all of you***,
> [7] ***But as man ye die***, and as one of the heads ye fall,
> [8] Rise, O God, judge the earth, ***For Thou hast inheritance among all the nations***! (Emphasis added.)

---

[d] Other ancient authorities read *in the law*

[e] Other ancient authorities lack *and understand*; others read *and believe*

While Jesus commonly refers to himself as son of God and even discusses others being and becoming sons and children of God, this appears different. This rather says that we are all, to some extent, gods. What does it mean to be made in the image of God? What creative powers might we have?

What does it mean to say that all living things are common in being an expression of God, or a form of God? The Psalms scripture says we are *all* gods, we are *all* sons of the most high, and upon judgment there are *inheritors* of God among *all* nations. This is as much as what Jesus has been trying to teach all along found in scripture that predates Jesus.

This also makes clear, that although all are sons of God, "as men" you die (verses 6-7).

It should be notable between the other points on translation and the translation of "only-begotten" in John 3:16, that even the superiority of the literal translation is compromised by long standing translational practice and bias that resulted from the influence of church-made doctrine *prior to* the earliest translations as further explored in the Appendix.

And what is written after Jesus' teachings?

See Galatians 3:19–4:7, YLT.

> 19 Why, then, the law? *on account of the transgressions it was added*, till the seed might come to which the promise hath been made, having been set in order through messengers in the hand of a mediator— 20and the mediator is not of one, and God is one— 21the law, then, *is* against the promises of God?—let it not be! for if a law was given that was able to *make alive*, truly by law there would have

been the righteousness, [22]but the Writing did shut up
the whole under sin, that the promise by faith of
Jesus Christ may be given to those believing. [23]And
before the coming of the faith, under law we were
being kept, shut up to the faith about to be revealed,
[24]so that the law became our child-conductor—to
Christ, that by faith we may be declared righteous,
[25]and the faith having come, no more under a child-
conductor are we, [26]*for ye are all sons of God*
through the faith in Christ Jesus, [27]for as many as to
Christ were baptized did put on Christ; [28]there is not
here Jew or Greek, there is not here servant nor
freeman, there is not here male and female, for all ye
are one in Christ Jesus; [29]and if ye *are* of Christ then
of Abraham ye are seed, and according to promise—
heirs.

Chapter 4

[1] And I say, so long time as the heir is a babe, he
differeth nothing from a servant—being lord of all,
[2]but is under tutors and stewards till the time
appointed of the father, [3]so also we, when we were
babes, under the elements of the world were in
servitude, [4]*and when the fulness of time did come,
God sent forth His Son, come of a woman, come
under law,* [5]*that those under law he may redeem,
that the adoption of sons we may receive;* [6]*and
because ye are sons, God did send forth the spirit of
His Son into your hearts, crying, 'Abba, Father!'* [7]*so
that thou art no more a servant, but a son, and if a
son, also an heir of God through Christ.* (Emphasis
added.)

Predating Jesus, the book of Obadiah tells of being cut off – to the age, because of our sin.

See Obadiah, verse 10, YLT.

> [10] For slaughter, for violence *to* thy brother Jacob, Cover thee doth shame, And thou hast been cut off—to the age.

Like the author of Obadiah, Jesus seems to be repeatedly telling us that there is a timing element involved with our opportunity to graduate, if we are ready. The opportunities for harvest, for out-resurrection sound like they come only at certain times (making "harvest" an apt term). Hence some are "cut off – to the age." This suggests, as do many other references to a "harvest," that if one is not yet worthy or aligned for graduating at the time of "harvest" or "reaping to the next age," that one will remain (cut off) in the cycle until the next harvest/reaping. "Harvests" and "crops" are cyclical, repetitive processes.

See Matthew 5:17-18, YLT.

> [17] 'Do not suppose that I came to throw down the law or the prophets—I did not come to throw down, but to fulfil; [18]for, verily I say to you, till that the heaven and the earth may pass away, one iota or one tittle may not pass away from the law, till that all may come to pass.

The timing element of a harvest appears to be further explained by Jesus in Matthew, Chapter 20.

See Matthew 20:1–13, YLT.

> [1]'For the reign of the heavens is like to a man, a

householder, who went forth with the morning to hire workmen for his vineyard, [2]and having agreed with the workmen for a denary a day, he sent them into his vineyard.

[3] 'And having gone forth about the third hour, he saw others standing in the market-place idle, [4]and to these he said, Go ye—also ye—to the vineyard, and whatever may be righteous I will give you; [5]and they went away. 'Again, having gone forth about the sixth and the ninth hour, he did in like manner. [6]And about the eleventh hour, having gone forth, he found others standing idle, and saith to them, Why here have ye stood all the day idle? [7]they say to him, Because no one did hire us; he saith to them, Go ye—ye also—to the vineyard, and whatever may be righteous ye shall receive.

[8]'And evening having come, the lord of the vineyard saith to his steward, Call the workmen, and pay them the reward, having begun from the last—unto the first. [9]And they of about the eleventh hour having come, did receive each a denary.

[10]'And the first having come, did suppose that they shall receive more, and they received, they also, each a denary, [11]and having received *it*, they were murmuring against the householder, saying, [12]that ***These, the last, wrought one hour, and thou didst make them equal to us, who were bearing the burden of the day—and the heat***.

[13]'And he answering said to one of them, Comrade, I do no unrighteousness to thee; for a denary didst not thou agree with me? [14]***take that whic is thine, and go; and I will to give to this, the last, also as to thee;*** [15]***is it not lawful to me to do***

what I will in mine own? is thine eye evil because I am good? [16]So the last shall be first, and the first last, for many are called, and few chosen.' (Emphasis added.)

Most of us could probably sympathize with the laborers who worked all day and got paid the same as the ones lately arrived. But Jesus says this is like the "reign of the heavens." How is that fair? If you align with the harvest you will be reaped. It matters not how long you (or others) may have been so. You either make the cut or you don't. You're either ready for the graduation or you're not. If you achieve the necessary frequency or vibration at the last hour, you will still be admitted. If the universe if energetic, then compatibility achieves automatic results. Isn't this why Jesus came to teach and illustrate "the way?" Isn't this why the disciples were told to go and spread the news? Even at the last hour, some may gain admittance. The parable is not really about payment for labor. It is about a functional result of a state of awareness and volitional conformity therewith that exists *at the time of harvest.* The conformity is that of the energetic equivalent of each of us, determined by the frequency of our thoughts, words, and deeds. The frequencies of gratitude, love, truth and authenticity are higher vibrations raising us to a higher existence, the kingdom of heaven. The frequencies of hate, greed, lust, dishonesty and inauthenticity are lower vibrations and keep us embedded in a lower existence, meeting the less than ideal circumstances such lower vibrations bring or attract into life at that energetic level.

As the appendix hereto will demonstrate, there is good evidence that early Church leaders and teachers also held many of these beliefs until they were outlawed *several hundred years* ***after*** the death of Jesus, in some instances not as much by even Church authority as secular authority.

Why would that be the case? Why would some who understood the real meaning of Jesus' teachings hide them from the masses? There is power and opportunity in the knowledge brought by Jesus' original teachings. There is also perpetual spiritual poverty in keeping people looking for the power of God not only outside of themselves but to the very institutions that hid, withheld, and safeguarded the information for themselves. This allowed, and continues to allow some to lord over others with the hidden truth and mislead them into a perpetual slumber that keeps them easily controlled with little opportunity to wake as we have been essentially lied to about the actual teachings.

CHAPTER FOUR

FURTHER EVIDENCE IN SCRIPTURE

In addition to the foregoing, there is yet further evidence in scripture of the teaching of reincarnation.

See Hebrews 11:35-40, YLT.

> 35 ***Women received by a rising again their dead***, and others were tortured, not accepting the redemption, *that a **better rising again** they might receive*, 36 and others of mockings and scourgings did receive trial, and yet of bonds and imprisonment; 37 they were stoned, they were sawn asunder, they were tried; in the killing of the sword they died; they went about in sheepskins, in goatskins—being destitute, afflicted, injuriously treated, 38 *of whom the world was not worthy*; in deserts wandering, and *in* mountains, and *in* caves, and *in* the holes of the earth; 39 and these all, having been testified to through the faith, did not receive the promise, 40 God for us something better having provided, that apart from us they might not be made perfect. (Emphasis added.)

What else can be meant by ***'Women received by a rising again their dead'*** than women bear the dead anew as babies? "***Others were tortured, not accepting the redemption, that a better rising again they might receive….***" What is "a better rising again?" What is a better rising again than being born anew as a baby? A rising again that is out of the cycle of death and rebirth.

And what is meant by "[39]and these all, having been testified to through the faith, did not receive the promise, [40]God for us something better having provided, that apart from us they might not be made perfect?" All these lives described of suffering and death are lives of people who "having been testified to through the faith, did not receive the promise, God for something better having provided." These people are the martyrs who attempted to teach but were tortured "of whom the world was not worthy." And "apart from us" "others may not be made perfect." If we do not teach this truth, what chance do others have of understanding the way to advance, to hear that there is a rising again out of the cycle of death and rebirth? "That apart from us they might not be made perfect." If we do not preach the gospel, they may never hear, may never know that a rising out of this cycle may be achieved.

The disciples encountered difficulty in spreading Jesus' teaching. See Acts 4:1-3, YLT.

> [1] And as they are speaking unto the people, there came to them the priests, and the magistrate of the temple, and the Sadducees— [2]being grieved *because of their teaching the people, and preaching in Jesus* ***the rising again out of the dead***— [3]and they laid hands upon them, and did put them in custody unto the morrow, for it was evening already; (Emphasis added.)

If the scripture is to be believed, Paul, as a Pharisee, already believed in resurrection/reincarnation before the events after Jesus' death. Only after Jesus' death did he come to learn of the out-resurrection. This provides important context for things that are attributed to Paul in scripture.

See also Acts 23:6-10, YLT.

> [6] ***And Paul having known that the one part are Sadducees, and the other Pharisees, cried out in the sanhedrim, 'Men, brethren, I am a Pharisee—son of a Pharisee—concerning hope and rising again of dead men I am judged.*'** [7]And he having spoken this, there came a dissension of the Pharisees and of the Sadducees, and the crowd was divided, [8]for Sadducees, indeed, say there is no rising again, nor messenger, nor spirit, but Pharisees confess both. [9]And there came a great cry, and the scribes of the Pharisees' part having arisen, were striving, saying, 'No evil do we find in this man; and if a spirit spake to him, or a messenger, we may not fight against God;' [10]and a great dissension having come, the chief captain having been afraid lest Paul may be pulled to pieces by them, commanded the soldiery, having gone down, to take him by force out of the midst of them, and to bring *him* to the castle. (Emphasis added).

Why does Paul appeal to the Pharisees *as* a Pharisee? Why does he tell them I am on trial ***concerning hope and rising again of dead men***? The Pharisees *and* Paul accept the rising again of the dead, i.e. reincarnation. He has common ground with them that he does not have with the Sadducees and he appeals to them. What is *the hope* of the resurrection of the dead - the hope of those who understand how reincarnation works? The hope is to graduate, to attain the rising OUT of the dead, the out-from-the-rising-again.

Paul appeals to the Pharisees because part of what he wants to teach necessarily relies on the teaching of and understanding of reincarnation. He is, in part, being tried for beliefs and teachings the Pharisees share. Thus, he appeals to them. And the Pharisees and Sadducees are divided on their view of Paul as they are divided in their beliefs.

See Acts 24:14-21, NRSV.

> [14] But this I admit to you, ***that according to the Way, which they call a sect***, I worship the God of our ancestors, believing everything laid down according to the law or written in the prophets. [15] I have a hope in God—a hope that they themselves also accept—***that there will be a resurrection of both***[e] ***the righteous and the unrighteous***. [16] Therefore I do my best always to have a clear conscience toward God and all people. [17] Now after some years I came to bring alms to my nation and to offer sacrifices. [18] While I was doing this, they found me in the temple, completing the rite of purification, without any crowd or disturbance. [19] But there were some Jews from Asia—they ought to be here before you to make an accusation, if they have anything against me. [20] Or let these men here tell what crime they had found when I stood before the council, [21] unless it was this one sentence that I called out while standing before them, ***'It is about the resurrection of the dead that I am on trial before you today***.'" (Emphasis added.)

[e] Other ancient authorities read *of the dead, both of*

See the literal translation of the same scripture, Acts 24:14-21, YLT.

> [14]'And I confess this to thee, that, according to ***the way that they call a sect***, so serve I the God of the fathers, believing all things that in the law and the prophets have been written, [15]*having hope* toward God, which *they themselves also wait for, that there is about to be a rising again of the dead, both of righteous and unrighteous*; [16]and in this I do exercise myself, to have a conscience void of offence toward God and men always.
>
> [17] 'And after many years I came, about to do kind acts to my nation, and offerings, [18]in which certain Jews from Asia did find me purified in the temple, not with multitude, nor with tumult, [19]whom it behoveth to be present before thee, and to accuse, if they had anything against me, [20]or let these same say if they found any unrighteousness in me in my standing before the sanhedrim, [21]except concerning this one voice, in which I cried, standing among them—***Concerning a rising again of the dead*** I am judged to-day by you.'

The text states that Paul worships "according to the way, which they call a sect." We know that followers of Jesus were known as followers of "The Way." We are told that Paul states "there is about to be a rising again of the dead, **both** of righteous and unrighteous" (emphasis added). Both the righteous and the unrighteous rise again through reincarnation, because all are subject to the natural law of reaping what is sown.

When Paul is forced to defend himself to authorities, it is

noted that one, Felix, is familiar with this particular sect, "the way."

See Acts 24:22, YLT.

> 22 And having heard these things, Felix delayed
> them—***having known more exactly of the things***
> ***concerning the way***—saying, 'When Lysias the chief
> captain may come down, I will know fully the things
> concerning you;' (Emphasis added.)

Why are they called followers of "the way," instead of Christians, or followers of Jesus? The way to where? The way to what? They way out of the cycle to become children of God. Jesus doesn't teach of a religion, but a recognition and awareness of the properties of an energetic universe and a process that is difficult to achieve in ignorance.

See Acts 13:26-37, YLT.

> 26 'Men, brethren, sons of the race of Abraham,
> and those among you fearing God, to you was the
> word of this salvation sent, 27 for those dwelling in
> Jerusalem, and their chiefs, this one not having
> known, also the voices of the prophets, which every
> sabbath are being read—having judged *him*—did
> fulfil, 28 and ***no cause of death having found***, they
> did ask of Pilate that he should be slain, 29 and when
> they did complete all the things written about him,
> having taken *him* down from the tree, they laid him
> in a tomb; 30 and God ***did raise him out of the dead***,
> 31 and he was seen for many days of those who did
> come up with him from Galilee to Jerusalem, who
> are his witnesses unto the people.
>
> 32 'And we to you do proclaim good news—that

the promise made unto the fathers, [33]God hath in full completed this to us their children, having raised up Jesus, as also in the second Psalm it hath been written, ***My Son thou art—I*** **to-day** ***have begotten thee***.

> [34] 'And that He did raise him up ***out of the dead, no more to return to corruption***, he hath said thus—I will give to you the faithful kindnesses of David; [35]wherefore also in another *place* he saith, Thou shalt not give Thy kind One to see corruption, [36]for David, indeed, his own generation having served by the will of God, ***did fall asleep***, and was added unto his fathers, and ***saw corruption, [37]but he whom God did raise up, did not see corruption***. (Emphasis added.)

Jesus achieved the out-resurrection because he was worthy, because he was energetically compatible based on the frequency he embodied, determined by his thoughts, words, and deeds. David "fell asleep," but his body still suffered corruption as is the natural state within the death and rebirth cycle. Presumably, David had not yet achieved the out-resurrection. Moreover, Jesus tells us one is ***beget*** as a son of God upon rising again ***out*** of the dead, as are any others who achieve the out-resurrection. It is no accident the Greek texts state that individuals 'fall asleep' rather than die. It is an error or intentional perversion of translation to substitute 'death' for 'sleep' which is repeatedly used by writers far closer to the time of Jesus than subsequent translators.

CHAPTER FIVE

THE BAPTISM IN THE GOSPELS

Scholars and students of the Bible have long noted the repetition and questions caused by both the similarities as well as the differences among the four canonical Gospels: Matthew, Mark, Luke, and John.

Many experts claim that all of them were likely written after the time of Jesus' generation and are likely not authored by the persons they claim to be.

Two of the books, Mark and John, make no mention whatsoever of Jesus' early life *or birth*. Matthew and Luke do discuss Jesus' birth which they relate as a miraculous birth to a virgin. The similarity of the Gospels create questions of their interdependence. Given some remarkable similarity in content as well as sequence and structure, particularly among Mark, Matthew, and Luke, what accounts for their differences? Surely if Jesus were the result of a miraculous virgin birth, that would not only be noteworthy, but *require* inclusion in a Gospel as highly relevant, conferring special status and authority. We have already examined scripture which is attributed to the mouth of Jesus which not only does *not* claim to be the *only* son of God, but gives instructions and qualifications on how to *become* a son of God. Given that Jesus himself (per the written texts of the New Testament) does not claim to be an *only* son of God, what other methods can be employed to make Jesus the "only" son of God, and different from all "others"? Making God (in the form of a Spirit, or the Holy Spirit) Jesus' "physical" father by conception is certainly one way to set him apart and bolster his status in a way that is inconsistent with what Jesus actually taught. It is an assertion that really cannot be "proven" one way or another. While such a birth would not be common in nature, it is also undoubtedly the case that there is much that we do not understand and cannot explain. Without attacking the status, it is clear from passages that have already been reviewed herein that such a status runs contrary to what Jesus himself represented. Furthermore, it is inconceivable that a virgin birth and such a claim to paternity would be omitted by no less than *half*, or fifty percent, of the four gospels.

The differences in the Gospels are noteworthy. But so are matters that are consistent in all four Gospels. It is clear in all four gospel accounts that the baptism of Jesus is a central and seminal event. Why exactly is that?

In all four gospels Jesus' ministry does not begin until *after* his baptism. Most Christians know and understand that Jesus was baptized by John the Baptist, but so, according to texts, were many other people. In fact, scripture states that Jesus' disciples were also baptizing people while he was still alive. (See John 3:22 and John 4:1-2, YLT.)

What made Jesus' baptism central to his narrative and the beginning of his ministry? What made his baptism different from others? Why is Jesus' baptism so seminal that all four gospels contain it, but the virgin birth only makes two of the four?

All four gospel accounts tell of a "Spirit" descending upon Jesus at the moment of his baptism, and remaining with him.

MATTHEW

The book of Matthew begins with a genealogy. An incredible contradiction is present with the form of written scripture we are presented with. Matthew is one of the two gospels (along with Luke) that recounts a virgin birth. Yet here, juxtaposed right next to the virgin birth claiming God as the "Holy Spirit" has conceived the child Jesus with Mary, is the account of the bloodline of the Messiah being traced back to the house and bloodline of King David, both prophesied and affirmed, *through Joseph as Jesus' father.*

Obviously, if the Messiah is prophesied to be from the bloodline and house of King David and Jesus himself is affirmed to fulfill the prophesy and be from the bloodline and house of King David, *through his father Joseph* as stated in the text, that prophesy *cannot* be true, through Joseph, if Joseph is denied to be the actual father in favor of the Holy Spirit.

If Jesus is not the child of Joseph he cannot be of the house of David – at least through Joseph as claimed in the text - and *cannot fulfill the prophecy* regarding the Messiah. These two assertions are contradictory and cannot both be correct. The text – the Gospel of Matthew – disagrees *with itself.* These two concepts are mutually exclusive and may well be considered not to have both been in the original version of the text. This is even further supported by the fact that two other gospels give no such account of a virgin birth.

Given such discrepancies, common elements to all four gospels may well be considered to have some possibility of greater reliability. All four gospels discuss a "Spirit" descending on Jesus at his baptism.

See Matthew 3:16, YLT.

> [16]And having been baptized, Jesus went up immediately from the water, and lo, opened to him were the heavens, and he saw *the Spirit of God descending as* a dove, and coming *upon* him (Emphasis added.)

According to Thayer's Greek Lexicon, the word translated here as "coming" upon him, the Greek word "*erchomenon,*" a version of "*erchomai,*" Strong's Concordance Number 2064, is fairly translated as "coming," and, according to Strong's, conveys a meaning of "to come from one place *into* another" when referring to persons (emphasis added). It can also be, and frequently is translated as "lighting" upon him.

The Greek word used here for "upon" is '*ep,'* a form of *epi,* Strong's Greek Concordance number 1909, a preposition, and is defined in Strong's Concordance as "on, to, against, on the basis of, at."

The scripture in Matthew goes on to make clear that the "Spirit" (here referred to as "the Spirit of God") *remained* with Jesus.

See Matthew 4:1, YLT.

> [1] Then Jesus was led up to the wilderness *by the Spirit*
> (Emphasis added.)

The verse clearly states that Jesus was "led" "by *the Spirit*" into the wilderness away from the people. The Spirit *remained* with Jesus *after descending upon him at his baptism,* and after its descent, influenced his actions and behavior.

MARK

The Gospel of Mark begins with an affirmation that John the Baptist is the foretold *messenger* sent to clear the way. See Mark 1:2-8, YLT.

> [2]As it hath been written in the prophets, 'Lo, I send ***My messenger*** before thy face, who shall *prepare thy way* before thee,'— [3]*'A voice of one calling in the wilderness, Prepare ye the way of the Lord, straight make ye his paths,'*— [4]***John** came baptizing in the wilderness*, and proclaiming a baptism of reformation—to remission of sins, [5]and there were going forth to him all the region of Judea, and they of Jerusalem, and they were all baptized by him in the river Jordan, confessing their sins. [6]*And John was clothed with camel's hair, and a girdle of skin around his loins, and eating locusts and honey of the field*, [7]and he proclaimed, saying, 'He doth come—who is mightier than I—after me, of whom I am not worthy—having stooped down—to loose the latchet of his sandals; [8]I indeed did baptize you with water, but he shall baptize you with the Holy Spirit.'

This passage confirms what Jesus told the disciples about John being the reincarnation of Elijah by both confirming John as "the messenger" and also giving him the same physical description of appearance as Elijah. The word translated here as "messenger" is the same word usually translated as "angel" in nonliteral translations. By calling and confirming John as "the messenger," the author is also confirming that messengers (angels, higher beings) may come into the world by birth for special purposes. John's special status, importance and purpose as a "messenger" is given first so that the baptism may be recounted, with its special importance.

In Mark, no narrative is given of Jesus' life before the baptism, and no account of his birth, much less a virgin birth is given. *In Mark, the gospel begins with the baptism.*

The wording of Jesus' baptism is given in Mark 1:9–11, YLT.

> 9 And it came to pass in those days, Jesus came
> from Nazareth of Galilee, and was baptized by John
> at the Jordan; 10and immediately coming up from the
> water, he saw the heavens dividing, and ***the Spirit*** *as*
> *a dove coming down upon him*; 11and a voice came
> out of the heavens, 'Thou art My Son—the Beloved,
> in whom I did delight.

In this verse, we are told simply that "the Spirit" came down upon him. It is not named as the Holy Spirit, or otherwise defined or named. The Greek word used for "upon" is different than in the previous Gospel (Matthew). Here, the Greek word used is *eis*, Strong's Greek Concordance number 1519. Strong's Concordance translates the word as "into" and "in" as well as "upon."

Thayer's Greek Lexicon gives an additional definition of *eis* as "of a place entered, or of entrance into a place, into; and a. it stands before nouns designating an open place, a hollow thing, or one in which an object can be hidden."

The Gospel of Mark also says *the Spirit* drove Jesus into the wilderness. See Mark 1:12, YLT.

> 12And immediately doth *the Spirit* put him forth to

the wilderness

The Spirit described that descended upon Jesus, and perhaps rather *into* Jesus, that wasn't there prior to the Baptism, *stays with* Jesus and is responsible for compelling him into the wilderness.

The Gospel of Mark (like the Gospel of John) says nothing of Jesus' life before the Baptism. Mark says nothing of Jesus' birth and does not recount a virgin birth or the Holy Spirit as Jesus' father and gives no claims of genealogy.

All of Jesus' ministry, miracles and healings occur *after* his baptism.

LUKE

Luke begins with the account of the foretold birth of John the Baptist. Luke (like Matthew) does give account of a virgin birth via the Holy Spirit. Luke also gives an account of genealogy which follows *immediately after* the account of the baptism. This genealogy is most interesting.

See Luke 3:23-38, YLT.

> 23 And Jesus himself was beginning to be about
> thirty years of age, **being, as was supposed, son of**
> **Joseph**, 24 the *son* of Eli, the *son* of Matthat, the *son*
> of Levi, the *son* of Melchi, the *son* of Janna, the *son*
> of Joseph, 25 the *son* of Mattathias, the *son* of Amos,
> the *son* of Naum, the *son* of Esli, 26 the *son* of
> Naggai, the *son* of Maath, the *son* of Mattathias, the
> *son* of Semei, the *son* of Joseph, the *son* of Juda,
> 27 the *son* of Joanna, the *son* of Rhesa, the *son* of
> Zerubbabel, the *son* of Shealtiel, 28 the *son* of Neri,

> the *son* of Melchi, the *son* of Addi, the *son* of
> Cosam, the *son* of Elmodam, the *son* of Er, 29the *son*
> of Jose, the *son* of Eliezer, the *son* of Jorim, the *son*
> of Matthat, 30the *son* of Levi, the *son* of Simeon, the
> *son* of Juda, the *son* of Joseph, the *son* of Jonan, the
> *son* of Eliakim, 31the *son* of Melea, the *son* of
> Mainan, the *son* of Mattatha, the *son* of Nathan, 32the
> *son* of **David**, the *son* of Jesse, the *son* of Obed, the
> *son* of Booz, the *son* of Salmon, the *son* of Nahshon,
> 33the *son* of Amminadab, the *son* of Aram, the *son* of
> Esrom, the *son* of Pharez, 34the *son* of Judah, the *son*
> of Jacob, the *son* of Isaac, the *son* of **Abraham**, the
> *son* of Terah, the *son* of Nahor, 35the *son* of Serug,
> the *son* of Reu, the *son* of Peleg, the *son* of Eber,
> 36the *son* of Salah, the *son* of Cainan, the *son* of
> Arphaxad, the *son* of Shem, the *son* of Noah, the *son*
> of Lamech, 37the *son* of Methuselah, the *son* of
> Enoch, the *son* of Jared, the *son* of Mahalaleel, 38the
> *son* of Cainan, the *son* of Enos, the *son* of Seth, **the
> *son* of Adam, the *son* of God.** (Emphasis added in
> bold only.)

Here Jesus is the "son of Joseph" "as was supposed." Like the Gospel of Matthew, Jesus' genealogy is traced back to King David, but again if Jesus is stated to not be the son of Joseph, but is only *supposed* to be the son of Joseph (though not in fact) he cannot claim a bloodline back to David through Joseph and cannot fulfill the prophesy regarding the Messiah. In addition, the conclusion of the genealogy reads "...the *son* of Adam, the *son* of God." Adam is referred to as "the son of God."

Not only is Jesus' genealogy traced back through Joseph to David, but it also carried all the way back to Adam who is referred to as *the Son of God.* This too does not comport with Jesus being the *only* son of God. The translation also has all of the words "son" in the phrase "son of" italicized except for where Jesus is referred to as the "son" of Joseph which is not italicized, differentiating his "sonship" from Joseph, from all of the others and making the entire genealogy counterfeit. Just prior to the genealogy, the account of the baptism is given.

See Luke 3:21-22, YLT.

> [21] And it came to pass, in all the people being baptised, Jesus also being baptised, and praying, *the heaven was opened, [22]and the Holy Spirit came down in a bodily appearance*, as if a dove, upon him, and a voice came out of heaven, saying, 'Thou art My Son—the Beloved, in thee I did delight. (Emphasis added.)

In Luke, unlike all the other Gospels, the "Spirit" is named as the "Holy Spirit" who descends in "bodily appearance." What accounts for the differences in these very similar accounts? Luke, like all of the Gospels, not only makes clear that that "Spirit" is distinct from the man Jesus, but also that the Spirit was not present prior to the baptism, descended at the baptism, and also stays with Jesus after the baptism and influences his actions.

See Luke 4:1, YLT.

> [1] And Jesus, full of the Holy Spirit, turned back from the Jordan, and was brought in the Spirit to the wilderness.

JOHN

The Gospel of John, like that of Mark, does not discuss Jesus' birth, nor make any claims of a virgin birth or Godly paternity, or give genealogies. John's account of the baptism is even more interesting.

The Gospel of John begins with a discussion of the Logos, or the Word.

See John 1:1-5, YLT.

> 1In the beginning was the Word, and the Word was with God, and the Word was God; 2this one was in the beginning with God; 3all things through him did happen, and without him happened not even one thing that hath happened. 4In him was life, and the life was the *light* of men.
>
> 5And the *light* in the darkness did shine, and the darkness did not perceive it. (Emphasis added.)

While the Logos, or the Word, is often seen and spoken of as synonymous with Jesus, that is not clearly stated in the text. The Word is equated with "light."

Next is a discussion of, or introduction to, John the Baptist.

See John 1:6-8, YLT.

> 6There came **a man—having been sent from God—whose name *is* John, 7this one came for testimony, that he might testify about the Light**, that all might believe through him; 8that one was not the Light, but—that he might testify about the Light. (Emphasis added in bold only.)

We are told John was sent from God to testify *about the Light (the Logos or the Word). But John does not testify until after the baptism, not before.*

See John 1:12-14, YLT.

> [12]but as many as did receive him to them he gave authority to become sons of God—to those believing in his name, [13]who—not of blood nor of a will of flesh, nor of a will of man but—of God were begotten. [14]And *the Word* became flesh, and *did tabernacle among us*, and we beheld his glory, glory as *of an only begotten of a father*, full of grace and truth. (Emphasis added.)

The Greek word translated as 'tabernacle' here, Strong's Greek Concordance number 4637, denotes "dwell as in a tent, encamp, have my tabernacle," according to the concordance, not simply 'to live.' Since Jesus himself appears to have had no fixed residence but appears to roam from place to place teaching and himself famously bemoaned "no place to lay his head" (See Matthew 8:20; Luke 9:58, YLT). What can be the tabernacle here? Doesn't this suggest a different type of 'dwelling,' a dwelling of the spirit that came down, rather than a man living without his own dwelling? Is it possible that Jesus the man becomes the "tabernacle" for the Word that descended upon him at the baptism?

The Gospel of John states that John the Baptist's purpose is to "testify" as to the Word (Logos), and his testimony *relates to the baptism.* Jesus existed prior to his baptism and John could have testified to Jesus' authority prior to the baptism, but he did not do so. If the Word is what descended at the baptism, then it makes sense that John's testimony would relate to the descent of the Word at the baptism. Such descent would have conferred special authority to Jesus and his actions.

See John 1:15, YLT.

> [29] On the morrow John seeth Jesus coming unto him, and saith, 'Lo, the Lamb of God, who is taking away the sin of the world; [30]this is he concerning whom I said, After me doth come ***a man***, who hath come before me, because he was before me: [31]***and I knew him not***, but, that he might be manifested to Israel, because of this I came with the water baptizing. ***[32]And John testified, saying—'I have seen the Spirit coming down, as a dove, out of heaven, and it remained on him; [33]and I did not know him, but he who sent me to baptize with water, He said to me, On whomsoever thou mayest see the Spirit coming down, and remaining on him, this is he who is baptizing with the Holy Spirit; [34]and I have seen, and have testified, that this is the Son of God.'*** [35]On the morrow, again, John was standing, and two of his disciples, [36]and having looked on Jesus walking, he saith, 'Lo, the Lamb of God;'

None of the gospels state that the descent was by an actual dove or that the descent of the Spirit was in the form of a dove. Rather the term given is that the descent of the Spirit was *as* the descent of a dove, comparatively. Traditionally, Christians understand and acknowledge that John the Baptist confirms Jesus as the Messiah. Traditionally, Christians interpret and understand the descent of the "Spirit" as a *sign* of Jesus' status as the Messiah and Son of God. But a careful reading of the scripture suggests something more.

John says "I did not know him" even though we know from scripture that John and Jesus are related as their mothers are related and were pregnant together (Luke Chapter 1). Verse 33 also makes very clear that the Spirit that descended *remained* on him. Is John testifying regarding Jesus the man or the Spirit that descended and remained on him? He is not testifying of a virgin birth, or paternity by the Holy Spirit or God; he is not testifying by virtue of miracles or acts since the ministry and miracles occur after the baptism. In fact, the book of John begins with a discussion of "the Word," after which follows a discussion of "John the Baptist," and the baptism that occurs with "the Spirit" that descended and remained with Jesus.

Many commentators have come to equate Jesus the man with the Logos or the Word, but John's testimony regarding the Word is of the Spirit that descends upon the Baptism. If Jesus and the Word were one and the same always, Jesus would have been the Word *prior* to the baptism, rather than being united after the baptism. Isn't John's testimony an affirmation that the Word, the Spirit that was separate from Jesus, joins with Jesus at his baptism? Isn't this why Jesus' ministry and works begin after the baptism, after he is united with the Word, after the Word descends and tabernacles, or abides with him and dwells in the flesh among us? Isn't this why the gospel of John fails to discuss Jesus' life before the baptism?

Granted, it is confusing to study Gospels that don't agree, sometimes even within themselves, but when presented with contradictions, what makes sense in light of the whole? Can't it be the case that the Spirit that descends and remains is the Logos, not Jesus himself, but subsequently united with him? Why does Jesus find himself attributed with multiple names, "Jesus," "Christ," and "Logos" or the "Word"? Can they denote different things that became merged over time?

John 1:32 (YLT) says, "***And John testified, saying—'I have seen the Spirit coming down, as a dove, out of heaven, and it remained on him."*** (Emphasis added.)

John's account again gives us just "the Spirit," not the Holy Spirit that descends. And John says clearly what all three other accounts confirm with their statements that the descended Spirit remained with Jesus to drive or lead him into the wilderness.

The Greek word used in John for 'remained' is *emeinen*, a form of the verb *menó*, Strong's Greek concordance number 3306, whose definition is given not only as "remain" but also as "abide" and "stay." The text here is clearly indicating that the Spirit that joined with the man Jesus at the baptism and wasn't present prior to the baptism, *abided* with Jesus.

Further Thayer's Greek Lexicon even puts forth a definition "equivalent to tarry as a guest, lodge." The Book of John actually says that "the Spirit" *dwelled, abided, or lodged, as a guest, with Jesus*.

The Gospel of John says John bore witness to "the Word." It appears more than fair to say that, according to the text of the Gospel of John, John the Baptist bore witness to the *Word* as the *Spirit* which descended and *dwelled* with Jesus. The text itself specifies John the Baptist's testimony regarding "the Word" to be the event of the descending of the Spirit at the baptism.

See John 1:14-18, YLT.

> 14And ***the Word*** became flesh, and did tabernacle
> among us, and we beheld his glory, ***glory as of an
> only begotten of a father***, full of grace and truth.
> 15***John doth testify concerning him***, and hath
> cried, saying, 'This was he of whom I said, He who
> after me is coming, hath come before me, for he was
> before me;' 16and out of his fulness did we all
> receive, and grace over-against grace; 17*for the law
> through Moses was given, the grace and the truth
> through Jesus Christ did come*; 18God no one hath
> ever seen; the only begotten Son, who is on the
> bosom of the Father—he did declare. (Emphasis
> added.)

John testifies as to the light, *the Word.* John states the truth comes *through* Jesus Christ. In verse 15 , "John doth testify concerning him" has the word "him" modifying the reference which directly precedes it, the reference to the "Word." Since the Gospel of John does not claim Jesus is the actual birth child of God, or the Holy Spirit, makes no mention of Jesus prior to the baptism, and bears witness to the Logos (or the Word) becoming flesh and dwelling among us *after* the baptism, this text testifies to the Spirit that came to dwell with Jesus after the baptism.

Reconsider part of the relevant text from John 1, YLT.

> 29 On the morrow John seeth Jesus coming unto
> him, and saith, 'Lo, the Lamb of God, who is taking
> away the sin of the world; 30this is he concerning
> whom I said, ***After me doth come a man, who hath
> come before me, because he was before me***: 31***and I
> knew him not, but, that he might be manifested to
> Israel, because of this I came with the water***

baptizing. [32]And John testified, saying—'I have seen the Spirit coming down, as a dove, out of heaven, and it remained on him; [33]and I did not know him, but he who sent me to baptize with water, He said to me, On whomsoever thou mayest see the Spirit coming down, and remaining on him, this is he who is baptizing with the Holy Spirit; [34]and I have seen, and have testified, that this is the Son of God.'
(Emphasis added.)

John confirms that "a man" is coming, but confirms Jesus' special status only after, and because of, the Spirit descending at the baptism and remaining with him. Recognition depends on the Spirit which is at first separate and apart from Jesus, was not with Jesus before the baptism, and which remains and abides with Jesus after the baptism.

Jesus' ministry, works and miracles are reported as happening after the baptism, beginning with the wedding in Cana (John Chapter 2).

There are a number of places where Jesus confirms that there is something spiritual with him that is distinct from him. Jesus describes something that is with him that will be separate from him when he departs.

See John 16:7, YLT.

> [7]'But I tell you the truth; it is better for you that I go away, for if I may not go away, ***the Comforter*** will not come unto you, and if I go on, ***I will send Him unto you***.....(Emphasis added.)

Whatever *the Comforter* is meant to denote, it is clear that it is *unavailable* while with Jesus, is available only if

Jesus goes away and that Jesus *will send Him* unto you. Jesus can only send something that is separate and distinct from himself.

See John 7:39, YLT.

> [39]and this he said of ***the Spirit***, which those believing in him were about to receive; for ***not yet was the Holy Spirit, because Jesus was not yet glorified***. (Emphasis added.)

See also 1 John 5:6-9, YLT.

> [6] This one is he who did come through water and blood—Jesus the Christ, not in the water only, but in the water and the blood; and ***the Spirit*** it is that is testifying, because ***the Spirit is the truth***, [7]because ***three are who are testifying (in the heaven, the Father, the Word, and the Holy Spirit, and these—the three—are one***; [8]and three are who are testifying in the earth), the Spirit, and the water, and the blood, and the three are into the one. [9]If the testimony of men we receive, the testimony of God is greater, ***because this is the testimony of God that He hath testified concerning His Son***.

Consider Matthew 11:1-6, YLT.

> [1] And it came to pass, when Jesus ended directing his twelve disciples, he departed thence to teach and to preach in their cities. [2]***And John having heard in the prison the works of the Christ***, having sent two of his disciples, [3]said to him, '***Art thou He who is coming, or for another do we look***?' [4]And Jesus

answering said to them, '***Having gone, declare to John the things that ye hear and see, [5]blind receive sight, and lame walk, lepers are cleansed, and deaf hear, dead are raised, and poor have good news proclaimed, [6]and happy is he who may not be stumbled in me.***'

John is thrown in prison *after* he baptizes Jesus, *after* the events concerning the Spirit that descended upon Jesus and remained to lead/drive him into the wilderness. (Chapter 3-4 in Matthew.) Why is he sending anyone to ask anything? Doesn't he know Jesus' status as he already declared it to others? How does Jesus answer him? Jesus confirms he is performing the works of the Christ with his miracles and delivery of the good news to the poor. John's question, and Jesus' understanding of the question and his response appear to confirm that the spirit that descended is still with him.

What does the text tell us Jesus says about his own authority and where it comes from?

See Mark 11:27–30, YLT.

> [27] And they come again to Jerusalem, and in the temple, as he is walking, there come unto him the chief priests, and the scribes, and the elders, [28]and they say to him, ***'By what authority dost thou these things? and who gave thee this authority that these things thou mayest do?***' [29]And Jesus answering said to them, 'I will question you—I also—one word; and answer me, and ***I will tell you by what authority I do these things; [30]the baptism of John—from heaven was it? or from men?*** answer me.' (Emphasis added.)

Jesus does *not* say his authority comes from a virgin birth, or paternity by God or even sonship. Jesus tells them his authority *comes from the baptism. All four gospels describe a Spirit descending from heaven and remaining with Jesus at the baptism.*

See also Acts 10:34-39, YLT.

> [34] And Peter having opened his mouth, said, 'Of a truth, I perceive that God is no respecter of persons, [35]but ***in every nation*** he who is fearing Him, and is working righteousness, ***is acceptable to Him***; [36]***the word*** *that he sent to the sons of Israel, proclaiming good news—peace* ***through*** Jesus Christ (this one is Lord of all,) [37]ye—ye have known;—***the word*** *that came throughout all Judea*, having begun from Galilee, ***after the baptism that John preached***; [38]Jesus who *is* from Nazareth—how *God did* ***anoint him with*** *the Holy Spirit and power*; who went through, doing good, and healing all those oppressed by the devil, *because God was* ***with*** *him*; [39]and we—we are witnesses of all things that he did, both in the country of the Jews, and in Jerusalem,—whom they did slay, having hanged upon a tree. (Emphasis added.)

Doesn't the above scripture state there are those "in every nation" that are acceptable to God? Doesn't the above passage state that "the word" was sent *through* Jesus *after* the baptism? Doesn't the above scripture state that "the word" made proclamations *through* Jesus, rather than being the same as the person of Jesus? Doesn't the above scripture state that God 'anointed' Jesus and was 'with'

Jesus? Doesn't this scripture reinforce and corroborate that "the Word," rather than being Jesus, was a separate entity from Jesus, was present with Jesus after the baptism, working through Jesus - and negate that Jesus the man is understood to be God himself?

Granted it gets confusing when the gospels do not agree and terms are blurred. We have "Jesus," "Christ," and "the Word." No wonder the whole matter has become a confused mess over 2000 years. But, given that, isn't it highly significant that we have the actual description of something spiritual descending and joining with Jesus at the baptism in all four gospel accounts? Isn't it significant that all four gospels agree that Jesus' works and ministry don't begin until after his baptism?

See Mark 15:33-39, YLT.

> [33] And the sixth hour having come, darkness came over the whole land till the ninth hour, [34]and at the ninth hour Jesus cried with a great voice, saying, 'Eloi, Eloi, lamma sabachthani?' which is, being interpreted, 'My God, my God, why didst Thou forsake me?' [35]And certain of those standing by, having heard, said, 'Lo, Elijah he doth call;' [36]and one having run, and having filled a spunge with vinegar, having put *it* also on a reed, was giving him to drink, saying, 'Let alone, let us see if Elijah doth come to take him down.' [37]***And Jesus having uttered a loud cry, yielded the spirit***, [38]and the veil of the sanctuary was rent in two, from top to bottom, [39]and the centurion who was standing over-against him, having seen that, having so cried out, ***he yielded the spirit***, said, 'Truly this man was Son of God.' (Emphasis added.)

What spirit did Jesus yield? Jesus himself laments the departure, evidencing it is not Jesus' own soul. Isn't this referring to the Spirit that descended at the baptism and had dwelled with him thereafter? It is referred to in the same way, as "the spirit," rather than "his" spirit? Wouldn't this explain Jesus' exclamation of "why didst Thou forsake me?," *when the Spirit that had been with him since the baptism, departed him on the cross*?

CHAPTER SIX

THE REIGN OF GOD and THE HARVEST

THE REIGN OF GOD

What is frequently translated as the "kingdom of God" or the "kingdom of heaven" is instead "the reign of God" in a literal translation (*Young's Literal Translation*) of the texts. This phrase is repeatedly used and even Jesus speaks of the "reign of God." But what does he mean? If the universe is energetic, what constitutes the kingdom of heaven, or the reign of God, that which is higher energetically? Jesus speaks of a harvest and first fruits. But what are they?

Many Jews expected the Messiah to be a warrior king and lead them to victory. But they wanted victory *in* this world and Jesus tried to help them achieve victory *over* this world, where one would not need to be subject to lessons anymore, and instead graduate to a higher existence. Per the texts as previously shown, achieving this victory makes one a child, or son of God, a higher existence possible for each of us.

Consider Matthew 5:43-48, YLT.

> 43 'Ye heard that it was said: Thou shalt love thy neighbour, and shalt hate thine enemy; 44but I—I say to you, Love your enemies, bless those cursing you, do good to those hating you, and pray for those accusing you falsely, and persecuting you, ***45that ye may be sons of your Father in the heavens***, because His sun He doth cause to rise on evil and good, and

> He doth send rain on righteous and unrighteous.
> 46 'For, if ye may love those loving you, what
> reward have ye? do not also the tax-gatherers the
> same? 47and if ye may salute your brethren only,
> what do ye abundant? do not also the tax-gatherers
> so? 48ye shall therefore be perfect, as your Father
> who *is* in the heavens is perfect. (Emphasis added.)

See also Luke 18:18-30, YLT.

> 18 And a certain ruler questioned him, saying,
> 'Good teacher, what having done—shall I inherit life
> age-during?' 19And Jesus said to him, ***'Why me dost***
> ***thou call good? no one is good, except One—God***;
> 20the commands thou hast known: Thou mayest not
> commit adultery, Thou mayest do no murder, Thou
> mayest not steal, Thou mayest not bear false witness,
> Honour thy father and thy mother.' 21And he said,
> 'All these I did keep from my youth;' 22and having
> heard these things, Jesus said to him, 'Yet one thing
> to thee is lacking; all things—as many as thou
> hast—sell, and distribute to the poor, and thou shalt
> have treasure in heaven, and come, be following
> me;' 23and he, having heard these things, became
> very sorrowful, for he was exceeding rich. 24And
> Jesus having seen him become very sorrowful, said,
> 'How hardly shall those having riches enter into the
> reign of God! 25for it is easier for a camel through
> the eye of a needle to enter, than for a rich man into
> the reign of God to enter.' 26And those who heard,
> said, 'And who is able to be saved?' 27and he said,
> 'The things impossible with men are possible with
> God.' 28And Peter said, 'Lo, we left all, and did

follow thee;' [29]and he said to them, 'Verily I say to you, that there is not one who left house, or parents, or brothers, or wife, or children, for the sake of the reign of God, [30]who may not receive back manifold more ***in this time, and in the coming age, life age-during***.' (Emphasis added.)

See Acts 13:34–37, YLT.

[34] 'And that He did raise him up **<u>out</u>** of the dead, ***no more <u>to return</u> to corruption***, he hath said thus—I will give to you the faithful kindnesses of David; [35]wherefore also in another *place* he saith, Thou shalt not give Thy kind One to see corruption, [36]for David, indeed, his own generation having served by the will of God, **did fall asleep**, and was added unto his fathers, **and saw corruption**, [37]**but he whom God did raise up, did not see corruption**. (Emphasis added.)

Why should the scripture read, "*no more* to return corruption" if death were a one-time event?

See also Acts 13:38-41, YLT.

[38] 'Let it therefore be known to you, men, brethren, that *through this one to you is the forgiveness of sins declared,* [39]*and from all things from which ye were not able in the law of Moses to be declared righteous, in this one every one who is believing is declared righteous*; (Emphasis added.)

The Greek word translated as "forgiveness" [of sins], Greek Concordance number 859, *aphesis*, can also be translated as "deliverance" [from sins], and can denote a release of a debt or obligation. This does not state that absolution is achieved for all *future* wrongs as well. Jesus himself told us repeatedly that everyone reaps what they sow. Through "this one" the way to "deliverance" from "debts and obligations" is "declared."

See Acts 13:46-50, YLT.

> [46]And speaking boldly, Paul and Barnabas said,
> 'To you it was necessary that first the word of God
> be spoken, and seeing ye do thrust it away, and do
> not judge yourselves ***worthy of the life age-during***,
> ***lo, we do turn to the nations***; [47]for so hath the Lord
> commanded us: I have set thee for a light of
> nations—for thy being for salvation unto the end of
> the earth.' [48]And the nations hearing were glad, and
> were glorifying the word of the Lord, and ***did***
> ***believe—as many as were appointed to life age-***
> ***during***; [49]and the word of the Lord was spread
> abroad through all the region. (Emphasis added.)

The good news or gospel is the way to overcome/master the cycle of death and rebirth that yields a life without death in the next age, graduation to a higher existence, at a higher energetic frequency. What does it mean that "many" "were appointed to life age-during"? Did some of the listeners achieve a state where they were no longer required to reincarnate, a higher frequency, compatible with a higher existence?

See Luke 9:26–27, YLT.

> [26] 'For whoever may be ashamed of me, and of my
> words, of this one shall the Son of Man be ashamed,

> when he may come in his glory, and the Father's, and the holy messengers'; [27]and I say to you, truly, there are certain of those here standing, who ***shall not taste of death till they may see the reign of God***.' (Emphasis added.)

What can Jesus mean by some 'shall not taste of death till they may *see* the reign of God'? In *Young's Literal Translation*, Luke 17:21 has Jesus saying that "the reign of God is within you."

See Luke 17:20-21, YLT.

> [20] And having been questioned by the Pharisees, when the reign of God doth come, he answered them, and said, 'The reign of God doth not come with observation; [21]nor shall they say, Lo, here; or lo, there; for lo, ***the reign of God is within you***.' (Emphasis added.)

See also Matthew 16:27-28, YLT.

> [27] 'For, *the* ***Son of Man is about to come in the glory of his Father, with his messengers****, and then he will reward each,* **according to his work**. [28]Verily I say to you, *there are certain of those standing here who shall not taste of death* ***till they may see the Son of Man coming in his reign***.'

What does Jesus mean for "each" to be rewarded "according to his work?" Doesn't this sound like the parable of the talents?

See Acts 17:24–33, YLT.

> 24 'God, who did make the world, and all things in it, this One, of heaven and of earth being Lord, in temples made with hands doth not dwell, 25 neither by the hands of men is He served—needing anything, ***He giving to all life, and breath, and all things***; 26 *He made also of one blood every nation of men*, to dwell upon all the face of the earth—having ordained times before appointed, and the bounds of their dwellings— 27 ***to seek the Lord, if perhaps they did feel after Him and find,—though, indeed, He is not far from each one of us, 28 for in Him we live, and move, and are***; as also certain of your poets have said: ***For of Him also we are offspring***.
>
> 29 'Being, therefore, offspring of God, we ought not to think the Godhead to be like to gold, or silver, or stone, graving of art and device of man; 30 the times, indeed, therefore, of the ignorance God having overlooked, doth now command all men everywhere to reform, ***31 because He did set a day in which He is about to judge the world*** in righteousness, by a man whom He did ordain, having given assurance to all, having raised him ***<u>out</u>*** of the dead.'
>
> 32 ***And having heard of a rising again of the dead, some, indeed, were mocking***, but others said, 'We will hear thee again concerning this;' 33 and so Paul went forth from the midst of them (Emphasis added).

According to the author of Acts, not only is God the Source of all life, living and moving in him, but *every nation of man* is also "of one blood," to "seek the lord," and "feel after Him and find" though "He is not far from each one of us." "For of Him also we are offspring." This text confirms a kinship and relationship to God beyond creed, nationality, or religion, which under the law of reincarnation could and would change from lifetime to lifetime, experience to experience. This text makes clear the way out of the cycle is not driven by, or dependent upon, religion.

Even at the time of the teaching some *mocked* the teaching of reincarnation, a necessary precept to understanding 'a rising *out'* of the cycle. Paul defends himself to Festus by defending belief in reincarnation – the rising again of the dead.

See Acts 26:4-8, YLT.

> [4] 'The manner of my life then, indeed, from youth—which from the beginning was among my nation, in Jerusalem—know do all the Jews, [5]knowing me before from the first, (if they may be willing to testify,) that after the most exact sect of our worship, *I lived a Pharisee*; [6]and now for the hope of the promise made to the fathers by God, I have stood judged, [7]to which our twelve tribes, intently night and day serving, do hope to come, concerning which hope I am accused, king Agrippa, by the Jews; [8]***why is it judged incredible with you, if God doth raise the dead?*** (Emphasis added.)

See also Acts 26:21-23, YLT.

> [21]because of these things the Jews—having caught me in the temple—were endeavouring to kill *me.*
>
> [22]'Having obtained, therefore, help from God, till this day, I have stood witnessing both to small and to

great, saying nothing besides the things that both the prophets and Moses spake of as about to come, [23]that the Christ is to suffer, whether first by a rising from the dead, he is about to proclaim light to the people and to the nations.'
(Emphasis added.)

Verse 23 states "whether first by a rising from the dead." The Greek text actually shows "ex anastaseōs" for what is translated as "rising from" which literally means, as we have seen, "out from" those "rising."

THE HARVEST

Jesus related the "next age" in his teaching about achieving life, without death, to a timing factor he repeatedly referred to as a "harvest." As harvests are seasonal and cyclical, Jesus' use of this term suggests there will eventually be another age, and harvest. The term eternity is not used by Jesus.

See Matthew 9:35-38, YLT.

> [35] And Jesus was going up and down all the cities and the villages, teaching in their synagogues, and proclaiming the good news of the reign, and healing every sickness and every malady among the people. [36]And having seen the multitudes, he was moved with compassion for them, that they were faint and cast aside, as sheep not having a shepherd, [37]then saith he to his disciples, 'The harvest indeed *is* abundant, but the workmen few; [38]beseech ye therefore the Lord of the harvest, that he may put forth workmen to His harvest.'

See Luke 10:1-5, YLT.

> 1 And after these things, the Lord did appoint also other seventy, and sent them by twos before his face, to every city and place whither he himself was about to come, 2 then said he unto them, ‘The harvest indeed *is* abundant, but the workmen few; beseech ye then the Lord of the harvest, that He may put forth workmen to His harvest.
>
> 3 ‘Go away; lo, I send you forth as lambs in the midst of wolves; 4 carry no bag, no scrip, nor sandals; and salute no one on the way; 5 and into whatever house ye do enter, first say, Peace to this house; 6 and if indeed there may be there the son of peace, rest on it shall your peace; and if not so, upon you it shall turn back.

See John 4:31-38, YLT.

> 31 And in the meanwhile his disciples were asking him, saying, ‘Rabbi, eat;’ 32 and he said to them, ‘I have food to eat that ye have not known.’ 33 The disciples then said one to another, ‘Did any one bring him anything to eat?’ 34 Jesus saith to them, ‘My food is, that I may do the will of Him who sent me, and may finish His work; 35 do not say that it is yet four months, and the harvest cometh; lo, I say to you, Lift up your eyes, and see the fields, that they are white unto harvest already.
>
> 36 ‘And he who is reaping doth receive a reward, and doth gather fruit to life age-during, that both he who is sowing and he who is reaping may rejoice

> together; [37]for in this the saying is the true one, that one is the sower and another the reaper. [38]I sent you to reap that on which ye have not laboured; others laboured, and ye into their labour have entered.

Lest anyone should think that the scriptures are all literal, and intended to be so, we are very clearly told that Jesus uses figurative devices in his teaching – symbols, similes and metaphors.

See Matthew 13:24-30, YLT.

> [24]*Another simile* he set before them, saying: 'The reign of the heavens was likened to a man sowing good seed in his field, [25]and, while men are sleeping, his enemy came and sowed darnel in the midst of the wheat, and went away, [26]and when the herb sprang up, and yielded fruit, then appeared also the darnel.
>
> [27]'And the servants of the householder, having come near, said to him, Sir, good seed didst thou not sow in thy field? whence then hath it the darnel? [28]And he saith to them, A man, an enemy, did this; and the servants said to him, Wilt thou, then, *that* having gone away we may gather it up?
>
> [29]'And he said, No, lest—gathering up the darnel—ye root up with it the wheat, [30]suffer both to grow together till the harvest, and in the time of the harvest I will say to the reapers, Gather up first the darnel, and bind it in bundles, to burn it, and the wheat gather up into my storehouse.' (Emphasis added.)

All are sowing, then sleeping, and their sowing yields

results - some useful, some not. These will be separated at the time of harvest. All are subject to the harvest, but only some will rise to a higher existence in the next age, depending upon their alignment.

See Galatians 6:7-10, YLT.

> [7]***Be not led astray; God is not mocked; for what a man may sow—that also he shall reap***, [8]***because he who is sowing to his own flesh, of the flesh shall reap corruption; and he who is sowing to the Spirit, of the Spirit shall reap life age-during***; [9]and in the doing good we may not be faint-hearted, ***for <u>at the proper time we shall reap</u>—not desponding***; [10]therefore, then, as we have opportunity, may we work the good to all, and especially unto those of the household of the faith. (Emphasis added.)

Although it may seem like sowing good (as judged by God) goes unrewarded, "at the proper time we shall reap – not desponding." Even though it may not appear to you that you – and others – are in fact reaping what you sow, "Be not led astray; God is not mocked." Everyone will reap what they sow eventually, in God's time.

Jesus spoke of a "harvest" at the "next age" over two thousand years ago to help souls understand the full import and effect of their thoughts, words, deeds and intentions. What is in your heart is as powerful as your deeds. These are all energy, frequency, and vibration that resonate in the energetic field of the universe. The universe recognizes the frequency emitted by each person, be it low or high, and responds accordingly, with circumstances and environment aligning with the frequency each of us emits. Low frequencies, which may consist of things such as hate, jealousy, deceit, manipulation, or ill-intent, will have the universe deliver a matching frequency external environment and circumstances. High frequencies, which may consist of gratitude, love, truth, and truth in how you present yourself, or authenticity, will have the universe likewise deliver an outer reality that matches and aligns with the energy of that inner reality. As within so without. If you wish your external environment to change, an internal shift must occur and it must occur on a frequency level that will align with the circumstances you wish to have. You receive what you are, not what you want. *You attract what you emit.* According to Jesus, God is within, and you not only have the power to create your own reality, *you are in fact already doing it whether you realize it or not*. Maintaining a reality based in a particular frequency requires not only achieving that frequency but also maintaining that frequency in order to maintain the circumstances that match or align with that frequency. When can we expect the harvest?

What if the next age is upon us, now. What if the harvest is now? What frequency do each of us embody?

CHAPTER SEVEN

RABBINICAL TEACHING AND UNIVERSAL RESTORATION

Custom and tradition held that some teachings remained hidden and were passed down orally, as opposed to those revealed, or written down. Furthermore, there was also a tradition of hidden teachings being allegorical and told in parable with multiple levels of meanings. These teachings were believed to hold great value and were not for the spiritually uninitiated, but for the more advanced student. The parables were meant to offer simplistic teachings for the novices with deeper meanings explained orally in rabbinic fashion to more advanced students. There is evidence in the Bible that Jesus utilized this approach and explained things to his disciples apart from the crowds. Reincarnation does have historic roots in Judaism. Jewish mystics, followers of the Kabbalah, Jewish secret teachings, did (and do) believe in reincarnation. Hasidic Jews believe in reincarnation. There may well have been a need to record teachings that had earlier been held orally after the destruction of the Temple by the Romans in 70 A.D. Christian Gnostics, followers of Christ who lived and wrote after Jesus' crucifixion, believed in reincarnation. Gnostic texts, among others, were suppressed by the early church.

In fact, many early church leaders believed in reincarnation and even in the concept of universal reconciliation. Universal reconciliation allows that the development of the soul is through reincarnation until the soul eventually develops sufficiently for the purpose of reunification with God and that all souls are intended for reunification. This concept holds there is no hell or permanent state of punishment. This was known as Universalism, or universal salvation. Evidence for the idea of universal reconciliation can be found in scripture.

See Acts 3:19-26, NRSV.

> [19] Repent therefore, and turn to God so that your sins may be wiped out, [20] so that times of refreshing may come from the presence of the Lord, and that he may send the Messiah[g] appointed for you, that is, Jesus, [21] who must remain in heaven ***until the time of universal restoration*** that God announced long ago through his holy prophets. [22] Moses said, 'The Lord your God will raise up for you from your own people[h] a prophet like me. You must listen to whatever he tells you. [23] And it will be that everyone who does not listen to that prophet will be utterly rooted out of the people.' [24] And all the prophets, as many as have spoken, from Samuel and those after him, also predicted these days. [25] You are the descendants of the prophets and of the covenant that God gave to your ancestors, saying to Abraham, 'And in your descendants all the families of the earth shall be blessed.' [26] When God raised up his servant,[i] he sent him first to you, to bless you by turning each of you from your wicked ways." (Emphasis added.)

---

[g] Or *the Christ*

[h] Gk *brothers*

[i] Or *child*

Note not only the phrase "until the time of universal restoration," but also that the Messiah is clearly a man, a "prophet like me."

This suggests not only did we begin/come from God, but so too did all of creation. See the literal translation of the above verse (Acts 3:21, YLT).

> [21]whom it behoveth heaven, indeed, to receive till times of a *restitution of all things* (Emphasis added.)

The Greek word translated here as "restitution" is *apokatastasis* Strong's Greek Concordance No. 605 and its meaning is shown as "restitution, reestablishment, restoration."

See 1 Tim. 2:3-7, NSRV.

> [3] This is right and is acceptable in the sight of God our Savior, [4] who desires ***everyone*** to be saved and to come to the knowledge of the truth. [5] For there is one God; there is also one mediator between God and humankind, Christ Jesus, ***himself human***,
> [6] who gave himself a ransom for all —this was attested at the right time. [7] For this I was appointed a herald and an apostle (I am telling the truth,[a] I am not lying), a teacher of the Gentiles in faith and truth. (Emphasis added.)

See 1 Timothy 2:1-8, YLT.

> [1] I exhort, then, first of all, there be made supplications, prayers, intercessions, thanksgivings,

---

[a] Other ancient authorities add *in Christ*

> for all men: 2for kings, and all who are in authority, that a quiet and peaceable life we may lead in all piety and gravity, 3for this *is* right and acceptable before God our Saviour, 4***who doth will all men to be saved***, and to come to the full knowledge of the truth; 5for one *is* God, one also *is* mediator of God and of men, ***the man Christ Jesus***, 6***who did give himself a ransom for all—the testimony in its own times***— 7in regard to which I was set a preacher and apostle—truth I say in Christ, I do not lie—a teacher of nations, in faith and truth. 8I wish, therefore, that men pray in every place, lifting up kind hands, apart from anger and reasoning. (Emphasis added.)

This scripture affirms Jesus is a man who gave himself as a ransom. The New Testament, as canonized, is written in Greek, not Aramaic, or even Hebrew. Were Greek Christians less knowledgeable about rabbinical teaching style? Issues regarding differences in language have been a contributing factor in how the greater meaning of some of the scriptures may have been lost, or purposefully exploited, in order to suppress the true nature of our energetic souls within an energetic universe.

The destruction of Jerusalem in 70 A.D. could not have helped this difficulty. Earlier versions of the gospels that may have been written in Hebrew or Aramaic may have been destroyed, secreted, or suppressed. It may be the case that with the influx of non-Jewish Christians came a growing reliance on written texts versus the practice of oral teachings - secret teachings - reserved for advanced students.

Over time, certain teachings appear to have been lost, or too little appreciated. The presence of evidence in the written texts of further teachings, oral teachings, and secret teachings certainly confirms that Jesus used this method. In that case, Jesus’ words of instruction to those closest to him, to his “advanced” students are particularly meaningful.

There is evidence that Jesus’ teachings were purposefully two-fold. There was one set of teachings for the masses, and secret teachings for those more advanced. The masses were uninitiated, and they received the parables. But the scriptures indicate that those who were able to receive more advanced teachings, received them, and clearly the passages showing Jesus’ revelations to the disciples demonstrate the presence of more advanced teachings. The Bible contains references that support these differences in teaching style to different groups.

Jesus’ teachings must have also included more advanced information. Otherwise he wouldn’t have had nor needed any of the private explanations given separately from what he spoke publicly as noted in the texts.

See Mark 4:3-34, YLT.

> 3‘Hearken, lo, the sower went forth to sow; 4and it
> came to pass, in the sowing, some fell by the way,
> and the fowls of the heaven did come and devour it;
> 5and other fell upon the rocky ground, where it had
> not much earth, and immediately it sprang forth,
> because of not having depth of earth, 6and the sun
> having risen, it was scorched, and because of not
> having root it did wither; 7and other fell toward the
> thorns, and the thorns did come up, and choke it, and
> fruit it gave not; 8and other fell to the good ground,
> and was giving fruit, coming up and increasing, and
> it bare, one thirty-fold, and one sixty, and one an
> hundred.’ 9And he said to them, ‘He who is having

ears to hear—let him hear.' [10]***And when he was
alone, those about him, with the twelve, did ask him
of the simile, [11]and he said to them, 'To you it hath
been given to know the secret of the reign of God,
but to those who are without, in similes are all the
things done***; [12]that seeing they may see and not
perceive, and hearing they may hear and not
understand, lest they may turn, and the sins may be
forgiven them.' [13]And he saith to them, 'Have ye not
known this simile? and how shall ye know all the
similes? [14]He who is sowing doth sow the word;
[15]and these are they by the way where the word is
sown: and whenever they may hear, immediately
cometh the Adversary, and he taketh away the word
that hath been sown in their hearts.

[16] 'And these are they, in like manner, who on the
rocky ground are sown: who, whenever they may
hear the word, immediately with joy do receive it,
[17]and have not root in themselves, but are temporary;
afterward tribulation or persecution having come
because of the word, immediately they are stumbled.

[18] 'And these are they who toward the thorns are
sown: these are they who are hearing the word, [19]and
the anxieties of this age, and the deceitfulness of the
riches, and the desires concerning the other things,
entering in, choke the word, and it becometh
unfruitful.

[20] 'And these are they who on the good ground
have been sown: who do hear the word, and receive,
and do bear fruit, one thirty-fold, and one sixty, and
one an hundred.'

[21] And he said to them, 'Doth the lamp come that
under the measure it may be put, or under the

couch—not that it may be put on the lamp-stand? [22]for there is not anything hid that may not be manifested, nor was anything kept hid but that it may come to light. [23]***If any hath ears to hear—let him hear***.' [24]And he said to them, ***'Take heed what ye hear; in what measure ye measure, it shall be measured to you;*** and to you who hear it shall be added; [25]for whoever may have, there shall be given to him, and whoever hath not, also that which he hath shall be taken from him.' [26]And he said, '*Thus is the reign of God: as if a man may cast the seed on the earth, [27]and may sleep, and may rise night and day, and the seed spring up and grow, he hath not known how; [28]for of itself doth the earth bear fruit, first a blade, afterwards an ear, afterwards full corn in the ear; [29]and whenever the fruit may yield itself, immediately he doth send forth the sickle, because the harvest hath come.*' [30]And he said, 'To what may we liken the reign of God, or in what simile may we compare it? [31]As a grain of mustard, which, whenever it may be sown on the earth, is less than any of the seeds that are on the earth; [32]and whenever it may be sown, it cometh up, and doth become greater than any of the herbs, and doth make great branches, so that under its shade the fowls of the heaven are able to rest.' [33]***And with many such similes he was speaking to them the word, as they were able to hear, [34]and without a simile he was not speaking to them, and by themselves, to his disciples he was expounding all.*** (Emphasis added.)

This is proof enough that the teachings given in the canonical scripture are not necessarily literal and are not always given in full. They are given as the listeners are able to receive. This would appear to give what Jesus tells more knowledgeable listeners like the disciples, and even Nicodemus or other Pharisees, even greater importance. In Jesus' example, the man who sowed the seed *sleeps* (dies or is unconscious of the period between lives and of his prior lives in which he sowed the seed) and he knows not how the seed sprang up ***even though he himself had sown it***. What better definition of reincarnation can be given - as we sow, sleep, and rise and live again in circumstances we do not know the origin of, but which we ourselves have previously germinated. The parable illustrates the progress that may be made by successive lifetimes by comparing them to successive days in which, progressively, the blade, ear, and then full corn emerges. Telling too, are the terms Jesus uses, which mirror the phrases regarding what you sow, you will reap.

We are also told some followers are nourished by "milk" and others should be ready for "solid food."

Consider Hebrews 5:10-14, YLT.

> [10] Having been addressed by God a chief priest, according to the order of Melchisedek, [11]concerning whom we have much discourse and of hard explanation to say, since ye have become dull of hearing, [12]for even owing to be teachers, because of the time, again ye have need that one teach you what *are* the elements of the beginning of the oracles of God, and ye have become having need of milk, and not of strong food, [13]for every one who is partaking of milk *is* unskilled in the word of righteousness—for he is an infant, [14]and of perfect men is the strong food, who because of the use are having the senses

exercised, unto the discernment both of good and of evil.

See Luke 8:1-18, YLT.

1 And it came to pass thereafter, that he was going
through every city and village, ***preaching and
proclaiming good news <u>of the reign of God</u>***, and the
twelve *are* with him, 2and certain women, who were
healed of evil spirits and infirmities, Mary who is
called Magdalene, from whom seven demons had
gone forth, 3and Joanna wife of Chuza, steward of
Herod, and Susanna, and many others, who were
ministering to him from their substance.
4 And a great multitude having gathered, and
those who from city and city were coming unto him,
he spake by a simile: 5'The sower went forth to sow
his seed, and in his sowing some indeed fell beside
the way, and it was trodden down, and the fowls of
the heaven did devour it.
6 'And other fell upon the rock, and having
sprung up, it did wither, through not having
moisture.
7'And other fell amidst the thorns, and the thorns
having sprung up with it, did choke it.
8'And other fell upon the good ground, and
having sprung up, it made fruit an hundred fold.'
These things saying, he was calling, 'He having ears
to hear—let him hear.' 9And his disciples were
questioning him, saying, 'What may this simile be?'
10And he said, '***To you it hath been given to know
<u>the secrets of the reign of God</u>, and <u>to the rest in
similes</u>***; that seeing they may not see, and hearing

they may not understand.

[11] 'And this is the simile: The seed is the word of God, [12]and those beside the way are those hearing, then cometh the Devil, and taketh up the word from their heart, lest having believed, they may be saved.

[13] 'And those upon the rock: They who, when they may hear, with joy do receive the word, and these have no root, who for a time believe, and in time of temptation fall away.

[14] 'And that which fell to the thorns: These are they who have heard, and going forth, through anxieties, and riches, and pleasures of life, are choked, and bear not to completion.

[15] 'And that in the good ground: These are they, who in an upright and good heart, having heard the word, do retain *it*, and bear fruit in continuance.

[16] 'And no one having lighted a lamp doth cover it with a vessel, or under a couch doth put *it*; but upon a lamp-stand he doth put *it*, that those coming in may see the light, [17]for nothing is secret, that shall not become manifest, nor hid, that shall not be known, and become manifest.

[18] 'See, therefore, how ye hear, for whoever may have, there shall be given to him, and whoever may not have, also what he seemeth to have, shall be taken from him.' (Emphasis added.)

Not only is the parable explained to the disciples, but also a cautionary declaration, "nothing is secret, that shall not become manifest, nor hid, that shall not be known." The word repeatedly translated as "secrets" is mustérion, Strong's Greek Concordance number 3466, translated as "mysteries" in the literal translation.

Jesus himself gave some explanation of why he gave two approaches to teaching.

See Matthew 13:10-23, YLT.

> [10]And the disciples having come near, said to him, 'Wherefore ***in similes*** dost thou speak to them?' [11]And he answering said to them that—'To you it hath been given to know the secrets of the reign of the heavens, and to these it hath not been given, [12]for whoever hath, it shall be given to him, and he shall have overabundance, and whoever hath not, even that which he hath shall be taken from him.
>
> [13]***'Because of this, in similes do I speak to them, because seeing they do not see, and hearing they do not hear, nor understand,*** [14]and fulfilled on them is the prophecy of Isaiah, that saith, With hearing ye shall hear, and ye shall not understand, and seeing ye shall see, and ye shall not perceive, [15]for made gross was the heart of this people, and with the ears they heard heavily, and their eyes they did close, lest they might see with the eyes, and with the ears might hear, and with the heart understand, and turn back, and I might heal them.
>
> [16] 'And happy are your eyes because they see, and your ears because they hear, [17]for verily I say to you, that many prophets and righteous men did desire to see that which ye look on, and they did not see, and to hear that which ye hear, and they did not hear.
>
> [18] 'Ye, therefore, hear ye the simile of the sower: [19]Every one hearing the word of the reign, and not understanding—the evil one doth come, and doth catch that which hath been sown in his heart; this is

that sown by the way.

[20] 'And that sown on the rocky places, this is he who is hearing the word, and immediately with joy is receiving it, [21]and he hath not root in himself, but is temporary, and persecution or tribulation having happened because of the word, immediately he is stumbled.

[22] 'And that sown toward the thorns, this is he who is hearing the word, and the anxiety of this age, and the deceitfulness of the riches, do choke the word, and it becometh unfruitful.

[23] 'And that sown on the good ground: this is he who is hearing the word, and is understanding, who indeed doth bear fruit, and doth make, some indeed a hundredfold, and some sixty, and some thirty.' (Emphasis added.)

How many of us fail to see and hear today? How many of us today would only rate instruction by parable if Jesus were here today, despite the modern convenience of widespread literacy and access to scripture and historical commentary and research?

Consider Matthew 7:1, YLT.

> [1]'Judge not, that ye may not be judged, [2]for in what judgment ye judge, ye shall be judged, and in what measure ye measure, it shall be measured to you.

We receive the judgment, condemnation, or mercy that we give to others through the lessons of reincarnation, attracting the same energy and intention that we emit. We are met by circumstances and experiences of the same frequency that we are, which determines the course of our life and which levels of creation we may occupy. This determination is by virtue of automatic and energetic alignment. None of us can occupy, inhabit, or experience levels of creation with which we are incompatible, much like the same ends of a magnet repel one another and cannot be joined as they do not attract one another.

> 3 'And why dost thou behold the mote that *is* in thy brother's eye, and the beam that *is* in thine own eye dost not consider? 4 or, how wilt thou say to thy brother, Suffer I may cast out the mote from thine eye, and lo, the beam *is* in thine own eye?
> 5 Hypocrite, cast out first the beam out of thine own eye, and then thou shalt see clearly to cast out the mote out of thy brother's eye

We do better to work on ourselves and work toward improvement than to judge our brother.

> 6 'Ye may not give that which is *holy* to the dogs, nor cast your pearls before the swine, that they may not trample them among their feet, and having turned—may rend you.

If we do get to a point where we can help others advance, only attempt to do so where they are ready to receive the assistance and are seeking such assistance. Any attempts to force teaching violates free will and may result in attacks.

> 7 'Ask, and it shall be given to you; seek, and ye shall find; knock, and it shall be opened to you; 8 for

every one who is asking doth receive, and he who is seeking doth find, and to him who is knocking it shall be opened.

This is how growth is achieved. It is easier to find something when we seek, easier to learn when we ask. If we wish to know, a sincere heart will be lead to answers. This is the reason for the method of the parables. They are designed for listeners to ponder and question and seek a deeper meaning. If they do so, they will be led to greater knowledge.

9 'Or what man is of you, of whom, if his son may
ask a loaf—a stone will he present to him? 10and if a
fish he may ask—a serpent will he present to him?
11if, therefore, ye being evil, have known good gifts
to give to your children, how much more shall your
Father who *is* in the heavens give good things to
those asking him?

Ask, to receive; seek, to find.

12 'All things, therefore, whatever ye may will that
men may be doing to you, so also do to them, for
this is the law and the prophets.

Do unto others as we would have them do unto us. This is the seed to plant in order to yield a desirable outcome. We will (eventually) reap what we sow.

21 'Not every one who is saying to me Lord, lord,
shall come into the reign of the heavens; but he who
is doing the will of my Father who is in the heavens.

Doesn't this state that it is not enough to make an oral profession? Rather, it is what we actually do and practice that determines who comes into the reign. Jesus full well knows that many will listen and not hear and not realize their failure.

CHAPTER EIGHT

ILLUSORY CONTRADICTION IN SCRIPTURE

As has been seen in the foregoing, there is much contained in scripture that supports the teaching of reincarnation. Is there content in the text which appears to oppose reincarnation?

Hebrews contains a well-known passage that many would point to in order to refute the many and varied references to, and explanations of, reincarnation made by Jesus himself.

See Hebrews 9:23-28, NRSV.

> 23 Thus it was necessary for the sketches of the heavenly things to be purified with these rites, but the heavenly things themselves need better sacrifices than these. 24 For Christ did not enter a sanctuary made by human hands, a mere copy of the true one, but he entered into heaven itself, now to appear in the presence of God on our behalf. 25 Nor was it to offer himself again and again, as the high priest enters the Holy Place year after year with blood that is not his own; 26 for then he would have had to suffer again and again since the foundation of the world. But as it is, he has appeared once for all ***at the end of the age to remove sin*** by the sacrifice of himself. 27 ***And just as it is appointed for mortals to die once, and after that the judgment***, 28 so Christ, having been offered once to bear the sins of many, will appear a second time, not to deal with sin, but to

save those who are eagerly waiting for him. (Emphasis added.)

See also this same passage from *Young's Literal Translation*:

> [23] *It is* necessary, therefore, the pattern indeed of the things in the heavens to be purified with these, and the heavenly things themselves with better sacrifices than these; [24]for not into holy places made with hands did the Christ enter—figures of the true—but into the heaven itself, now to be manifested in the presence of God for us; [25]nor that he may many times offer himself, even as the chief priest doth enter into the holy places every year with blood of others; [26]since it had behooved him many times to suffer from the foundation of the world, ***but now once, at the full end of the ages, for putting away of sin through his sacrifice***, he hath been manifested; [27]***and as it is laid up to men once to die, and after this—judgment***, [28]so also the Christ, once having been offered to bear the sins of many, a second time, apart from a sin-offering, shall appear, to those waiting for him—to salvation! (Emphasis added.)

Why would this be in here? What does it really say? An important difference between the nonliteral translation and the literal translation has to do with the word order in the most pertinent sentence as shown in *Young's Literal Translation* below.

Let us compare the nonliteral (NSRV) and literal (YLT) translations.

The YLT states-

and as it is laid up to men <u>once to die</u>, and after this—judgment

-and the NRSV states-

And just as it is appointed for mortals <u>to die once</u>, and after that the judgment.

Consider the difference between "men once to die," essentially "men once dead" versus "mortals to die once." The difference is essentially that between 'once you die, then judgment' versus 'mortals die once then the judgment.'

The difference is significant when the question is, do we die only once or more than once?

The Greek word translated as "once" is apax (hapax) and can actually mean "once and for all," not just a one and only time. It can mean the conclusive, last, time.

This verse is shown below with the Greek transliteration, along with the Strong's Greek Concordance numbers and concordance definitions.

Each Greek word is given a number in Strong's Greek Concordance which can then be consulted for the meaning of each Greek word/term. (The concordance also allows each word's use and occurrence in other scriptures to be catalogued.)

The Greek text is more fully defined, per Strong's Exhaustive Greek Concordance as follows:

(2532) kai - and, even,also

(2596) kath (kata) -	down from, against, according to, throughout, during;
(3745) oson (hosos) -	how much, how many,
(606) apokeitai (apokeimai) -	to be laid away, be laid up in store, reserved for
(3588) tois (ho, he, to) -	the
(444) anthropois (anthropos) -	man, mankind, the human race
(530) apax (hapax) -	once, once for all, (conclusively)
(599) apothanein (apothnesko) -	to die, dying, die, wither, decay (from "apo" (Strong's # 575) = "away from" and "thnesko" (Strong's # 2348) = "to die"), - yielding "die off/away from, a separation that goes with "dying off (away from)"

(3326) meta -	with, after ("*after* with"),
(1161) de -	but, and, now
(5124) touto -	this; he, she, it
(2920) krisis -	judging, judgment, decision, sentence; generally: divine judgment; accusation

Let us examine the Greek sentence again in light of full word definitions.

(And/even/ also) ("down from", throughout, during) (how much, how many) (be laid up in store, reserved for) (the) (mankind, human race) **(once for all, (conclusively))** (die off **(away from)**) (*with* ("*after* with") (but, and, now) (this/it) (judgment, decision) (Emphasis added.)

Or rather-

And during how many be reserved once (and) for all (the conclusive time) to die off (away from) the human race (mankind) after with now this judgment.

How can we die *the conclusive time* if we die only once? We can't, and the context suggests otherwise. How can we die "away from" the human race? Jesus says the conclusive death which occurs when we are harvested out of the cycle of death and rebirth yields messengers, heavenly beings, not men. The harvest yields a move away from men for those that are ready, or reserved, for such a change.

Greek grammar does not mirror English grammar. For context let us look at the preceding sentence again:

> [26]**since it had behoved him many times to suffer from the foundation of the world, but now *once, at the full end of the ages, for putting away of sin* through his sacrifice, he hath been manifested**; (Emphasis added.)

How had Jesus suffered *many times* from the foundation of the world if not through reincarnation? Look at this "once" given as "now once, at the full end of the ages," used not as a once and only occurrence but as a conclusive occurrence. What is the putting away of sin? Other scripture denotes that the sacrifice and ransom of Jesus was to redeem us from *past* sin. (See Romans 3:25, YLT, ***because of the passing over of the bygone sins*** in the ***forbearance*** of God.) Once Jesus died, did people err no more? Clearly not, sin, or error, did, and has, continued to occur. Jesus' life and teachings are the illustration of the way to graduate from the lessons of the reincarnation cycle. This cycle is driven by wrongful actions in an attempt to have us learn from meeting the experiences we have determined for ourselves through previous conduct and decisions.

Consider the following passage again.

> **since it behooved him** (Jesus) **many** (life)**times to suffer from the foundation of the world, but**

now once, at the full end of the ages, for putting away of (past) **sin through his sacrifice, he hath been manifested;**

Even during/throughout (the age) **how many** (of) **the human race** (mankind) **be reserved once for all to die away from** (the rest) **after this judgment.** (Clarification parentheticals and bolded emphasis added.)

How many of us have been reserved and judged as worthy to be separated out at the harvest? How many will remain subject to the law of reincarnation? How many will make the graduation?

The resurrection taught by Jesus from *out* of the dead has a timing element. One age ends and a new one begins and a harvest occurs. This passage does not confirm only one lifetime and negate reincarnation. It affirms that just as Jesus suffered and graduated out of the cycle, so will those who are reserved to do the same. This is what makes the teaching so relevant. Not only is there a timing element involved but the whole hope of those who rise again is in understanding the graduation out of the cycle to "a better resurrection." There is a reason why the very early followers of Jesus believed Jesus' resurrection to be a triumph over sin and death. The two are bound together in the reincarnation cycle and those followers understood that cycle to have been broken and overcome by Jesus.

If this still seems unconvincing, look at the book of Hebrews itself, in which the following passages appear.

See Hebrews 1:4–6, YLT.

[4] Having become so much better than the

> messengers, as he did inherit a more excellent name than they. [5]For to which of the messengers said He ever, 'My Son thou art—**I to-day have begotten thee?**' and again, 'I will be to him for a father, and he shall be to Me for a son?' [6]and when again He may bring in the **first-born** to the world (Emphasis added.)

See also Hebrews 2:10–12, YLT.

> [10] For it was becoming to Him, because of whom *are* the all things, and through whom *are* the all things, **many sons to glory bringing**, **the author of their salvation through sufferings to make perfect**, [11]**for both he who is sanctifying and those sanctified *are* all of one**, for which cause ***he is not ashamed to call them brethren***, [12]saying, 'I will declare Thy name to my brethren (Emphasis added.)

Consider Hebrews 2:14–18, YLT.

> [14] Seeing, then, the children have partaken of flesh and blood, he himself also in like manner did take part of the same, **that through death he might destroy him having the power of death**—that is, the devil— [15]**and might deliver those, whoever, with fear of death, throughout all their life, were subjects of bondage**, [16]for, doubtless, of messengers it doth not lay hold, but of seed of Abraham it layeth hold, [17]wherefore it did behove him in all things to be made like to the brethren, **that he might become a kind and stedfast chief-priest in the things with God**, to make propitiation for the sins of the people,

[18]for in that he suffered, himself being tempted, he is able to help those who are tempted. (Emphasis added.)

See Hebrews 3:1–6, YLT.

[1] Wherefore, holy brethren, partakers of a heavenly calling, consider ***the apostle and chief priest*** of our profession, Christ Jesus, [2]being stedfast to Him who did appoint him, as also Moses in all his house, [3]for of more glory than Moses hath this one been counted worthy, inasmuch as more honour than the house hath he who doth build it, [4]for every house is builded by some one, and He who the all things did build *is* God, [5]and Moses indeed *was* stedfast in all his house, as an attendant, for a testimony of those things that were to be spoken, [6]and Christ, as a Son over his house, whose house are we, if the boldness and the rejoicing of the hope unto the end we hold fast. (Emphasis added.)

Here Jesus is called "the apostle and chief priest." One who is God himself is not an apostle or chief priest. Jesus is also compared to Moses, another prophet, a man. This scripture goes on to say Jesus, our chief priest, has lived as we have and can sympathize with us.

See Hebrews 5:1–9, YLT.

[1]For every chief priest—*out of men taken*—in behalf of men is set in things *pertaining* to God, that he may offer both gifts and sacrifices for sins, [2]able to be gentle to those ignorant and going astray, *since himself also is compassed with infirmity*; [3]and

> because of this infirmity he ought, as for the people, so also for himself to offer for sins; [4]and no one to himself doth take the honour, but he who is called by God, *as also Aaron*: [5]so also the Christ did not glorify himself to become chief priest, but He who spake unto him: 'My Son thou art, I to-day have begotten thee;'
>
> [6]as also in another *place* He saith, ***'Thou art a priest—to the age, according to the order of Melchisedek***;' [7]who in the days of his flesh both prayers and supplications unto Him who was able to save him from death—with strong crying and tears—having offered up, and having been heard in respect to that which he feared, ***[8]through being a Son, did learn by the things which he suffered—the obedience, [9]and having been made perfect, he did become to all those obeying him a cause of salvation age-during***. (Emphasis added except for "*pertaining*" in verse 1.)

Note that Jesus is a *cause* of salvation "age-during" at the harvest, to those who obeyed (not those just *professing* faith). The profession of faith has become distorted. Faith in Jesus and his teaching is supremely important as it was meant as the goal and a representation of the means to triumph over death. But that faith has been distorted to be the means itself, without the achievement of acting in harmony with that faith.

Every "chief priest" (including Jesus) is "out of men taken." Every chief priest (including Jesus) is "compassed with infirmity" and ought to offer for sins *of himself* and others. "I today have begotten thee" my Son. Today. When was that? Thou art a priest – ***to the age*** like Melchisedek, who..., ***through being a Son, did learn by the things which he suffered—the obedience, [9]and having been made perfect, he did become to all those obeying him a cause of salvation age-during***.

Just as Melchisedek was a chief priest to the age, Jesus is a chief priest to the age. Melchisedek also suffered (through reincarnation) and learned obedience, "having been made perfect" and became a Son.

See Hebrews 5:10–14, YLT.

> [10] Having been addressed by God a chief priest, according to the order of Melchisedek, [11]concerning whom we have much discourse and of hard explanation to say, since ye have become dull of hearing, [12]for even owing to be teachers, because of the time, again ye have need that one teach you what *are* the elements of the beginning of the oracles of God, and ye have become having need of milk, and not of strong food, [13]for every one who is partaking of milk *is* unskilled in the word of righteousness—for he is an infant, [14]and of perfect men is the strong food, who because of the use are having the senses exercised, unto the discernment both of good and of evil.

Are you content with milk, or are you trying to discern the strong food?

Consider Hebrews 6:1–8, YLT.

> [1]Wherefore, having left ***the word of the beginning of the Christ, <u>unto the perfection we may advance</u>, not again a foundation laying of reformation from dead works, and of faith on God,***

> [2]***of the teaching of baptisms, of laying on also of hands, of rising again also of the dead, and of judgment age-during***, [3]and this we will do, if God may permit, [4]for *it is* impossible for those once enlightened, having tasted also of the heavenly gift, and partakers having became of the Holy Spirit, [5]and did taste the good saying of God, the powers also of the coming age, [6]and having fallen away, again to renew *them* to reformation, having crucified again to themselves the Son of God, and exposed to public shame. [7]For earth, that is drinking in the rain many times coming upon it, and is bringing forth herbs fit for those because of whom also it is dressed, doth partake of blessing from God, [8]and that which is bearing thorns and briers *is* disapproved of, and nigh to cursing, whose end *is* for burning. (Emphasis added.)

The passage above states that the teaching of Jesus is the beginning ("having left the word of the beginning of the Christ"). We may ***advance*** into improvement ("unto the perfection we may advance"). The growing period closes and the harvest is at hand. We will become "herbs" that are "fit" or "thorns and briars" that are "disapproved of."

See Hebrews 6:9-20, YLT.

> [9] And we are persuaded, concerning you, beloved, the things that are better, and accompanying salvation, though even thus we speak, [10]*for God is not unrighteous to forget your work, and the labour of the love, that ye shewed to His name, having ministered to the saints and ministering;* [11]*and we desire each one of you the same diligence to shew,*

> *unto the full assurance of the hope unto the end, [12]that ye may not become slothful, but followers of those who through faith and patient endurance are inheriting the promises.* [13]For to Abraham God, having made promise, seeing He was able to swear by no greater, did swear by Himself, [14]saying, 'Blessing indeed I will bless thee, and multiplying I will multiply thee;' [15]and so, having patiently endured, he did obtain the promise; [16]for men indeed do swear by the greater, and an end of all controversy to them for confirmation *is* the oath, [17]in which God, more abundantly willing to shew to the heirs of the promise the immutability of his counsel, did interpose by an oath, [18]that through two immutable things, in which *it is* impossible for God to lie, a strong comfort we may have who did flee for refuge to lay hold on the hope set before *us*, [19]which we have, as an anchor of the soul, both sure and stedfast, and entering into that within the vail, ***[20]whither a forerunner for us did enter—Jesus, after the order of Melchisedek chief priest having become—to the age***. (Emphasis added.)

Your previous good works in previous lifetimes are given credit, are not forgotten by God. You must continue to show diligence, and through patience and faith you will inherit the promise. You can be assured of this because Jesus, a forerunner for us, did enter, having become chief-priest to the age.

The passage in Hebrews, Chapter Nine, has to do with sacrifice and that Jesus, having died his conclusive human death, in a manner, will not have to do so again. The following line from YLT Hebrews 9:27 is part of a larger context and reads as follows: "[27]and as it is laid up to men once to die, and after this—judgment, [28]so also the Christ, once having been offered to bear the sins of many, a second time, apart from a sin-offering, shall appear, to those waiting for him—to salvation!" The book is directed toward Hebrews, who, according to the practice of their religion are used to repeated, yearly sacrifices. Jesus came to light the way, to demonstrate the way out of the cycle. Having done so, he will not have to make that personal sacrifice to accomplish the illustration again. He has done so in preparation for, and in an attempt to aid others to achieve advancement in the harvest at the end of the age.

If reincarnation is a truth, your immortal self never dies. The conclusive 'end of the age judgment' is at the time of the harvest, determining if you are ready for a graduation to a higher existence in the 'next age.' If you are energetically aligned with a higher existence, you will not have to reincarnate and die a physical death again. Your last 'death' will have been conclusive. (Consistent with earlier discussions herein, this would not preclude advanced beings from reincarnating for the purpose of helping humanity rather than to engage in lessons or need to balance the scales of justice and karma, although presumably it would be possible to create new karma to have to answer.)

This passage is part of a specific epistle to a specific group who are being persecuted for their beliefs and the author urges them to stay firm to the teachings of Jesus in the face of it. It is not a general epistle and it is written within a certain context. It is written to address the perseverance of this specific group and point out that repeated sacrifices like that of Jesus will not be necessary or required. This makes sense if some of the group may be worried they will suffer the same fate as Jesus. It also makes sense given that the Jewish law required a blood sacrifice every year. This passage wasn't written to refute reincarnation.

The book of Hebrews goes on to explore priesthood and sacrifice. Chapter 11 discusses the faith of Abel, Enoch, Noah, Abraham, and Sarah in promises hoped for and things unseen.

See Hebrews 11:13-16, YLT.

> 13***In faith*** died all these, ***not*** having received the promises, but from afar having seen them, and having been persuaded, and having saluted *them*, and having confessed that ***strangers and sojourners they are upon the earth***, 14for those saying such things make manifest that they seek a country; 15and if, indeed, they had been mindful of that from which they came forth, they might have had an opportunity to return, 16but now they long for a better, that is, an heavenly, wherefore God is not ashamed of them, to be called their God, for He did prepare for them a city. (Emphasis added.)

Then Hebrews discusses the faith of Isaac, Jacob, Joseph, Moses, and of the many prophets, including Rahab, Samson, David, and Samuel.

Consider also Hebrews 11:35-40, YLT.

> 35***Women received by a rising again their dead***, ***and others were tortured, not accepting the redemption, that a better rising again they might receive***, 36and others of mockings and scourgings did receive trial, and yet of bonds and imprisonment; 37they were stoned, they were sawn asunder, they

> were tried; in the killing of the sword they died; they went about in sheepskins, in goatskins—being destitute, afflicted, injuriously treated, [38]of whom the world was not worthy; in deserts wandering, and *in* mountains, and *in* caves, and *in* the holes of the earth; [39]***and these all, having been testified to through the faith, did not receive the promise, [40]God for us something better having provided, that apart from us they might not be made perfect.*** (Emphasis added.)

What can be meant by "women receive their dead by a rising again" if not reincarnation? Women receive their dead by reincarnation. Why is it that it is only *the women* who receive the dead? Because only women give birth. Only women can give the dead rebirth. That is "a rising again." What is "a ***better*** rising again they might receive?" A better rising again is different from the first "rising again," the first meaning reincarnation. A 'better' rising again is the rising again that is *out* of the cycle of death and rebirth. But many have not received this teaching, this message, this promise, this redemption. That is why "that apart from us they might not be made perfect." Apart from us good-news-bringers, who are being horribly treated by the world, people might not hear and receive the message of how to achieve the resurrection out of the dead (out of the cycle of death and rebirth.

Is the book that proclaims, "women received by a rising again their dead" and reincarnation must be accepted so that "a better rising again may be received," also the book that claims men only live once and then are judged? No, it is a book that declares that at the end of the age, judgment comes that will lift some out of the cycle of death and

rebirth if they are aligned, if they are diligent and faithful.
See Hebrews 12:5-11, YLT.

> [5]and ye have forgotten the exhortation that doth speak fully with you as with sons, 'My son, be not despising chastening of the Lord, nor be faint, being reproved by Him, [6]for whom the Lord doth love He doth chasten, and He scourgeth every son whom He receiveth;' [7]if chastening ye endure, as to sons God beareth Himself to you, for who is a son whom a father doth not chasten? [8]and if ye are apart from chastening, of which all have become partakers, then bastards are ye, and not sons. [9]Then, indeed, fathers of our flesh we have had, chastising *us*, and we were reverencing *them*; shall we not much rather be subject to the Father of the spirits, and live? [10]for they, indeed, for a few days, according to what seemed good to them, were chastening, but He for profit, to be partakers of His separation; [11]and all chastening for the present, indeed, doth not seem to be of joy, but of sorrow, yet afterward the peaceable fruit of righteousness to those exercised through it—it doth yield.

According to the text in Hebrews, it is God who raises Jesus out of the dead.
See Hebrews 13:20-21, YLT.

> [20]*And the God of the peace, who did bring up* ***out of the dead*** *the great shepherd of the sheep*—in the blood of an age-during covenant—our Lord Jesus, [21]**make you perfect in every good work to do His will**, doing in you that which is well-pleasing before

Him, through Jesus Christ, to whom *is* the glory—to the ages of the ages! (Emphasis added.)

CHAPTER NINE

THE PREEXISTENCE OF THE SOUL
AND
THE QUESTION OF HELL

PREEXISTENCE OF THE SOUL

The Fifth Ecumenical Council held in 553 A.D. at Constantinople (also called the Second Council of Constantinople) outlawed belief in reincarnation in the 6th century after the crucifixion of Jesus. As we have seen in the foregoing, there is scripture that supports a reasonable basis for belief that Jesus taught reincarnation. In the 6th century, the Fifth Ecumenical Council also outlawed belief in the preexistence of the soul. If reincarnation is a reality and was taught by Jesus, then preexistence of the soul would also have to be a reality, and we would expect that concept to have some basis in scripture.

See Job 38:1–21, YLT.

> 1 And Jehovah answereth Job out of the
> whirlwind, and saith:— 2Who *is* this—darkening
> counsel, By words without knowledge? 3Gird, I pray
> thee, as a man, thy loins, And I ask thee, and cause
> thou Me to know.
>
> 4 Where wast thou when I founded earth?
> Declare, if thou hast known understanding. 5Who
> placed its measures—if thou knowest? Or who hath
> stretched out upon it a line? 6On what have its
> sockets been sunk? Or who hath cast its corner-

stone? [7]In the singing together of stars of morning,
And all sons of God shout for joy, [8]And He shutteth
up with doors the sea, In its coming forth, from the
womb it goeth out. [9]In My making a cloud its
clothing, And thick darkness its swaddling band,
[10]And I measure over it My statute, And place bar
and doors, [11]And say, ‘Hitherto come thou, and add
not, And a command is placed On the pride of thy
billows.’

[12] Hast thou commanded morning since thy days?
Causest thou the dawn to know its place? [13]To take
hold on the skirts of the earth, And the wicked are
shaken out of it, [14]It turneth itself as clay of a seal
And they station themselves as clothed. [15]And
withheld from the wicked is their light, And the arm
lifted up is broken. [16]Hast thou come in to springs of
the sea? And in searching the deep Hast thou walked
up and down? [17]Revealed to thee were the gates of
death? And the gates of death-shade dost thou see?
[18]Thou hast understanding, Even unto the broad
places of earth! Declare—if thou hast known it all.
[19]Where *is* this—the way light dwelleth? And
darkness, where *is* this—its place? [20]That thou dost
take it unto its boundary, And that thou dost
understand The paths of its house. [21]***Thou hast
known—for then thou art born And the number of
thy days are many!*** (Emphasis added.)

This is God’s answer to Job. How can Job have been born/in existence then? How could he have “known” and had “understanding?” In addition to these Old Testament verses, the story of the man blind from birth and the disciples’ question as to whether it was this man’s sin or his parents' that caused his blindness (John 9:1-3), confirms that Jesus and his disciples believed in the preexistence of the soul. Jesus' affirmation that John the Baptist is the same entity as the Old Testament prophet Elijah shows that John's soul did not originate with his birth or gestation in that lifetime.

THE QUESTION OF HELL

Many have been lead to believe the counterbalance to an eternal reward for the choices, decisions, and events born out in one short lifetime is eternal punishment in Hell. How does the concept of Hell square with the teaching of Jesus? Not so neatly, as it turns out. The Hebrews had a concept of where the dead were, Sheol, an underworld. The Greek concept of the underworld, Hades, seems to have taken over scripture with the influx of Greeks as followers and scholars. We have already seen that it was the case that while some Jews, the Pharisees, believed in 'resurrection' (reincarnation), some others, the Sadducees, did not. What did Jesus say on the matter?

In consulting the New Testament scripture it should be noted that Jesus appears most frequently to refer to Gehenna, rather than Sheol, or Hades. What is Gehenna?

The Hebrew phrase *ge* ("ravine" or "valley" of) *hinnom* became *geenna* in Greek and *Gehenna* in Latin and English. It refers to an actual place, a valley outside of Jerusalem.

The valley of Hinnom is mentioned in Nehemiah 11:30, and the valley of the son of Hinnom is mentioned at Joshua 15:8 in the Old Testament.

The valley of Hinnom became associated with the

worship of Moloch. See Jeremiah 32:34-35, YLT. The worship of Moloch included the burning sacrifice of children (or possibly a ritual where children were burned).

> [34]'And they set their abominations in the house over which My name is called, so as to defile it;
> [35]And they build the high places of Baal, that *are* in the *valley of the son of Hinnom*, to *cause their sons and their daughters to pass through to Molech*, which I did not command them, nor did it come up on my heart to do this abomination, so as to cause Judah to sin. (Emphasis added.)

The Israelites had already begun worshiping Moloch, an Ammonite god. See YLT, Lev. 18:21.

> [21]'And *of thy seed thou dost not give to pass over to the Molech*; nor dost thou pollute the name of thy God; I *am* Jehovah. (Emphasis added.)

See 1 Kings 11:7, YLT.

> [7]Then doth Solomon build a high place for Chemosh the abomination of Moab, in the hill that *is* on the front of Jerusalem, and for Molech the abomination of the sons of Ammon;

See also Acts 7:43, YLT.

> [43]and ye took up the tabernacle of Moloch, and the star of your god Remphan—the figures that ye made to bow before them, and I will remove your dwelling beyond Babylon.

Consider 2 Chron. 28:1-5, YLT.

> [1]A son of twenty years *is* Ahaz in his reigning, and sixteen years he hath reigned in Jerusalem, and he hath not done that which is right in the eyes of Jehovah, as David his father, [2]and walketh in the ways of the kings of Israel, and also, molten images hath made for Baalim, [3]*and himself hath made perfume in the valley of the son of Hinnom, and burneth his sons with fire according to the abominations of the nations that Jehovah dispossessed from the presence of the sons of Israel*, [4]and sacrificeth and maketh perfume in high places, and on the heights, and under every green tree. [5]And Jehovah his God giveth him into the hand of the king of Aram, and they smite him, and take captive from him a great captivity, and bring *them* in to Damascus, and also into the hand of the king of Israel he hath been given, and he smiteth him—a great smiting. (Emphasis added.)

See 2 Kings 23:10, YLT.

> [10]And he hath defiled Topheth, that *is* in **the valley of the son of Hinnom so that no man doth cause his son and his daughter to pass over through fire to Molech**. (Emphasis added.)

See also 2 Chron. 33:1-6, YLT.

> [1]A son of twelve years is Manasseh in his reigning, and fifty and five years he hath reigned in

> Jerusalem; [2]and he doth the evil thing in the eyes of Jehovah, like the abominations of the nations that Jehovah dispossessed from the presence of the sons of Israel, [3]and he turneth and buildeth the high places that Hezekiah his father hath broken down, and raiseth altars for Baalim, and maketh shrines, and boweth himself to all the host of the heavens, and serveth them. [4]And he hath built altars in the house of Jehovah of which Jehovah had said, 'In Jerusalem is My name to the age.' [5]And he buildeth altars to all the host of the heavens in the two courts of the house of Jehovah. [6]*And he hath caused his sons to pass over through fire in the valley of the son of Hinnom* (Emphasis added.)

See Matthew 5:21-22, YLT.

> [21]'Ye heard that it was said to the ancients: Thou shalt not kill, and whoever may kill shall be in danger of the judgment; [22]but I—I say to you, that every one who is angry at his brother without cause, shall be in danger of the judgment, and whoever may say to his brother, Empty fellow! shall be in danger of the sanhedrim, and whoever may say, Rebel! shall be in danger of the ***gehenna of the fire***. (Emphasis added.)

See Matthew 5:29–30, YLT:

> [29]'But, if thy right eye doth cause thee to stumble, pluck it out and cast from thee, for it is good to thee that one of thy members may perish, and not thy whole body be cast to **gehenna**.

> [30]'And, if thy right hand doth cause thee to stumble, cut it off, and cast from thee, for it is good to thee that one of thy members may perish, and not thy whole body be cast to **gehenna**. (Emphasis added.)

See Matthew 10:28, YLT.

> [28]'And be not afraid of those killing the body, and are not able to kill the soul, but fear rather Him who is able both soul and body to destroy in **gehenna**. (Emphasis added.)

See Matthew 18.9, YLT.

> [9]'And if thine eye doth cause thee to stumble, pluck it out and cast from thee; it is good for thee one-eyed to enter into the life, rather than having two eyes to be cast to the **gehenna** *of the fire*. (Emphasis added.)

See Matthew 23:15, YLT.

> [15]'Woe to you, Scribes and Pharisees, hypocrites! because ye go round the sea and the dry land to make one proselyte, and whenever it may happen—ye make him a *son of gehenna* twofold more than yourselves. (Emphasis added.)

See Matthew 23:33, YLT.

> [33]'Serpents! brood of vipers! how may ye escape from the judgment of the **gehenna**? (Emphasis

added.)

Strong's Greek Concordance shows that the word translated as "judgment" in the above scripture, kriseōs, Strong's number 2920, is equally translatable as "sentence," instead of "judgment."

See Mark 9:43-50, YLT.

> [43]'And if thy hand may cause thee to stumble, cut it off; it is better for thee maimed *to enter into the life*, than having the two hands, to go away to the gehenna, to the fire—the unquenchable— [44]where there worm is not dying, and the fire is not being quenched.
>
> [45]'And if thy foot may cause thee to stumble, cut it off; it is better for thee to enter into the life lame, than having the two feet to be cast to the *gehenna*, to the fire—the unquenchable— [46]where there worm is not dying, and the fire is not being quenched. [47]And if thine eye may cause thee to stumble, cast it out; it is better for thee one-eyed *to enter into the reign of God*, than having two eyes, to be cast to the *gehenna* of the fire— [48]where their worm is not dying, and the fire is not being quenched; [49]for every one with fire shall be salted, and every sacrifice with salt shall be salted. [50]The salt *is* good, but if the salt may become saltless, in what will ye season *it*? Have in yourselves salt, and have peace in one another.' (Emphasis added.)

Strong's Greek Concordance lists the definition of ***skōlēx***, Strong's word number 4663, the word translated here as "worm," as being "a gnawing worm" *or* "a gnawing *anguish.*" Not only that, but Strong's Greek Concordance clearly shows that the word in Greek translated in verses 44 and 46 as "there" is a personal pronoun, which should be translated as "their" or "of them," not "there", as it is properly translated in verse 48. What is the import of that? The Greek word, ***auton***, Strong's number, 846, actually signifies a personal pronoun, and Strong's Greek concordance shows the proper translation as "them", the "worm of them," or "their" worm. Does that suggest that each person not achieving the out-resurrection actually has their own personal gnawing worm, or their own personal gnawing *anguish*?

The Greek word translated as "dies", ***teleutaó***, Strong's Greek number 5053, is equally translatable as "*end*", "*finish*", or even "***complete***".

The Greek word translated as "fire" here, ***pyr***, Strong's number 4442, can be translated as "fire" but can also be translated as "***trials***".

The Greek word translated as "quenched" is *sbennumi*, Strong's number 4570, can also be translated as "suppressed" or "thwarted".

The Greek word translated as "cause to stumble" [9:47], ***skandalizē*** , Strong's number 4624, is closely related to *skandalon*, Strong's #4625, meaning "a snare" or trap, suggesting "***to fall into a trap.***"

The Greek word for "will/shall be salted" here is ***halisthēsetai***, Strong's number 233, and also means "***keep fresh and sound, and so acceptable to God,***" figuratively, God preserving and seasoning a believer as he grows.

Consider an examination of word meanings.

> [47]And if thine eye may ***cause thee to stumble***, cast it out; it is better for thee one-eyed *to enter into the*

> *reign of God*, than having two eyes, to be cast to the *gehenna* of the ***fire***— [48]where ***their worm*** is not ***dying***, and the ***fire*** is not beng ***quenched***; [49]for every one with ***fire*** shall be ***salted*** (Emphasis added.)

Becomes:

> And if thy eye may cause thee to ***fall into a trap***, cast it out; it is better for thee one-eyed to enter into the reign of God, than having two eyes, to be cast to the gehenna of the ***trial*** – where ***their anguish*** is not ***complete***, and the ***trial*** is not being ***thwarted/suppressed***; for every one with ***trials*** shall be **kept fresh and sound, and so acceptable to God**

If we examine the above scripture again, seeking the most accurate translation and the one that makes the most sense given the context, what the Greek words of the older, translated text actually speak of is not a place of undying worms and eternal fire, but a cycle of trials not completed and the gnawing anguish of being held in the cycle, not having achieved a graduation from the cycle of death and rebirth in learning and perfecting through trials. *The only hell any of us endures is circumstances which we make ourselves, the one we have right here and right now in our trials on earth.* Why do we have these trials? We have them to become salted, or acceptable to God. You cannot achieve the out-resurrection until you are capable of appropriately dwelling in a "higher" realm. You have to be energetically aligned by attaining higher frequency.

The reference in the above scripture to the worm and the fire is a reference by Jesus to Isaiah 66:23-24, YLT, which reads as follows.

> [23]And it hath been from month to month, And from sabbath to sabbath, Come do all flesh to bow themselves before Me, Said Jehovah. [24]And they have gone forth, And looked on the carcases of the men *Who are transgressing against me*, For their worm dieth not, And their fire is not quenched, And they have been an abhorrence to all flesh!
> (Emphasis added.)

Jesus references the Old Testament scripture about carcasses of men who are transgressing against me, for their worm dieth not. They are stuck in a perpetual cycle of death for the worms to feed on (their carcasses) *because they are transgressing against me.* This is a state of being wherein one is unproductive, unimproved, and even degrading perpetually, stuck in a cycle with no advancement. The cycle is repetitive if we do not make the efforts to learn from experience and become worthy. Understanding the presence of a cycle is immensely useful in making attempts to overcome it rather than being held in it due to errors.

See Luke 12:4-5, YLT.

> [4]'And I say to you, my friends, be not afraid of those killing the body, and after these things are not having anything over to do; [5]but I will show to you, whom ye may fear; Fear him who, after the killing, is having authority to cast to the gehenna; yes, I say to you, Fear ye Him.

Who determines who advances and who remains (even after the death of the body) to be born anew in the cycle? Fear ye Him, or rather, revere him – enough to pay attention to what you do.

See James 3:1-18, YLT.

> [1]Many teachers become not, my brethren, having known that greater judgment we shall receive, [2]for we all make many stumbles; ***if any one in word doth not stumble, this one is a perfect man, able to bridle also the whole body; [3]lo, the bits we put into the mouths of the horses for their obeying us, and their whole body we turn about***; [4]lo, also the ships, being so great, and by fierce winds being driven, *are led about by a very small helm*, whithersoever the impulse of the helmsman doth counsel, [5]so also the tongue is a little member, and doth boast greatly; lo, a little fire how much wood it doth kindle! [6]and the tongue *is* a fire, the world of the unrighteousness, so the tongue is set in our members, which is spotting our whole body, and is setting on fire the course of nature, and ***is set on fire by the gehenna***. [7]For every nature, both of beasts and of fowls, both of creeping things and things of the sea, is subdued, and hath been subdued, by the human nature, [8]and the tongue no one of men is able to subdue, *it is* an unruly evil, full of deadly poison, [9]with it we do bless the God and Father, and with it we do curse the men made according to the similitude of God; [10]out of the same mouth doth come forth blessing and cursing; it doth not need, my brethren, these things so to happen; [11]doth the fountain out of the same opening pour forth the sweet and the bitter? [12]is a fig-tree able, my brethren, olives to make? or a vine figs? so no fountain salt and sweet water *is able* to make.
>
> [13] Who *is* wise and intelligent among you? let him

shew out of the good behaviour his works in meekness of wisdom, [14]and if bitter zeal ye have, and rivalry in your heart, glory not, nor lie against the truth; [15]this wisdom is not descending from above, but earthly, physical, demon-like, [16]for where zeal and rivalry *are*, there is insurrection and every evil matter; [17]and the wisdom from above, first, indeed, is pure, then peaceable, gentle, easily entreated, full of kindness and good fruits, uncontentious, and unhypocritical:— [18]and the fruit of the righteousness in peace is sown to those making peace. (Emphasis added.)

Words appear to be as important in making our works good or evil as any other sort of deed, perhaps even more so, according to this author, because the mouth functions as a lead. Consider this carefully. That gives serious import to untruths someone may tell – to ourselves as well as to others. It dictates that telling untruths to mislead others or create false impressions or illusions is particularly grievous. Others can be seriously injured on their paths by the import and ripple effect of purposefully saying things that are untrue and intentionally trying to create a belief in another that is untrue.

In Matthew 13:37-44, YLT, the imagery is that of sowing and reaping a field.

> [37] And he answering said to them, 'He who is sowing the good seed is the Son of Man, [38]and the field is the world, and the good seed, these are the sons of the reign, and the darnel are the sons of the evil one, [39]and the enemy who sowed them is the devil, and the harvest is a full end of the age, and the

reapers are messengers.

[40] 'As, then, the darnel is gathered up, and is burned with fire, so shall it be in the full end of this age, [41]the Son of Man shall send forth his messengers, and they shall gather up out of his kingdom all the stumbling-blocks, and those doing the unlawlessness, [42]and shall cast them to the furnace of the fire; there shall be the weeping and the gnashing of the teeth.

[43] 'Then shall the righteous shine forth as the sun in the reign of their Father. He who is having ears to hear—let him hear.

[44]'Again, the reign of the heavens is like to treasure hid in the field, which a man having found did hide, and from his joy goeth, and all, as much as he hath, he selleth, and buyeth that field.

The Kingdom is hidden (treasure in the field) and each person must discover it, find it, arrive at it on their own, individually and once found, discovered, realized, has worth far greater than material possessions.

The imagery of the gathering of the harvest and of the fire in the furnace is not a punishment for all time. The imagery is of a field harvested at the end of the age, the separation of the productive yield from the unproductive yield. Harvests are cyclical and reoccur. What happens if one doesn't make the harvest at the end of the age? Do we not remain in the cycle for another age, until the next harvest, at the end of the next age, in hopes of being productive yield at that point? The fire is transformative, a trial, that a furnace uses to yield bread or earthen ware or to smelt metals. It is productive.

Matthew 13:49, YLT, states judgment is limited to the

duration, and conclusion, “of the age.”

> 49***so shall it be in the full end of the age***, the
> messengers shall come forth and ***separate the evil***
> ***out of the midst of the righteous***, 50and shall cast
> them to the furnace of the fire, there shall be the
> weeping and the gnashing of the teeth.’ 51Jesus saith
> to them, ‘Did ye understand all these?’ They say to
> him, ‘Yes, sir.’ 52And he said to them, ‘Because of
> this every scribe having been discipled in regard to
> the reign of the heavens, is like to a man, a
> householder, who doth bring forth out of his treasure
> things new and old.’
> 53And it came to pass, ***when Jesus finished these***
> ***similes***, he removed thence (Emphasis added.)

WE ARE MANY TIMES TOLD THAT JESUS SPEAKS IN SIMILES. If there is no “hell” in the Bible, to what then does all the talk of punishment and eternal punishment, torment, etc. refer? The Bible, in a *literal* translation, does not speak of the end of the world. It speaks of the *end of the age.* It makes reference to a coming age. Ages begin, endure, and end, followed by a successive age. The language in the texts regarding “ages” and “harvests” are spoken of as cyclical and repetitive. A mistranslation of *aión*, the Greek word meaning “age” or “age-during,” is responsible for much of the problem. It is wrongly translated as “eternal,” and “world,” and “never ending.” Strong’s Greek Concordance shows this word, *aión*, Strong’s Concordance number 165, means “a space of time, an age” and “an age, a cycle (of time), especially of the present age as contrasted with the future age, and of one of a series of ages stretching to infinity.” Isn’t this variance in translation an effort to gain power over people and keep people ensnared in fear?

What about all the language about punishment? There appear to be two common Greek words for "punishment." One is "*kolasin,*" the other, "*timoria.*" *Kolasin* is a form of *Kolasis*, Strong's Greek Concordance number 2851. Strong's Concordance gives the meaning of kolasis as "chastisement, punishment, torment." Strong's also notes a cognate, "*kólasis* (from *kolaphos*, "a buffeting, a blow") – properly, punishment that "fits" (matches) the one punished. The NAS Exhaustive Concordance shows the Word Origin is from kolazó which is defined as "correction." Strong's shows kolazó, number 2848, as meaning "chastisement", and "properly, to dwarf, mutilate (curtail)" "i.e. in a way that restrains (impedes, restricts)." The use of this particular word suggests chastisement *not as punitive but as corrective, a pruning to prevent growth in an undesired direction.* This fits the teaching of Jesus that we are in a reincarnation cycle to learn lessons and improve or raise our energetic frequency. The idea of an everlasting punishment is not taught except to the extent we ourselves determine our circumstances and lessons through our own willfulness or lack of appropriate effort. The goal of chastisement is a lesson. The goal of curtailing or restricting would apply when the use of free will has been used in a destructive manner. The goal is improvement not endless punishment.

This is the word given in Greek attributed to Jesus in Matthew 25:46, YLT, which is inexactly translated as "punishment."

> 46And these shall go away to punishment age-during, but the righteous to life age-during.'

Matthew 25:46, YLT, limits the 'punishment' to the duration of an age...until the next harvest, at the end of the age. While this scripture is frequently translated as speaking of "eternal" punishment, and "eternal" life, a correct literal translation makes clear that it isn't the case. The scripture speaks to correction, rather than punishment, *during the age* (rather than eternally) through the cycle of death and rebirth and *life during the age* with the absence of physical death for the righteous because the cycle is no longer needed as a form of growth and/or correction.

The Greek word translated as eternal is actually aionion, an adjective, Strong's Concordance word number 166, *aiṓnios*, meaning "age-long." Although it is frequently translated as eternal, it's meaning is age-long, or age-during. It derives from the word aión, Strong's Exhaustive Concordance word number 165, a noun. Aión means "a space of time, an age," "an age, a cycle of time," and "a cycle (of time), especially of the present age as contrasted with the future age, and of one of a series of ages stretching to infinity." A term that means "a cycle of time" is obviously inexact. An adjective describing something as being age-long cannot be more exact, or longer than the noun that gives the word its descriptive quality, particularly when it relates to time. Weekly isn't construed to mean eternal. Neither is yearly or every century, or rather it shouldn't be. It is obvious in numerous passages that Jesus speaks of cycles of time. The terms ages, this age, next age, and coming age all denote something very different than the concept of eternity, a yawning stretching seamless gap of time so infinite it is non-time. Rather, these terms denote regular cycles, or intervals of time, quite unlike an infinite expanse. The repeated use of the symbol, metaphor, and comparison of harvest iterates the same concept used by

Jesus of regular, cyclical intervals. The next age, even the one without death, where those worthy are to be like angels/messengers/heavenly beings (Luke 20:36) is not said by Jesus to be endless or eternal. Likewise, the "punishment" in the form of "correction" and the "life" he speaks of are never said by Jesus to be eternal, but to be for an "age." Jesus also speaks of the "end of the age," not the end of the world as is usually translated.

This word *kolasin*, a concept that is closer to "correction" is translated as "punishment" in Matthew 25:46 and in 1 John 4:18, YLT.

> [18]fear is not in the love, but the perfect love doth cast out the fear, because the fear hath punishment, and he who is fearing hath not been made perfect in the love;

What punishment (i.e. correction) does fear have? Fear of future consequences from wrongful acts is corrective in and of itself. If you understand how correction works, then you are less likely to willfully do things that are hurtful to others and can understand that whatever lessons are coming to you are ones that you need to improve. Pruning a tree may mutilate it temporarily, but it will help it grow in a more productive direction and bear more fruit.

This is the word for correction that Jesus used, translated as "punishment." Jesus does in fact tell us very directly that the Father cleanses by pruning to yield more fruit.

See John 15:1-2, YLT.

> [1]'I am the true vine, and my Father is the husbandman; [2]every branch in me not bearing fruit, He doth take it away, and every one bearing fruit, *He*

doth cleanse by pruning it, that it may bear more fruit; (Emphasis added.)

Contrast that for another Greek word used in the New Testament for punishment. Strong's Concordance shows ***timóreó***, Strong's Number 5097, to mean, "to punish, avenge," a verb. This word occurs twice in the New Testament. It appears once in Acts 22:5, YLT.

> [4]'And this way I persecuted unto death, binding and delivering up to prisons both men and women, [5]as also the chief priest doth testify to me, and all the eldership; from whom also having received letters unto the brethren, to Damascus, I was going on, to bring also those there bound to Jerusalem that they might be ***punished***, (Emphasis added.)

Paul, or rather Saul, the Pharisee, is giving his account of how he sought to punish or seek vengeance against the followers of Jesus and his teachings before his conversion to Christianity (and from Saul to Paul).

The word appears again in Acts 26:9-11, YLT.

> [9]'I, indeed, therefore, thought with myself, that against the name of Jesus of Nazareth it behoved *me* many things to do, [10]which also I did in Jerusalem, and many of the saints I in prison did shut up, from the chief priests having received the authority; they also being put to death, I gave my vote against them, [11]and in every synagogue, often ***punishing*** them, I was constraining *them* to speak evil, being also exceedingly mad against them, I was also persecuting *them* even unto strange cities. (Emphasis

added.)

Again, Saul/Paul gives further account of his previous punishment against Jesus' followers. Paul does not pretend to be seeking to correct anyone. Rather he is very honestly telling of his aim (and achievement) of torturing them in a brutal fashion.

The same word in noun form, timória, given in Strong's Exhaustive Concordance as word number 5098, meaning "punishment, vengeance," is used in Hebrews 10:29-32, YLT.

> 29of how much sorer ***punishment*** shall he be counted worthy who the Son of God did trample on, and the blood of the covenant did count a common thing, in which he was sanctified, and to the Spirit of the grace did despite? 30for we have known Him who is saying, 'Vengeance *is* Mine, I will recompense, saith the Lord;' and again, 'The Lord shall judge His people;'— 31fearful *is* the falling into the hands of a living God. 32And call to your remembrance the former days, in which, having been enlightened, ye did endure much conflict of sufferings,.... (Emphasis added.)

This scripture is citing retributive punishment, not correction, for those who trample on the teachings of Jesus. Yet, Jesus himself did not use this word for vengeful punishment. Rather he used a different word, arguably, more closely resembling correction, correction for a better direction of future growth. Which word is compatible with the modern concept of hell? Which word is compatible with the cycle of reincarnation?

The word choice attributed to Jesus is far more compatible with universal reconciliation than with eternal damnation and torture.

See also Corinthians 15:22, YLT.

> [22]for even as in Adam ***all die***, so also in the Christ ***all shall be made alive***, [23]and each in his proper order, ***a first-fruit*** Christ, (Emphasis added).

In Adam (mankind), and sin, humanity is caught in a reincarnation cycle of death and rebirth, but through Christ, the way out of the cycle may be shown to others. This is why Jesus is the first-fruit, but not the *only* fruit. It is especially noted that all die within the cycle and all are expected to overcome the cycle to life without death in due time.

Consider I Timothy 2:1-6, YLT.

> [1]I exhort, then, first of all, there be made supplications, prayers, intercessions, thanksgivings, for all men: [2]for kings, and all who are in authority, that a quiet and peaceable life we may lead in all piety and gravity, [3]for this *is* right and acceptable before God our Saviour, [4]***who doth will all men to be saved, and to come to the full knowledge of the truth***; [5]for one *is* God, one also *is* mediator of God and of men, the man Christ Jesus, [6]who did give himself a ransom for all—***the testimony in its own times***—.... (Emphasis added.)

All men are to be saved. Wouldn't achieving the goal be somewhat more realistic if one had "the full knowledge of the truth?" The testimony of how to achieve salvation from the cycle is Jesus' teaching and example.

Although we have already examined parts of 1 Corinthians Chapter 15, consider it again. It is divided into three sections titled, "The Resurrection of Christ," "The Resurrection of the Dead," and "The Resurrection Body."

If the resurrection of the dead is meant to be reincarnation, then the resurrection of the Christ is the resurrection OUT of the dead (death and rebirth cycle). A logical question would then be what is our out-resurrection body to be?

Consider 1 Corinthians 15:1–11, YLT.

> *The Resurrection of Christ*
>
> 1 And I make known to you, brethren, the good
> news that I proclaimed to you, which also ye did
> receive, in which also ye have stood, 2 through which
> also ye are being saved, in what words I proclaimed
> good news to you, if ye hold fast, except ye did
> believe in vain, 3 for I delivered to you first, what also
> I did receive, that Christ died for our sins, according
> to the Writings, 4 and that he was buried, and that *he*
> *hath risen on the third day, according to the*
> *Writings, 5 and that he appeared to Cephas, then to*
> *the twelve, 6 afterwards he appeared to above five*
> *hundred brethren at once, of whom the greater part*
> *remain till now, and* ***certain also did fall asleep***;
> 7 afterwards he appeared to James, then to all the
> apostles. 8 And last of all—as to the untimely birth—
> he appeared also to me, 9 for I am the least of the
> apostles, who am not worthy to be called an apostle,
> because I did persecute the assembly of God, 10 and
> by the grace of God I am what I am, and His grace

that *is* towards me came not in vain, but more abundantly than they all did I labour, yet not I, but the grace of God that *is* with me; [11]whether, then, I or they, so we preach, and so ye did believe. (Emphasis added.)

[The author affirms that Jesus overcame death in his (out) resurrection and that he appeared to the many (as enumerated) after his death on the cross.]

See 1 Corinthians 15:12–34, YLT.

> [12] And if Christ is preached, that ***<u>out</u> of the dead he hath risen, how say certain among you, that there is <u>no rising again of dead persons</u>***? ***[13]and if there be no rising again of dead persons, neither hath Christ risen; [14]and if Christ hath not risen, then void is our preaching, and void also your faith, [15]and we also are found false witnesses of God, because we did testify of God that He raised up the Christ, whom He did not raise if then dead persons do not rise; [16]for if dead persons do not rise, neither hath Christ risen, [17]and if Christ hath not risen, vain is your faith, ye are yet in your sins; [18]then, also, those having fallen asleep in Christ did perish; [19]if in this life we have hope in Christ only, of all men we are most to be pitied.***
>
> [20] And now, ***Christ hath risen out of the dead—the first-fruits of those sleeping he became, [21]for since through man is the death, also through man is a rising again of the dead, [22]for even as in Adam all die, so also in the Christ all shall be made alive, [23]and each in his proper order, a first-fruit Christ***, afterwards those who are the Christ's, in his

> presence, [24]then—the end, when he may deliver up the reign to God, even the Father, when he may have made useless all rule, and all authority and power—[25]for it behoveth him to reign till he may have put all the enemies under his feet—[26]the last enemy is done away—death; [27]for all things He did put under his feet, and, when one may say that all things have been subjected, *it is* evident that He is excepted who did subject the all things to him, [28]and when the all things may be subjected to him, then the Son also himself shall be subject to Him, who did subject to him the all things, that God may be the all in all. [29]Seeing what shall they do who are baptized for the dead, if the dead do not rise at all? why also are they baptized for the dead? [30]why also do we stand in peril every hour? [31]***Every day do I die***, by the glorying of you that I have in Christ Jesus our Lord: [32]if after the manner of a man with wild beasts I fought in Ephesus, ***what the advantage to me if the dead do not rise? let us eat and drink, for to-morrow we die!*** [33]Be not led astray; evil communications corrupt good manners; [34]awake up, as is right, and sin not; for certain have an ignorance of God; for shame to you I say *it*. (Emphasis added.)

Verse twelve states, "And if Christ is preached, that ***out of the dead he hath risen, how say certain among you, that there is no rising again of dead persons***?" Having told how Christ died but overcame death out of the cycle of death and rebirth, the Author asks how can one believe the escape from the death and rebirth cycle and question the cycle of death and rebirth, reincarnation itself. If there were no cycle, then an escape or overcoming is far less meaningful as you would otherwise only die once, and only have one effort in your experience. Are we to celebrate a graduation from a one and only try?

> ***[13]and if there be no rising again of dead persons, neither hath Christ risen; [14]and if Christ hath not risen, then void is our preaching, and void also your faith, [15]and we also are found false witnesses of God, because we did testify of God that He raised up the Christ, whom He did not raise if then dead persons do not rise; [16]for if dead persons do not rise, neither hath Christ risen, [17]and if Christ hath not risen, vain is your faith, ye are yet in your sins; [18]then, also, those having fallen asleep in Christ did perish; [19]if in this life we have hope in Christ only, of all men we are most to be pitied.***

If there is no reincarnation, Jesus could not have perfected himself in one lifetime and become worthy of the out-resurrection and all believers are doomed since we too cannot achieve the mark in one lifetime.

The author of this scripture affirms that reincarnation is how we manage to perfect our imperfect selves to achieve the out-resurrection triumph over death. If there is no reincarnation (rising again of dead persons, plural), then there can be no out-resurrection, (rising out of the cycle of reincarnation). If you do not believe and understand the rising again of dead persons (reincarnation), how can you understand and believe Jesus' lesson and example of escaping the cycle and achieving a resurrection *out* of the cycle? If we must make the harvest cut in this one lifetime we are all in for disappointment.

Jesus is not the only son of God, but the *first fruit* of the harvest *out* from the dead.

> "[20]And now, ***Christ hath risen out of the dead—the first-fruits of those sleeping he became"....***

All have died. All have reincarnated. All are intended to eventually become sons of God. How else to be the "first fruits of those sleeping?" Those sleeping are already dead – already destined to die repeatedly due to being in the cycle, under the law of reincarnation.

> "[22]***for even as in Adam all die, so also in the Christ all shall be made alive***"

> "[32]***... what the advantage to me if the dead do not rise? let us eat and drink, for to-morrow we die!*** [33]Be not led astray; evil communications corrupt good manners; [34]awake up, as is right, and sin not; for certain have an ignorance of God; for shame to you I say *it*."

The author states that if there is no reincarnation (if the dead are not raised) then do what you like (let us eat and drink) for you will *truly* die (for tomorrow we die). The author states, but that is not true (Be not led astray). Death is but sleep (I die every day). Do not be deceived. What you do today matters to you tomorrow (evil communications corrupt good manners).

Jesus himself purposely and plainly referred to death as merely sleep – an impermanent state, before he raises the very dead Lazarus.

See John 11:11-15, YLT.

> [11]These things he said, and after this he saith to them, 'Lazarus our friend *hath fallen asleep*, but I go on *that I may awake him*;' [12]therefore said his disciples, 'Sir, if he hath fallen asleep, he will be saved;' [13]*but Jesus had spoken about his death, but they thought that about the repose of sleep he speaketh.* [14]*Then, therefore, Jesus said to them freely, 'Lazarus hath died*; [15]and I rejoice, for your sake, (that ye may believe,) that I was not there; but we may go to him;' (Emphasis added.)

The scripture goes on to make clear that Lazarus had already been four days in the tomb.

Reincarnation is a truth, a law. And it is the mechanism that gives one the opportunity, through the application of will and intent toward an ideal to improve oneself and become worthy of achieving the out-resurrection. But what are we once the out-resurrection is achieved?

The Resurrection Body

> 1 Corinthians 15:35-58, YLT.
>
> [35]***But some one will say, 'How do the dead rise?*** [36]***unwise! thou—what thou dost sow is not quickened except it may die***; [37]and that which thou dost sow, *not the body that shall be dost thou sow, but bare grain*, it may be of wheat, or of some one of the others, [38]and God doth give to it a body according as He willed, and to each of the seeds its proper body. [39]All flesh *is* not the same flesh, but

there is one flesh of men, and another flesh of beasts,
and another of fishes, and another of birds; [40]and
there are heavenly bodies, and earthly bodies; but
one *is* the glory of the heavenly, and another that of
the earthly; [41]one glory of sun, and another glory of
moon, and another glory of stars, for star from star
doth differ in glory. [42]So also *is* the rising again of
the dead: it is sown in corruption, it is raised in
incorruption; [43]it is sown in dishonour, it is raised in
glory; it is sown in weakness, it is raised in power;
[44]it is sown a natural body, it is raised a spiritual
body; ***there is a natural body, and there is a
spiritual body;*** [45]so also it hath been written, 'The
first man Adam became a living creature,' the last
Adam *is* for a life-giving spirit, [46]but that which is
spiritual *is* not first, but that which *was* natural,
afterwards that which *is* spiritual. [47]The first man *is*
out of the earth, earthy; the second man *is* the Lord
out of heaven; [48]as *is* the earthy, such *are* also the
earthy; and as *is* the heavenly, such *are* also the
heavenly; [49]and, according as we did bear the image
of the earthy, we shall bear also the image of the
heavenly. [50]And this I say, brethren, that ***flesh and
blood the reign of God is not able to inherit***, nor
doth the corruption inherit the incorruption.

[51]Lo, I tell you a secret; we indeed shall not all
sleep, and we all shall be changed; [52]in a moment, in
the twinkling of an eye, in the last trumpet, for it
shall sound, and the dead shall be raised
incorruptible, and we—we shall be changed: [53]for it
behoveth this corruptible to put on incorruption, and
this mortal to put on immortality; [54]and when this
corruptible may have put on incorruption, and this

> mortal may have put on immortality, then shall be brought to pass the word that hath been written, '***The Death was swallowed up—to victory;*** [55]***where, O Death, thy sting? where, O Hades, thy victory?'*** [56]***and the sting of the death is the sin, and the power of the sin the law***; [57]and to God—thanks, to Him who is giving us the victory through our Lord Jesus Christ.
>
> [58]So that, my brethren beloved, become ye stedfast, unmovable, abounding in the work of the Lord at all times, knowing that your labour is not vain in the Lord. (Emphasis added.)

The passage states, [35]***But some one will say, 'How do the dead rise?*** [36]***unwise! thou—what thou dost sow is not quickened except it may die***"....

Why would anyone be called unwise who asks "how do the dead rise?" Because that teaching has been around for a while. The Pharisees already understood and believed in reincarnation. What is new? The way to achieve the rising again that is *out* of the cycle as taught by Jesus, victory over earthly death, victory over the physical reincarnation cycle.

> '***The Death was swallowed up—to victory;*** [55]***where, O Death, thy sting? where, O Hades, thy victory?'*** [56]***and the sting of the death is the sin, and the power of the sin the law***;
>
> ***"Death has been swallowed up in victory."***

"The sting of death is sin." Our manner of living keeps us in the cycle of death and rebirth. "The power of sin is the law." You become the recipient of that which you do to others. "But thanks be to God who gives us victory through our Lord Jesus Christ." Jesus has *shown us the way* to victory, what we must do, how we must live and strive to be worthy of the rising *out* of the cycle of death and rebirth. Jesus has not done the task for you, but illustrated and illuminated the road you must travel. He has shown the way. "Therefore, my beloved, be steadfast, immovable, always excelling in the work of the Lord, because you know that in the Lord your labor is not in vain." We will answer to the law and reap what we sow.

Jesus said that after the out-resurrection we are like messengers ("and the rising again that is out of the dead, neither marry, nor are they given in marriage; [36]for neither are they able to die any more—for they are like messengers—and they are sons of God,"). The literal translation does not speak of angels but messengers. *Jesus also said that messengers will return at the end of the age to reap the harvest.*

CHAPTER TEN

DISPARITY OF CIRCUMSTANCES AND THE LAW

Who among us has not pondered the great disparity of circumstances into which human beings are born? How are we to be judged following a single lifetime when some of us have had advantages or difficulties so much greater than others? What about the enormous disparity of circumstances people are born into, hardship or tragedy, privilege or opportunity? What about the short-lived? What about the handicapped? What about the mentally infirm? What about the poor? What about the abused? How is this fair? It simply isn't. But modern-day Christians ignore this unfairness, ignore that this makes God's judgment, as currently commonly interpreted, inherently and grossly unfair. For any who seek righteousness, this has been a bitter pill to swallow. Many have been unable to swallow it and with good reason. What accounts for the moral justice of judgment on such varied circumstance and, ultimately, experience? Many of these circumstances are received and experienced to one's benefit or detriment while still very young. This is inherently inequitable. 'Pull yourself up by your bootstraps' does not mean as much when one of us has to dig down six feet to find a pair and another's look like hip waders.

But reincarnation explains this most equitably. This is a result of something that has gone before, of reaping what you sow, or perhaps, a choice to achieve a certain condition in the growth of the soul. It serves a purpose, and is not a state of permanence.

We are born into circumstances we have ourselves determined by our own actions and choices. That too may be a bitter pill to swallow at times, but at least it is not random and chance and it has meaning and purpose for your soul's development. What could be a more fitting mechanism for the working of the world as set forth by Jesus himself?

See Matthew 22:34–40, YLT.

> [34] And the Pharisees, having heard that he did silence the Sadducees, were gathered together unto him; [35]and one of them, a lawyer, did question, tempting him, and saying, [36]'Teacher, which *is* the great command in the Law?' [37]And Jesus said to him, *'Thou shalt love the Lord thy God with all thy heart, and with all thy soul, and with all thine understanding*— [38]this is a first and great command; [39]and the second *is* like to it, ***Thou shalt love thy neighbour as thyself***; [40]on these—the two commands—all the law and the prophcts do hang.' (Emphasis added.)

See Mark 12:28-34, YLT.

> [28] And one of the scribes having come near, having heard them disputing, knowing that he answered them well, questioned him, 'Which is the first command of all?' [29]and Jesus answered him—'The first of all the commands *is*, Hear, O Israel, *the Lord is our God, the Lord is one*; [30]and *thou shalt love the Lord thy God out of all thy heart, and out of thy soul, and out of all thine understanding, and out of all thy strength*—this *is* the first command; [31]and

> the second *is* like *it*, this, ***Thou shalt love thy neighbour as thyself***;—greater than these there is no other command.' [32]And the scribe said to him, 'Well, Teacher, in truth thou hast spoken that there is one God, and there is none other but He; [33]and to love Him out of all the heart, and out of all the understanding, and out of all the soul, and out of all the strength, and to love one's neighbour as one's self, is more than all the whole burnt-offerings and the sacrifices.' [34]And Jesus, having seen him that he answered with understanding, said to him, ***'Thou art not far from the reign of God;'*** and no one any more durst question him. (Emphasis added.)

See Luke 10:25–28, YLT.

> [25] And lo, a certain lawyer stood up, trying him, and saying, *'Teacher, what having done, life age-during shall I inherit?'* [26]And he said unto him, *'In the law what hath been written? how dost thou read?'* [27]And he answering said, '*Thou shalt love the Lord thy God out of all thy heart, and out of all thy soul, and out of all thy strength, and out of all thy understanding, and thy neighbour as thyself.*' [28]And he said to him, '*Rightly thou didst answer; this do,* ***and thou shalt live***.' (Emphasis added.)

Why does Jesus tell this lawyer, "this do, and thou shalt live." Isn't the lawyer alive when he asks Jesus the question? The answer indicates more than "living" as we know it, it indicates "living" without death.

And the lawyer continued. See Luke 10:29-37, YLT.

[29]And he, willing to declare himself righteous, said unto Jesus, ***'And who is my neighbour?'*** [30]and Jesus having taken up *the word,* said, 'A certain man was going down from Jerusalem to Jericho, and fell among robbers, and having stripped him and inflicted blows, they went away, leaving *him* half dead.

[31]'And by a coincidence a certain priest was going down in that way, and having seen him, he passed over on the opposite side; [32]and in like manner also, a Levite, having been about the place, having come and seen, passed over on the opposite side.

[33]'But a certain Samaritan, journeying, came along him, and having seen him, he was moved with compassion, [34]and having come near, he bound up his wounds, pouring on oil and wine, and having lifted him up on his own beast, he brought him to an inn, and was careful of him; [35]and on the morrow, going forth, taking out two denaries, he gave to the innkeeper, and said to him, Be careful of him, and whatever thou mayest spend more, I, in my coming again, will give back to thee.

[36]'Who, then, of these three, seemeth to thee to have become neighbour of him who fell among the robbers?' [37]and he said, 'He who did the kindness with him,' then Jesus said to him, 'Be going on, and thou be doing in like manner.' (Emphasis added.)

Jesus' answer tells that strangers and even those who might be considered enemies, are included as your neighbors, to whom you owe a duty of love under the law. Love is a higher frequency. We are to consider strangers never met, even those in dire need, to be neighbors to whom a duty of love is owed under the law.

If in fact you follow this law, then you will be the recipient of what you give others, and if that is good, then you shall receive good. Is this not fairness itself? And if it be bad acts, or selfishness, or indifference, that you give others, then what better way to learn compassion and empathy than meeting with that gift yourself? Our neighbors are not just those who are like us, but rather, as given in Jesus' example, those who may be considered very unlike us. "Neighbor" appears to refer to *anyone* near enough to you to be affected by you at any given time.

Why does treatment of your neighbor encapsulate the law? Because the law (of reincarnation) ensures that you will reap what you sow and receive the very treatment you give to others around you. *We are all derivative of God. We are one being even if we appear to be separate. This means that what we do to another we actually do to ourselves.*

Consider as an example, that John the Baptist, a revered figure in the New Testament, and one that even Herod believes to be a righteous man, is in fact beheaded and meets with a horrible demise at the hands of a seemingly treacherous woman. What is the meaning and purpose of this? What were events in one of John's previous lives as Elijah?

See 1 Kings 18:17-20, YLT.

> [17] And it cometh to pass at Ahab's seeing Elijah, that Ahab saith unto him, 'Art thou he—the troubler of Israel?' [18]And he saith, 'I have not troubled Israel, but thou and the house of thy father, in your forsaking the commands of Jehovah, and thou goest

> after the Baalim; [19]and now, send, gather unto me all Israel, unto the mount of Carmel, *and the prophets of Baal four hundred and fifty, and the prophets of the shrine, four hundred—eating at the table of Jezebel.*' [20]And Ahab sendeth among all the sons of Israel, and gathereth the prophets unto the mount of Carmel. (Emphasis added.)

See 1 Kings 18:40, YLT.

> [40]And Elijah saith to them, 'Catch ye the prophets of Baal; let not a man escape of them;' and they catch them, ***and Elijah bringeth them down unto the stream Kishon, and doth slaughter them there.*** (Emphasis added.)

See 1 Kings 19:1-2, YLT.

> [1] And Ahab declareth to Jezebel all that Elijah did, and all how he slew all the prophets by the sword, [2]and Jezebel sendeth a messenger unto Elijah, saying, 'Thus doth the gods, and thus do they add, surely about this time to-morrow, I make thy life as the life of one of them.'

Elijah had the prophets of Baal murdered and heads rolled.

What is the law? What happened to Elijah, arisen again as John the Baptist?

Elijah lopped off the heads of others and lost his own in this incarnation as John the Baptist. Yes, he was a servant of the Lord, a righteous man, and he reaped what he sowed. No greater man born to woman, according to Jesus himself, and still subject to the law.

THE LAW

Why is it so important to understand reincarnation? Because it is near impossible to understand the working of the law (reaping what you sow) without understanding reincarnation. ***Reincarnation is the mechanism by which you learn lessons and reap what you sow.*** Without an understanding of reincarnation and the law, there is little understanding of why we are here in our particular circumstances, or how to improve our circumstances.

See Matthew 26:52, YLT.

> 52Then saith Jesus to him, 'Turn back thy sword to its place; for all who did take the sword, by the sword shall perish;

See Matthew 7:1–2, YLT.

> 1'Judge not, that ye may not be judged, 2for in what judgment ye judge, ye shall be judged, and in what measure ye measure, it shall be measured to you.

See Matthew 12:36-37, YLT.

> 36'And I say to you, that every idle word that men may speak, they shall give for it a reckoning in a day of judgment; 37for from thy words thou shalt be declared righteous, and from thy words thou shalt be declared unrighteous.'

See Galatians 6:7–9, YLT.

> [7]Be not led astray; God is not mocked; for what a man may sow—that also he shall reap, [8]because he who is sowing to his own flesh, of the flesh shall reap corruption; and he who is sowing to the Spirit, of the Spirit ***shall reap life age-during***; [9]***and in the doing good we may not be faint-hearted, for at the proper time we shall reap***—not desponding; (Emphasis added.)

See Revelations 13:9–10, YLT.

> [9]if any one hath an ear—let him hear: [10]if any one a captivity doth gather, into captivity he doth go away; if any one by sword doth kill, it behoveth him by sword to be killed; here is the endurance and the faith of the saints.

See Matthew 7:12, YLT.

> [12] 'All things, therefore, whatever ye may will that men may be doing to you, so also do to them, for ***this is the law*** and the prophets.

Do any of us know individuals who have done things but not appeared to receive like treatment in this lifetime? Yes, we all do. How can these many verses, all emphatically setting forth the same idea – that you will receive what you do to others – be true, unless the receipt occurs in a future lifetime?

See Luke 6:27-37, YLT.

27 'But I say to you who are hearing, Love your enemies, do good to those hating you, 28bless those cursing you, and pray for those accusing you falsely; 29and to him smiting thee upon the cheek, give also the other, and from him taking away from thee the mantle, also the coat thou mayest not keep back.

30 'And to every one who is asking of thee, be giving; and from him who is taking away thy goods, be not asking again; 31***and as ye wish that men may do to you, do ye also to them in like manner***; 32and—if ye love those loving you, what grace have ye? for also the sinful love those loving them; 33and if ye do good to those doing good to you, what grace have ye? for also the sinful do the same; 34and if ye lend *to those* of whom ye hope to receive back, what grace have ye? for also the sinful lend to sinners—that they may receive again as much.

35 '***But love your enemies, and do good, and lend, hoping for nothing again, and your reward will be great***, and ***ye shall be sons of the Highest***, because He is kind unto the ungracious and evil; 36be ye therefore merciful, as also your Father is merciful.

37 '***And judge not, and ye may not be judged; condemn not, and ye may not be condemned; release, and ye shall be released***. (Emphasis added.)

How do we get to be sons of the Highest? By doing good, even to those who are evil to us, and hoping for nothing in return; by doing unto others as we wish them to do unto us.

"Judge not, and ye may not be judged; condemn not, and ye may not be condemned; release, and ye shall be

released. ***"*** What are we to be released from? From the obligations we create through our wrongful thoughts, words, and deeds – sin. From the requirement to come back again to meet the circumstances we have directed toward another. When we forgive others and release them from wrongs they may have done, we actually secure our own release. You attain forgiveness by giving it away, releasing, not holding onto wrongs, pain, other emotions caused by wrongs. Many people think that forgiveness is release for the other person, but failing to release keeps *us* bound.

If we believe these words, then we don't get an easy out from belief or faith. We are held accountable for every action and these effects are sometimes not seen until coming lifetimes when circumstances will meet us with just what we have earned for ourselves. The reason and purpose for reincarnation is why it is so pivotal to understand the workings of "the law."

A release from our own obligations is only achieved when we have released others, when we have given that which we would like to receive. By being gracious with others, we ourselves may receive grace and its benefits. Sometimes actions do not appear to be answered with consequences. Many do not believe they will have to reap what they sow because they believe in Jesus' personal sacrifice alone will absolve them of sins. But this is NOT what Jesus clearly states.

See Matthew 22:34-40, YLT.

> 34 And the Pharisees, having heard that he did
> silence the Sadducees, were gathered together unto
> him; 35 and one of them, a lawyer, did question,
> tempting him, and saying, 36 'Teacher, which *is* the
> great command in the Law?' 37 And Jesus said to

> him, '*Thou shalt love the Lord* thy God with all thy heart, and with all thine understanding— [38]this is a first and great command; [39]and the second *is* like to it, ***Thou shalt love thy neighbour*** as thyself; [40]on these—the two commands—all the law and the prophets do hang.' (Emphasis added.)

See Matthew 5:17-20.

> [17]'***Do not suppose that I came to throw down the law or the prophets—I did not come to throw down, but to fulfil; [18]for, verily I say to you, till that the heaven and the earth may pass away, one iota or one tittle may not pass away from the law, till that all may come to pass***. (Emphasis added.)

Jesus very clearly states that he is not abolishing the law. He is fulfilling the prophecy that foretold of him, the Messiah, but you will still reap what you sow. Not one letter, not one stroke of a letter will be removed. He is the light and the way. Whosoever believeth in him will not die. But he is your example, not your absolution. If you believe in him then believe his plain-spoken words. Follow his instruction and you have the way. ***"The way" is not the task done. "The way" is what you must do to accomplish the task. "The light" does not perform tasks. "The light" illuminates the path so you may move forward. It does not circumvent the need for any of us to traverse the path, or go the way, or perform the task.***

But what of the scripture that assures us that our good works will not save us?

See Ephesians 2:1–10, YLT.

> [1] Also you—***being dead in the trespasses and the sins***, [2]in which once ye did walk according to the age of this world, according to the ruler of the authority of the air, of the spirit that is now working in the sons of disobedience, [3]among whom also we all did walk once in the desires of our flesh, doing the wishes of the flesh and of the thoughts, and were by nature children of wrath—as also the others.
>
> [4] And God, being rich in kindness, because of His great love with which He loved us, [5]even being dead in the trespasses, did make us to live together with the Christ, (by grace ye are having been saved,) [6]and did raise *us* up together, and did seat *us* together in the heavenly *places* in Christ Jesus, [7]that He might show, in the ages that are coming, the exceeding riches of His grace in kindness toward us in Christ Jesus, [8]***for by grace ye are having been saved, through faith, and this not of you—of God the gift,*** [9]***not of works, that no one may boast;*** [10]***for of Him we are workmanship, created in Christ Jesus to good works***, which God did before prepare, that in them we may walk. (Emphasis added.)

The author, attributed as Paul, states that good works are necessary and will be present for the saved. Jesus attempted to illustrate the "way" to salvation, but you will still have to have good works, and you will still answer for your deeds. This scripture states you are created in Christ Jesus ***to good works,*** and that the reason it is "***not of works***" that any are saved is so "***that no one may boast.***" If you are a follower of Jesus, good works *are* the lesson. If you don't get the lesson, do you think you will be "saved," that you will be commensurate with a graduation at "the next age?" Jesus' sacrifice should not be used to abolish the law (reincarnation and personal accountability) that Jesus stated he came to fulfill. Reincarnation, personal responsibility, accountability, and correction are the way to the rising *out* of the cycle. During Jesus' time it was well understood that sacrifices were offered to atone for *past, "bygone,"* sins not for absolution against future sins (see Romans 3:25, YLT).

Each of us receives the equivalent of our deeds. What about all the scriptures about forgiveness? Aren't I forgiven, as Jesus states, for my misdeeds? Yes, but a sincere desire for forgiveness necessitates an awareness of the error and repentance for wrongful actions. The release of forgiveness does not work one-way. If you desire forgiveness, a release from your misdeeds, you must also willingly give forgiveness and release others whose misdeeds have been directed toward you. If you truly repent, do you continue to do the same misdeeds again and again? No, you don't. And if you have a problem with doing certain misdeeds again and again, then you must learn by meeting yourself, by meeting the circumstances you have inflicted on or sent to another. If your awareness or will, your heart, is changed and you no longer commit that sin then further lesson is not needed.

Scripture states that even the man who was Jesus learned obedience.

See Hebrews 5:7–10, YLT.

> [5]so also the Christ did not glorify himself to become chief priest, but He who spake unto him: '***My Son thou art, I <u>to-day</u> have begotten thee***;' [6]as also in another *place* He saith, 'Thou *art* a priest—***to the age***, according to the order of Melchisedek;'

> [7]***who in the days of his flesh both prayers and supplications unto Him who was able to save him from death***—with strong crying and tears—having offered up, and having been heard in respect to that which he feared, [8]***through being a Son, did learn by the things which he suffered—the obedience,*** [9]***and having been made perfect, he did become to all those obeying him a cause of salvation age-during.*** (Emphasis added.)

Jesus became a son. "Today I have begotten thee." "In the days of his flesh" Jesus "did learn by the things which he suffered" "and having been made perfect" "did become to all those obeying him a cause of salvation age-during."

Jesus is a cause of salvation during this age for all those who obey him (not just those who profess faith).

This passage states clearly that Jesus suffered and was "made perfect."

See John 8:56-59, YLT.

> [56]Abraham, your father, was glad that he might see my day; and he saw, and did rejoice.' [57]The Jews, therefore, said unto him, 'Thou art not yet fifty years old, and Abraham hast thou seen?' [58]Jesus said to them, 'Verily, verily, I say to you, ***Before Abraham's coming—I am***;' [59]they took up, therefore, stones that they may cast at him, but Jesus hid himself, and went forth out of the temple, going through the midst of them, and so passed by. (Emphasis added.)

Jesus himself professed to have lived before and seen Abraham. And his listeners attempted to stone him for the claim. The Jews believed the Messiah would be a man, not a God. Jesus, a Jew, believed himself to be the Messiah, a son of God, but he did not profess to be God. He believed his brothers may claim their status as sons upon the out-resurrection. Jesus taught the law of reincarnation and the way to graduate from the lessons taught by reincarnation, the way to become a son of God. Jesus specifically separated himself from God, the Father, and did not equate himself and God/the Father, something the evolving church eventually refused to acknowledge and strove to eradicate.

See John 14:28, YLT.

> 28 Ye heard that I said to you—I go away, and I come unto you; if ye did love me, ye would have rejoiced that I said—I go on to the Father, ***because my Father is greater than I***. (Emphasis added.)

Jesus said he was a son of God, but he talked of other sons of God and told us how others could become children of God. The raising of the vibrational self through choices and actions in successive reincarnations, learning to apply will and intention leads to the reign of God.

This is the real failing of Christianity – teaching comfort for all that no matter what you do, all is absolved without consequence to yourself. There are many who do not appear to be reaping what they sow, good or bad. But if the mechanism of reincarnation is understood, then the law becomes far more pertinent, in a way that really isn't currently understood. People are not worried about receiving in the future the energy they are directing toward others. Many are not worried about judgment because they believe that they are saved through their belief, that they will not have to be subject to the law, and that they will not have to reap what they sow. Jesus clearly states otherwise over and over again. Most do not understand they are meting out their own judgment even though Jesus stated as much.

See Matthew 7:1, YLT.

> 1 'Judge not, that ye may not be judged, 2 for in what judgment ye judge, ye shall be judged, and in what measure ye measure, it shall be measured to you.

Many are familiar with this scripture, but they don't really believe this. They do not believe the law is as exacting as Jesus keeps trying to tell them. If they did, people would be conducting themselves in a far higher manner than they actually do.

See Luke 6:37-38, YLT.

> 37 '***And judge not, and ye may not be judged; condemn not, and ye may not be condemned; release, and ye shall be released***.
>
> 38 'Give, and it shall be given to you; good measure, pressed, and shaken, and running over, they shall give into your bosom; for with that measure with which ye measure, it shall be measured to you again.' (Emphasis added.)

What you do to your fellow man, you will eventually receive yourself. The salvation Jesus offers is in learning the truth, the way the mechanism of reincarnation/the law operates, the way to become a son of God. It is the way to salvation that is offered but it still requires some effort of each of us.

The workings of the law, as facilitated by reincarnation, aren't punitive, they are a mechanism for learning. Do you have little compassion for those less fortunate, less able? Then experience it and you may yet learn compassion. Do you lack forgiveness for certain kinds of conduct or certain kinds of people? Then you may come to know circumstances desperate enough to cause you to take whatever actions you have difficulty forgiving. Or perhaps there is some conduct that you inflict on others with impunity, without seeing the effects, until the same conduct happens to you and you are the receiver of the conduct instead of the sender.

It may seem odd that you could have learned things and not remember the lesson, or that you could have to endure things and not remember the reasons why, but this *is* how learning works. Most of us know how to read, spell, add, subtract, and multiply, but we can't recall all of the lessons we spent learning those skills. For correction to be effective, memory is necessary, for learning to be effective, a forgotten learning process does not erase the knowledge. The law is educational, not punitive. It may produce suffering, but it is a suffering of our own creation and one that can be avoided if Jesus' words of assistance and caution are heeded. Wouldn't it be easier if each of us realized our circumstances were no accident, not random and that we are creating our circumstances of tomorrow?

How many 'devout' and 'faithful' have wondered bitterly why a just and omniscient God would allow such perversity, tragedy, and sorrow to continue in the world, seemingly unanswered. How humbling to realize God has only allowed all our ills to the extent we have created them ourselves and that they are not in fact unanswered, but answered again and again by ourselves. God has not made the world imperfect, we have, through our own thoughts, words, and deeds.

Under this law there is no need for jealousy. What skills your neighbor possesses or talents he has, he has acquired through doing, in this lifetime or previously. Therefore with patience and practice you may acquire whatever skill you are willing to practice enough to master. Virtuosos and prodigies may not be simply born advanced, but may be bringing forward talents, skills and interests from previous experience.

This is not to assert that Jesus, in his incarnation as Jesus, was not divine. Each of our souls inhabits our bodies for a time and purpose. The body is called a temple. Something that dwells within each of us is, in fact, part of Source/God.

See 1 Corinthians 3:16-17, YLT.

> 16 Have ye not known that ye are a sanctuary of God, ***and the Spirit of God doth dwell in you***? 17if any one the sanctuary of God doth waste, him shall God waste; for the sanctuary of God is holy, the which ye are. (Emphasis added.)

If the Spirit of God dwells in each of us, then to sin against another is a sin against God and against that part of ourselves that is the same as the "other."

See 2 Corinthians 6:14-18, YLT.

> 14Become not yoked with others—unbelievers, for what partaking *is there* to righteousness and lawlessness? 15and what fellowship to light with darkness? and what concord to Christ with Belial? or what part to a believer with an unbeliever? 16and what agreement to the sanctuary of God with idols?

> ***for ye are a sanctuary of the living God***, according as God said—'I will dwell in them, and will walk among *them*, and I will be their God, and they shall be My people, [17]wherefore, come ye forth out of the midst of them, and be separated, saith the Lord, and an unclean thing do not touch, and I—I will receive you, [18]***and I will be to you for a Father, and ye—ye shall be to Me for sons and daughters, saith the Lord Almighty.'*** (Emphasis added.)

Doesn't the affirmation that we are each a "sanctuary of the living God" support Jesus' assertions that we can all become sons of God? Wouldn't common divinity, and the same creative source, bring new meaning to the ideas of praying for your enemy and turn the other cheek? Don't *all living things* share a spark of the creator as their living spirit? If God is the energy behind all living matter, then it's not just that all are from God but all *are* God. Why is God so often referred to as a *living* God? What import does this bring to not only the manner in which we treat one another but also animals, plants, and the Earth itself?

Consider for a moment the scene in Mark 11:15, and Matthew 21:12, the example of Jesus' anger – acted upon at the temple, with the money changers, where animals were sold for sacrifice, for slaughter. Even if we believe we are held accountable for our treatment of other people – this illustrates the importance Jesus gives to the treatment of God's creatures. Isn't it unrighteous to abuse or ill use animals also created by God? Wouldn't this also be action for which we are held accountable, reaping what we sow?

The proposition that good works are required is not new. Good works performed only to achieve an end without being an outgrowth of right motivations and intentions would not appear to be the same as good works performed for the simple purpose of being helpful or beneficial to another. This seems to be where Paul diverges from other apostles insisting that works do not get you to the reign of God. This philosophy of faith alone became the bedrock of christian doctrine, and yet it appears false, and not in alignment with Jesus' teachings. There are plenty of scriptures which illustrate that good works are, in fact, necessary, and are the natural and logical result of following Jesus' admonitions. Jesus himself is given credit for telling us so.

See John 5:28, YLT.

> [28] 'Wonder not at this, because there doth come an hour in which ***all*** those in the tombs shall hear his voice, [29]and they shall come forth; ***those who did the good things to a rising again of <u>life</u>***, and ***those who practised the evil things to a rising again of <u>judgment</u>***. (Emphasis added.)

Jesus is *not* reported to say that all die and are judged and some rise to life. Judgment as stated above is reserved for those "who practiced the evil things." The word translated here from the Greek as judgment could also be translated as "sentence." The "sentence" for them is rendered by their own hand. They will endure what they have visited upon others. They will continue in the reincarnation death and rebirth cycle. But those who have done good, have no need of "judgment," or "sentence," of enduring their treatment of others, for their treatment of others was good. The "law" would mean that good things come to/return to those who send good energy to others. If energy is sufficiently raised to align, they rise to an existence without death, to "life" having graduated from the lessons taught in the reincarnation cycle. The mechanism of the cycle being that truly, what you do to others, returns to you.

If you reject your kinship to Jesus and his journey, then you deprive yourself of what "the way" is, you fail to hear or benefit from his life's divine mission and the grace you are offered to set you free from the workings of the law you have not understood or appreciated. It is enough to read the many repetitions of the law as given by Jesus and his assertion that he came not to abolish it to pay heed to its workings.

If we answer for all we do and say, and even think, and if we don't get a free pass by professing belief in Jesus, then how did the message get so distorted? What about the passages cited herein makes us uncomfortable?

See John 10:31-38, YLT.

> 31Therefore, again, did the Jews take up stones that
> they may stone him; 32Jesus answered them, 'Many
> good works did I shew you from my Father; because
> of which work of them do ye stone me?' 33The Jews
> answered him, saying, 'For a good work we do not
> stone thee, but for evil speaking, and because thou,
> being a man, dost make thyself God.' 34Jesus
> answered them, 'Is it not having been written in your
> law: I said, ***ye are gods***? 35if them he did call gods
> unto whom the word of God came, (and the Writing
> is not able to be broken,) 36of him whom the Father
> did sanctify, and send to the world, do ye say—Thou
> speakest evil, because I said, ***Son of God I am***? 37if I
> do not the works of my Father, do not believe me;
> 38and if I do, even if me ye may not believe, the
> works believe, that ye may know and may believe

that in me *is* the Father, and I in Him.'
(Emphasis added.)

Jesus' reference to, "I said, ye are gods" being written in the law appears to be a reference to Psalm 82.

See Psalm 82, YLT.

Psalm 82 1.—A Psalm of Asaph. God hath stood in the company of God, In the midst God doth judge.
2 Till when do ye judge perversely? *And the face of the wicked lift up*? Selah.
3 Judge ye the weak and fatherless, *The afflicted and the poor declare righteous*.
4 *Let the weak and needy escape, From the hand of the wicked deliver them*.
5 ***They knew not, nor do they understand, In darkness they walk habitually***, Moved are all the foundations of earth.
6 I—I have said, ***'Gods ye are, And sons of the Most High—all of you***,
7 ***But as man ye die***, and as one of the heads ye fall,
8 *Rise, O God, judge the earth,* ***For Thou hast inheritance among all the nations***! (Emphasis added.)

What does this say? How long will you *judge perversely and the face of the wicked lift up*? *Declare the afflicted and the poor righteous* (worthy of resurrection out of the cycle of death and rebirth). *Let the weak and the needy escape the hand of the wicked. Deliver them from the hand of the wicked* (which they are forced to endure within the cycle).

The wicked know not, nor do they understand, they habitually walk in darkness (they do not know they are here to learn lessons, they do not understand what they need to do to progress, and they habitually continue their errors in their lack of knowledge and understanding).

All of you are gods and sons of the most high, but as men you die. Judge the earth, God, for you have inheritance in <u>all</u> nations. Some individuals in *all* nations, not just Hebrews, Jews, or followers of Jesus, are worthy of resurrection out of the cycle of death and rebirth, some are worthy of inheriting their status as sons of God and leaving behind their lessons as men.

What is the import of Jesus citing this scripture? Jesus believed *all* were sons of the most high, and there were those ready to inherit in *all* nations. Jesus does not believe or advocate that only belief in him leads to resurrection out of the cycle. Jesus believes that worth determined through choices and actions, words and intentions, will mean some in every nation are worthy of their inheritance to become sons of God, being worthy of the resurrection out of the cycle.

Jesus affirmed "in me *is* the Father, and I in Him" (John 10:38). If Jesus himself believes we are all gods, we are all capable of becoming sons of the most high and if Jesus himself does not set himself apart from us except as an example, a mediary to what we are to achieve and become, then what does it mean for Jesus to say the father is in him and he is in the father? The father is in us and we are in the father. Isn't that required for us to all "be gods?" Don't we have some latent, undeveloped capabilities or at least, possibilities that Jesus is trying to help us grow toward?

What does it mean that Jesus himself, even though *his* power did not vary from locale to locale, could not heal in his hometown, *because of the nonbelief of those there*?

See Mark 6:1-5, YLT.

> [1] And he went forth thence, and came to his own country, and his disciples do follow him, [2]and sabbath having come, he began in the synagogue to teach, and many hearing were astonished, saying, 'Whence hath this one these things? and what the wisdom that was given to him, that also such mighty works through his hands are done? [3]***Is not this the carpenter, the son of Mary, and brother of James, and Joses, and Judas, and Simon? and are not his sisters here with us?***'—and they were being stumbled at him. [4]And Jesus said to them—'A prophet is not without honour, except in his own country, and among his kindred, and in his own house;' [5]***and he was not able there any mighty work to do, except on a few infirm people having put hands he did heal them;*** [6]***and he wondered because of their unbelief.*** And he was going round the villages, in a circle, teaching. (Emphasis added.)

See Matthew 13:54-58, YLT.

> [54]and having come to his own country, he was teaching them in their synagogue, so that they were astonished, and were saying, 'Whence to this one this wisdom and the mighty works? [55]is not this the carpenter's son? is not his mother called Mary, and his brethren James, and Joses, and Simon, and Judas? [56]and his sisters—are they not all with us? whence, then, to this one all these?' [57]and they were stumbled at him. And Jesus said to them, 'A prophet

> is not without honour except in his own country, and in his own house:' [58]***and he did not there many mighty works, because of their unbelief.*** (Emphasis added.)

There is something within each of us, the prospective recipient of healing, that must participate and help effectuate our own healing, even with Jesus there to perform great works, of which many were reported. There must be a central component of that work separate and apart from Jesus himself that each person he was working with, and maybe even those around them, contributed toward a successful or unsuccessful result. What is the mechanism of Jesus' healing if unbelief on the part of those being healed prevented Jesus from performing any might works?

What was the reason for the authorities' persecution of Jesus and his message? He challenged the concepts of religious teachings, authority, and order of the time. He and his teachings threatened those with power and sought to empower everyone, even the powerless. In truth, his teaching reveals a different power, not external, which comes from a larger, broader awareness or consciousness regarding ourselves and others. It also held those with power responsible for their use of power, their actions, and their treatment of others, making them directly answerable for it. During Jesus' time, some believed illness and malady were earned. Such conditions may have been believed to be karmic results by groups such as the Pharisees familiar with reincarnation. As a consequence, the ill and infirm were excluded from society and shunned from temple. Jesus' healing of the infirm challenged the authority of those doing the excluding and shunning by allowing them to rejoin the mainstream. Such healing also raised the question whether

Jesus had the authority to release the infirm person from what may have been perceived as just consequences.

Jesus said "ye are gods" (John 10:34, YLT). He also said even more.

See John 14:12, YLT.

> [12] 'Verily, verily, I say to you, he who is believing in me, the works that I do—that one also shall do, *and greater than these he shall do*, because I go on to my Father; (Emphasis added.)

Jesus tells us that those who believe in him, in his works shall do greater works than he, *because* I go on to my Father.

What is it about his "going on" to the father that will enable those who trust Jesus to perform better works? Jesus intends to illustrate the way out of the cycle. If you have testimony or an illustration of one having graduated out of the cycle, and you know what you must do to get out of the cycle, then you can achieve that and more.

Jesus tells us he is our example, the way, the light. Jesus is the illustration, example, and way shower, but he never claimed to exempt us from the law, rather he clearly proclaimed that he came to fulfill the law. The law is you reap what you sow. Following Jesus' teaching doesn't mean you get to escape the reaping of what you have sown, rather it helps you achieve a better reaping, a "better" resurrection.

Consider again Jesus' conversation with Nicodemus.

See John 3:1 -10, YLT.

> [1] And there was a man of the Pharisees, Nicodemus his name, a ruler of the Jews, [2]this one

> came unto him by night, and said to him, 'Rabbi, we have known that from God thou hast come—a teacher, for no one these signs is able to do that thou dost, if God may not be with him.' [3]Jesus answered and said to him, 'Verily, verily, I say to thee, ***If any one may not be born from above, he is not able to see the reign of God;*** ' [4]Nicodemus saith unto him, 'How is a man able to be born, being old? is he able into the womb of his mother a second time to enter, and to be born?' [5]Jesus answered, 'Verily, verily, I say to thee, ***If any one may not be born of water, and the Spirit, he is not able to enter into the reign of God; [6]that which hath been born of the flesh is flesh, and that which hath been born of the Spirit is spirit.***
>
> [7] 'Thou mayest not wonder that I said to thee, It behoveth you to be born from above; [8]the Spirit where he willeth doth blow, and his voice thou dost hear, but thou hast not known whence he cometh, and whither he goeth; thus is every one who hath been born of the Spirit.' [9]Nicodemus answered and said to him, 'How are these things able to happen?' [10]Jesus answered and said to him, '***Thou art the teacher of Israel—and these things thou dost not know***! (Emphasis added.)

This is a strange and interesting conversation between Nicodemus, a Pharisee, and Jesus. We have already seen that Pharisees believed in the resurrection that is reincarnation although the Sadducees did not. We have already seen that the form of resurrection they could be expected to be familiar with is reincarnation, a concept believed in many parts of the ancient world. So Nicodemus, who the scripture is careful to identify as a Pharisee, could be expected to already be familiar with the concept of reincarnation. Yet, he seems not to understand what Jesus is talking to him about. What is Jesus talking to him about?

The Greek word, *anóthen* translated here as "from above" is also shown by Greek language sources to mean "from above," "from the beginning," and "again" (Strong's Concordance word number 509). Thayer's Greek Lexicon states this Greek word means "from above, from a higher place" Matthew 27:51; Mark 15:38; "from the upper part, from the top," John 19:23, "Often (also in Greek writings) used of things which come from heaven, or from God as dwelling in heaven": John 3:31; John 19:11; James 1:17; James 3:15, 17, "from the first": Luke 1:3; "from the beginning on, from the very first": Acts 26:5. "anew, over again, indicating repetition (a use somewhat rare, but wrongly denied by many....)" (Thayer's Greek Lexicon).

If Nicodemus should already believe in reincarnation, as a Pharisee, what about Jesus' statement denotes something other than, or more than being born again or anew (as would happen with reincarnation)? The definition indicating from above would be something other than just again or anew. What is Nicodemus questioning and what do the rest of Jesus statements tell him?

> *If any one may not be born from above, he is not able to see the reign of God.*

Nicodemus asks:

> *'How is a man able to be born, being old? is he able into the womb of his mother a second time to enter, and to be born?'*

We are already here, how do we manage to be born "from above." (I may understand we are in a cycle of death and rebirth but how can we be born from above?)

If any one may not be born of water, and the Spirit, he is not able to enter into the reign of God; [6]that which hath been born of the flesh is flesh, and that which hath been born of the Spirit is spirit.

Jesus answers that you cannot achieve the graduation unless you are already born of water and Spirit, unless you are already a being that is both physical and spiritual. The physical gives birth to your physical portion and the Spirit yields your spiritual portion. Your physical body is from here on Earth, but your Spiritual self is from above, from a higher place.

Jesus tells Nicodemus the following.

> *[8]the Spirit where he willeth doth blow, and his voice thou dost hear, but thou hast not known whence he cometh, and whither he goeth; thus is every one who hath been born of the Spirit*

Everyone's spiritual self is like the wind. As we live in our earthly bodies, many of us don't have conscious awareness of where our spiritual self was before birth or where it is going after death. In this life, it is like the wind. You may realize you are a spiritual being, like you may hear the wind, but many cannot remember or conceive its origin or destination. Furthermore, Jesus expects him to have some concept of the spiritual self as he is a teacher of Israel.

See John 3:11–21, YLT.

[11]'Verily, verily, I say to thee—What we have known we speak, and what we have seen we testify, and our testimony ye do not receive; [12]if the earthly things I said to you, and ye do not believe, how, if I shall say to you the heavenly things, will ye believe? [13]and ***no one hath gone up to the heaven, except he who out of the heaven came down—the Son of Man who is in the heaven***.

[14]'And as Moses did lift up the serpent in the wilderness, so ***it behoveth the Son of Man to be lifted up***, [15]that every one who is believing in him may not perish, but ***may have life age-during***, [16]for God did so love the world, that His Son—the only begotten [or rather as we have seen, *monogene* means one of a group, class]—He gave, that every one who is believing in him may not perish, but may have life age-during. [17]For ***God did not send His Son to the world that he may judge the world, but that the world may be saved through him***; [18]he who is believing in him is not judged, but ***he who is not believing hath been judged already***, because he hath not believed in the name of the only begotten [monogene] Son of God.

[19]***'And this is the judgment, that the light hath come to the world, and men did love the darkness rather than the light, for their works were evil; [20]for every one who is doing wicked things hateth the light, and doth not come unto the light, that his works may not be detected; [21]but he who is doing the truth doth come to the light, that his works may be manifested, that in God they are having been wrought***.' (Emphasis and *monogene* bracket added.)

Consider what Jesus tells Nicodemus.

What we have known we speak, and what we have seen we testify, and our testimony ye do not receive; [12]if the earthly things I said to you, and ye do not believe, how, if I shall say to you the heavenly things, will ye believe?

You have not believed or understood what we are teaching about how to escape the cycle of reincarnation, how are you supposed to believe or understand what I might teach about where your spirit comes from and where it goes?

If reincarnation is a truth, a mechanism of the law which all are subject to, Nicodemus, as a Pharisee, may be expected to know something of the concept as Herod and those around him do. The Sadducees, in being defined as those who do not believe in the resurrection that is reincarnation have been differentiated from another Jewish group that does believe in reincarnation - the Pharisees.

Consider again John:13, YLT.

> …***no one hath gone up to the heaven, except he who out of the heaven came down—the Son of Man who is in the heaven….***

No one can go to heaven except one who came down from heaven. The spiritual selves of men come from heaven to indwell physical bodies and they return up to a higher place. The use of a phrase meaning "from the top" further suggests that in the nonphysical realms some are higher than others. If the son of man is a reference that Jesus uses of himself and of mankind in general, and that is generally understood in Jewish usage to refer to man and his humble status, then all souls are spiritual selves that come down from heaven. But one born from the top might be advanced, might have special abilities, might be something like a messenger (angel) incarnate. And this idea of being born 'from the top' explains the response to Nicodemus's question, 'Rabbi, we have known that from God thou hast come—a teacher, for no one these signs is able to do that thou dost, if God may not be with him.'

CHAPTER ELEVEN

SYMBOLISM AND CHAKRAS

Portions of the Bible address matters with a meaning that appears to have been lost to many readers. Certain philosophies have long taught that the body has seven energy centers, or spiritual centers, called chakras that are aligned along the trunk of the body up to the crown. The chakra located on the forehead is commonly known as the "third eye" chakra.

Consider the following scripture, attributed to Christ.

See Matthew 6:22–23, YLT.

> 22 '***The lamp of the body is the eye***, if, therefore, thine eye may be perfect, all thy body shall be enlightened, 23but if thine *eye* may be evil, all thy body shall be dark; if, therefore, the light that *is* in thee is darkness—the darkness, how great! (Emphasis added.)

See Luke 11:34–36, YLT.

> 34 '***The lamp of the body is the eye***, when then thine *eye* may be simple, thy whole body also is lightened; and when it may be evil, thy body also is darkened; 35take heed, then, lest the light that *is* in thee be darkness; 36if then thy whole body is lightened, not having any part darkened, the whole shall be lightened, as when the lamp by the brightness may give thee light.' (Emphasis added.)

These scriptures, which are attributed to Jesus, only speak of one eye - "the" eye? The "third eye" is a reference that is commonly known. If the third eye chakra isn't what is being referred to, why use a distinctly singular and purposeful designation of only one eye?

What is the purpose of the chakra centers?

The seven chakra centers are the focus not only of bodily health, believed to correspond to certain glands of the endocrine system, they are also spiritual centers through which the life force (an energy) may be raised to higher levels of awareness. This is done through meditation.

The Bible refers to meditation as times of silence, stillness, listening for the Lord.

See Psalm 37:7, YLT.

> 7 ***Be silent for Jehovah, and stay thyself*** for Him, Do not fret because of him Who is making prosperous his way, Because of a man doing wicked devices. (Emphasis added.)

Some scripture also refers to meditation by stating that the speaker is "in the spirit" while meditating, and receives visions while "in the spirit," or meditating.

See Revelation 21:9-10, YLT.

> 9 And there came unto me one of the ***seven*** messengers, who have the ***seven*** vials that are full of the ***seven*** last plagues, and he spake with me, saying, 'Come, I will shew thee the bride of the Lamb—the wife,' 10 and he carried me away ***in the Spirit to a mountain great and high***, and did shew to me the great city, the holy Jerusalem, coming down out of

the heaven from God.... (Emphasis added.)

Seven is repeated and is significant. There are seven chakras, spiritual centers through which the life force energy can be raised. While "In the spirit," in a state of subjugation of the conscious mind, "he carried me away to a mountain great and high."

See Revelation 3:20-22, YLT.

> [19] *'As many as I love, I do convict* ***and chasten***; be zealous, then, and reform; [20]lo, ***I have stood at the door, and I knock***; ***if any one may hear my voice, and may open the door, I will come in unto him, and will sup with him, and he with me. [21]He who is overcoming—I will give to him to sit with me in my throne, as I also did overcome and did sit down with my Father in His throne***. [22]*He who is having an ear—let him hear* what the Spirit saith to the assemblies.' (Emphasis added.)

This says what Jesus told us, "the kingdom is within," or rather, in the literal translation, "the reign of god is within you."

See again Luke 17:20-21, YLT.

> [20] And having been questioned by the Pharisees, when the reign of God doth come, he answered them, and said, 'The reign of God doth not come with observation; [21]nor shall they say, Lo, here; or lo, there; for lo, ***the reign of God is within you***.' (Emphasis added.)

This is as plain as it gets. The reign of God is within

you. It is not an "other" place or an "other" time. It is a condition or state of being, of awareness, of consciousness. God is as close to you as to "stand knocking at the door," as to be able to "hear" his voice. But you must "open the door," to become aware of a higher existence. It exists at a higher level of energetic frequency and vibration. By raising the energetic life force through the seven chakra centers, one opens the door. This is how the kingdom where God dwells among us is achieved. God is within each of us. "To the one who conquers" himself, his ego, his willfulness, his conscious mind in a state of meditation, "I will give a place with me on the throne."

"He who is overcoming—I will give to him to sit with me in my throne, as I also did overcome and did sit down with my Father in His throne." I have overcome the physical and been resurrected out of the cycle of death and rebirth. He who also overcomes and achieves the out-resurrection can dwell with me in a higher place than this current one. Jesus does not elevate himself above us. He goes before us and tells us how to join him.

See Revelation 4:1-2, YLT.

> [1] After these things I saw, and lo, a door opened in the heaven, and the first voice that I heard *is* as of a trumpet speaking with me, saying, '***Come up hither***, and I will shew thee what it behoveth to come to pass after these things;' [2]and immediately I was ***in the Spirit***....(Emphasis added.)

Jesus is telling us that meditation is helpful, maybe even necessary, to having a healthy spiritual life, to commune with God, and that, when that occurs, and the third eye, the lamp, is filled with light, (the life force is raised to that level), the body too will be healthy. Ignore it if you like, but the message is in the text.

The replete imagery in the Bible regarding "the staff," "serpents," and references and groupings of seven are also purposeful references to the raising of the life force through the seven chakra centers in order to commune with God. The staff and the serpent are straight rods with curves at the top. These images refer to the raising of energy upward through the chakras. The chakra centers, when all are activated, would rise up the trunk (spine) and curve over the head, yielding a shape like a staff or a raised serpent. These references go completely unnoticed to many modern readers. This prompts an important and necessary question. Why would peoples' approach be so limiting? Because religion, in and of itself, limits belief in that it is a source of indoctrination, designed to convince people what to think and believe and what to reject. Consider that God himself places no such limitations on any of us.

Consider the words attributed to Jesus from John 9:11, YLT.

> [11] 'I am the good shepherd; the good shepherd his
> life layeth down for the sheep; [12]and the hireling, and
> not being a shepherd, whose own the sheep are not,
> doth behold the wolf coming, and doth leave the
> sheep, and doth flee; and the wolf catcheth them, and
> scattereth the sheep; [13]and the hireling doth flee
> because he is an hireling, and is not caring for the
> sheep.
>
> [14]'I am the good shepherd, and I know my *sheep*,
> and am known by mine, [15]according as the Father
> doth know me, and I know the Father, and my life I
> lay down for the sheep, [16]***and other sheep I have***

that are not of this fold, these also it behoveth me to bring, and my voice they will hear, and there shall become one flock—one shepherd.

[17]'Because of this doth the Father love me, because I lay down my life, that again I may take it; [18]no one doth take it from me, but I lay it down of myself; authority I have to lay it down, and authority I have again to take it; this command I received from my Father.' (Emphasis added.)

Doesn't "***and other sheep I have that are not of this fold***" suggest that we, however we may define ourselves, do not have a lock hold on how God may reveal himself? What does that say about institutions and practices that claim to have such ownership? Maybe some of us have been lied to about God and spiritual reality. Letting others translate for us is a dangerous prospect.

Jesus tells his disciples to not be troubled by the man who casts out demons in his name, though he is not one of them. Jesus states, "[40]for he who is not against us is for us" (Mark 9:40, YLT; Luke 9:50, YLT).

Why is Jesus not alarmed by this? Because the works performed are good works, they are helping people, and yield good fruit. Jesus is not alarmed because he does not seek power and authority for himself alone; because he knows that any man who could perform such works would have to be spiritually advanced. Additionally, he knows that this man could have acquired abilities and knowledge in previous lifetimes. He is not bothered that this man is different or not recognizable by the disciples. He does not undermine the person or his works but recognizes God's works through another, notwithstanding that person being different and unexpected, and Jesus can appreciate the works as ‘from God.’

CHAPTER TWELVE

BEYOND RELIGION
AND
JEWISH GROUPS OF THE DAY

The Bible speaks of Sadducees and Pharisees among the Jews. These are two divergent groups of Jews and their beliefs differ. Although not mentioned in the Bible there was another group of Jews during the time of Jesus known as Essenes. Biblically, Jesus is addressed as a rabbi, master, and teacher. Paul tells that he himself had been a Pharisee. No such information is given for Jesus. The Bible is famously silent about Jesus in childhood and between age 12 and adulthood. In fact, the story of his knowledge at 12, impressive enough to stump the teachers in the temple of Jerusalem certainly implies some pretty intense study of Jewish history, texts, and law of his day. Where did he gain this knowledge? We could probably ask the same about Jesus' close relative, John the Baptist, who was also a teacher with followers but was likewise not identified as Sadducee or Pharisee.

We know some things about Jewish life and history from the writings of Josephus, a Jewish historian who lived A.D. 37 – c.100 and wrote in the first century. He was born the son of a Jewish priest, was associated for a time with the Essenes and eventually joined the Pharisees.

Who were the Essenes and why might they be relevant to this discussion? Josephus tells us in his written work, *The Antiquities of the Jews*, that the Jewish community had *three* sects, the Pharisees, the Sadducees, and the Essenes (Book

13.5.9 (171)). He goes on to tell us that the Essenes believe that the circumstances that befall us are ordained by fate, the Sadducees believe nothing is ordained by fate, and the Pharisees are somewhat in between with some things being attributable to fate and some not (172-173).

Josephus writes, in *Antiquities*, Book 18.1.2-5, that the ***Pharisees believe that souls are immortal*** and that those who have lived virtuously ***are able to revive and live again*** (14). Josephus also writes that the ***Pharisees say that all souls are immortal***, the souls of bad men being subject to punishment, and ***the souls of good men being only removed into different bodies*** (*The Wars of the Jews,* 2.8.14, (163). This agrees with the biblical assertion that the Pharisees believed in the "rising again" of dead persons, or reincarnation, given in Acts 23:8, YLT.

Josephus further writes that the doctrine of the **Sadducees** is that ***souls are not immortal*** and ***die with their bodies*** (*Antiquities* 18.1.4(16). This assertion agrees with the biblical assertion that Sadducees do not believe in the "rising again" of dead persons, or reincarnation, given in Acts 23:8, YLT. Josephus also writes in *The Wars of the Jews*, 2.8.14, that the Sadducees believe God is unconcerned with whether we do or do not do evil (*Wars*, 164), that it is men's choice to act good or evil, and that men may act as they please, not believing in the immortality of the soul, or in punishments or rewards after a mortal life (*Wars*, 165). It is worth noting that the Sadducees were the wealthy and ruling class. How convenient for them it must have been to believe they could do as they pleased.

According to Josephus, the ***Essenes ascribe all things to God and teach that souls are immortal.*** They believe one should earnestly strive for the rewards of righteousness (*Antiquities* 18.1.5(18)). The Essenes send what they have dedicated to God into the temple, but they ***do not offer animal sacrifices and because of this they are excluded from the common court of the temple*** (19). They exceed all other virtuous men in righteousness as is shown by ***their practice in holding all things in common, which the rich and the poor enjoy equally*** (20).

Josephus confirms that the ***Essenes do not believe in masters and servants or slaves***, holding all in their group in the same inclusion and equality (21). While Josephus states that many do not marry wives (21) he also tells us in *The Wars of the Jews*, (Book 2, Chapter 8.2) that some Essenes do not completely deny that men should marry, so that mankind may be carried forward by succession (121).

According to Josephus, the Essenes despise riches, and ***those who join them must give what they have to be held in common for the whole group*** (*Wars*, 2.8.2 (122)). They do not live in one city or place but many live in every city. ***They take nothing with them when they travel and their fellow Essenes share everything with Essene travelers as if well acquainted*** (124 – 125). ***They ritually immerse themselves in water*** (129). ***They take meals together*** (131-132). ***They consider swearing worse than lying and it is to be avoided*** (136). They study ancient writings (136).

Anyone who wishes to join them must go through rigors and pains to do so for at least three years (138) ***and then they are bound to never release Essene doctrines to others even unto hazard to one's own life*** (142). Josephus writes that even during the war with the Romans they would smile in their pain, laughed to their tormentors and ***resigned their souls with cheerful willingness, as anticipating to receive them again*** (153). Josephus states that the ***Essenes believe the body is corruptible and impermanent but that the souls continue forever, immortal*** (154). They believe their bodies are prisons (154) and that ***when they are freed from their prison of flesh and released from their bondage, they rejoice and go upward*** (155). Good men improve in their life's conduct due to the hope they have of reward after death and bad men are restrained from bad acts by fear and anticipation that they should suffer immortal punishment after their death even though their vices may be presently concealed (157).

As is made clear by Josephus, Jesus is not the only Jew during his time who believes the soul is immortal and reincarnation is a truth. According to Josephus, both the Pharisees and the Essenes believed this, even though the Sadducees did not. This comports with what is stated about the Pharisees and the Sadducees in the New Testament. Why is there nothing about the Essenes in the Bible? Is it because, as Josephus states, they were excluded in the common court of the temple and did not make animal sacrifices? Are there other reasons why the Essenes might have gone unmentioned in the New Testament?

What similarities can we see in the practices of the Essenes and the teachings of Jesus? According to Josephus, the Essenes had the following practices.

Essenes forbade swearing;

Essenes held all property in common and joiners surrendered their property to the group;

Essenes did not sacrifice animals in the temple;

Essenes ritually immersed themselves in water as a purification;

Essenes took meals together as a group;

Essenes traveled without provisions because provision is made by others in their group at their destination;

Essenes believed their souls are immortal and incorruptible although the body is corruptible;

Essenes believed in rewards and punishments for lives lived; and

Essenes believed that good men would live again in different bodies through reincarnation.

Jesus' teachings differed from the Essenes in that he sought to teach everyone. He did not separate himself from those who did not believe as he did. Rather he sought to teach everyone a better way. But the above similarities are more than a little striking. Is it possible Jesus had studied with Essenes or himself been an Essene? Jesus certainly seems to be teaching a lot of the same ideas as those held by the Essenes. But the Essenes didn't teach publicly or to the masses. Their teachings were far more secreted and protected. Jesus is clearly trying to get his message to the masses. Maybe this is why Jesus does not seem to be aligned with any group by the texts. While texts could certainly have been whitewashed, it could also be that Jesus attempted to avoid being identified with certain groups so that he could be accessible, identifiable and ultimately, a symbol, to everyone. If that is the case, how ironic that his message to all should be reduced to a religion that there appears to be no evidence he intended.

There is every indication that Jesus attempted to take

people beyond religion and beyond the boundaries and groups that most used to separate themselves from others. Jesus was critical of and diverged sharply from religious leaders in his day. How tragic that Jesus has not only been made a symbol for limiting religious concepts and doctrine, but his message and teachings regarding reincarnation have also been stolen altogether by the very religion that brandishes him as a symbol for their own agenda.

See Luke 17:20–21, YLT.

> [20] And having been questioned by the Pharisees, when the reign of God doth come, he answered them, and said, 'The reign of God doth not come with observation; [21]nor shall they say, Lo, here; or lo, there; for lo, *the reign of God is within you.*'

The revelation that '*the reign of God is within you*' does not require anyone to have an intermediary or be part of a particular group or community. Everyone has the same access. 'Doing unto others' draws no exceptions. 'Reaping what you sow' applies to all – equally.

The Christian Church appears to base much of its doctrine on the approach taken by Paul, rather than the followers that remained in Jerusalem after the crucifixion, including James, Jesus' brother.

Why do writings attributed to Paul so often state that he is not lying and that it is acceptable to eat meat? Who is questioning if it is not acceptable to eat meat and who is accusing him of lying? Paul didn't know Jesus in life, never heard him teach, persecuted Jesus' followers horribly as Saul, but then becomes himself a follower of Jesus and teacher. The texts certainly indicate the disciples were untrusting of him and Paul spends a lot of time defending himself and giving proofs of his authority. How and why did the Church come to settle in the West after the temple was destroyed in 70 A.D.?

How does Jesus tell us to evaluate if a thing be good or evil? Jesus himself did not encourage a narrow perspective. Rather, he admonished his followers to be open to things that may not fit their expectations or currently held concepts and judge them by the fruit they produce.

See Mark 9:38-41, YLT.

> 38 And John did answer him, saying, 'Teacher, we saw a certain one in thy name casting out demons, who doth not follow us, and we forbade him, because he doth not follow us.' 39 And Jesus said, '***Forbid him not***, for there is no one who shall do a mighty work in my name, and shall be able readily to speak evil of me: 40 ***for he who is not against us is for us***.
>
> 41 For whoever may give you to drink a cup of water in my name, because ye are Christ's, verily I say to you, he may not lose his reward; (Emphasis added.)

Even Jesus himself was rejected by religious leaders *because no prophet was foretold from Galilee.*

See John 7:45-52, YLT.

> 45 The officers came, therefore, unto the chief priests and Pharisees, and they said to them, 'Wherefore did ye not bring him?' 46 The officers answered, 'Never so spake man—as this man.' 47 The Pharisees, therefore, answered them, 'Have ye also been led astray? 48 did any one out of the rulers

> believe in him? or out of the Pharisees? [49]but this multitude, that is not knowing the law, is accursed.' [50]Nicodemus saith unto them—he who came by night unto him—being one of them, [51]'Doth our law judge the man, if it may not hear from him first, and know what he doth?' [52]They answered and said to him, 'Art thou also out of Galilee? *search and see, that a prophet out of Galilee hath not risen*;' (Emphasis added.)

If we carefully examine the words attributed to Jesus in the canonical texts, what are we left with? Someone who never declared himself God, never purported to start a religion, never endorsed a group or religion, received a Spirit upon baptism that remained until it departed on the cross before death, never stated he was the *only* son, but clearly discussed *others* becoming sons/children of God, taught or delivered gospel – good news - to the masses, urged his followers to spread the good news, and gave others the same relation to God as himself.

See John 20:17, YLT.

> [17]Jesus saith to her, 'Be not touching me, for I have not yet ascended unto my Father; and *be going on to* ***my brethren***, and say to them, ***I ascend unto my Father, and your Father, and to my God, and to your God***.' (Emphasis added.)

Jesus said the reign of God is *within each of us* and attempted to lead people beyond religion with his message. Jesus was openly critical of the Pharisees and Sadducees and diverged from the Essenes in sharing knowledge of overcoming the cycle of birth and death with the masses.

He endorsed no group and instructed one to recognize the wolf from the sheep *by their fruits*.

See Matthew 7:15–20, YLT.

> [15] 'But, take heed of the false prophets, who come unto you in sheep's clothing, and inwardly are ravening wolves. [16]***From their fruits ye shall know them***; do *men* gather from thorns grapes? or from thistles figs? [17]so every good tree doth yield good fruits, but the bad tree doth yield evil fruits. [18]A good tree is not able to yield evil fruits, nor a bad tree to yield good fruits. [19]Every tree not yielding good fruit is cut down and is cast to fire: [20]***therefore from their fruits ye shall know them***. (Emphasis added.)

How do we ultimately evaluate this message? What is the fruit of expecting to receive what you mete out? Does that lead one to do, think, speak evil? Or good?

Truth may come in different forms from different sources particularly when dealing with an incomplete picture. Why would "church" doctrine attempt to narrow what may be spiritually legitimate if Jesus did not? Why do we expect spiritual revelation to be set and dead with nothing new, and no progression if Jesus proclaims God the God of *the living*? Do you believe God capable of revelation, to others as well as yourself?

To whose advantage does it work if you close off your mind and heart to further spiritual revelation and insight? Why has church doctrine taken a dim view of most everything that falls outside their purview or control? How does a doctrine of 'you have but one lifetime and you must spend it the way we say, following our dictates if you want to reach an eternal heaven and avoid an eternal hell,' compare with a doctrine or teaching of caution that 'what you reap you will sow,' eventually, and the meeting of these circumstances is meant to be an opportunity to grow, learn, improve, and become more aware? Which doctrine attempts to exert more power and control over your person, your life, and your soul? Which doctrine empowers each of us as a child of God? Which doctrine is congruent with a God who has given us complete freedom of choice and will?

If you knew yourself to be subject to the law of reincarnation, then you would know that good efforts yield good results. You would know that the time-line of your existence is longer than you may have realized, and that your efforts, both good and bad, create far reaching effects. Fear of death would be greatly, if not completely, reduced if you understood that you could take your talents and skills with you, if you knew you didn't have to try to squeeze everything into one lifetime. Rather we could make each lifetime count as progress in the rungs of a ladder, understanding that neither our failures nor our successes in one singular lifetime are our ultimate destinies.

Science informs us that matter and energy are interchangeable. Einstein's formula of general relativity $E=mc^2$, equates Energy (E) to the mass (m) of an object times the speed of light (c) squared (times itself). While advances in science continue, this formula simply means that every bit of matter is transferable or equivalent to some amount of energy. It also establishes or presupposes that a form of energy lays at the root of how matter comes into being. It is an assertion that the universe is energetic, frequency, vibration. Isn't that energy God? If this is the case, not only is all of matter traceable back to the energetic Source or God, but all of creation would, in a sense, be a form or expression of God as that energy took varying forms, frequencies, and vibrations. Is this what is meant by the scriptural term "*living God?*" How is God *living* in our three-dimensional existence? We think of some parts of creation being alive and others being inanimate, but the truth is all of matter is made of atoms which contain within them active, moving energetic particles. What we think of as inanimate is not without energy and movement. Energy can be transformed into matter, the physical stuff of our daily lives, and vice versa. This means also that matter should be transformable back into energy (or some nonphysical form that we may not currently understand as energy). We know that particles can behave as waves in some instances and under certain conditions. Matter is not nearly as fixed or solid as environmental observation would lead us to believe. Could physical anomalies be explained by the energies of higher awareness and consciousness if we but understood more about it?

Science informs us that space and time are an illusion that appears to serve a purpose. Science informs us that the observer changes the outcome of particle/wave experiments, simply by observing, by bringing consciousness to the situation, without *otherwise* physically participating (as shown in bucky ball, or double-slit experiments demonstrating quantum mechanics). This attests that consciousness affects matter, and its energetic wave equivalent. What if our "religious" or "spiritual" experiences or insights are simply glimpses into a higher dimension/dimensions that we do not have the sensory apparatus to normally be aware of, dimensions we have no language with which to express or gain understanding, dimensions which would have to appear to us only partly, imperfectly, or not at all? What if these may nevertheless be real dimensions that Jesus tried to inform us of and help us to grow toward? If our senses limit our perceptions of such higher dimensional realms, is it at all surprising that language is inept to express the nature of such things verbally?

And thus exists the crux of spiritual belief. Some feel it real, some do not. None seem to be able to conclusively "prove" spirituality although science is currently getting some intriguing results. Science supports that the believer, the seeker, is far more likely to have such an experience, no matter how slight or imperfect that glimpse because of their consciousness, expectation, state of mind or openness to possibility as shown in the observer experiments. So, the more you believe or question or seek, the more likely you are to have an affirming experience. The less you believe, or question, or seek, the less likely you are to have any experience at all because you expect none and doubt its possibility.

What are the larger truths of the universe? Science informs us that you live in a multidimensional universe. If the truth is that a great intelligence is at work here, then things are not as finite as some would have us believe. Atheists don't believe in God or a higher power because they believe it is unlikely, an impossible likelihood. They believe God does not exist and rely on their rationality for not believing in something that cannot be proven. But the logical conclusion of an inability to prove the existence of God is not that God does not exist, but rather that the existence of God is an unknown. Lack of proof, if one believes this, does not prove that God does *not* exist. In its most objective form, a lack of proof, at the very least, should lead to the conclusion that God *may or may not* exist. "I cannot know for sure there is a God" can never mean the same thing as - or be proof for - "I can know for sure there is not a God." Under this perspective, the possible existence of God simply remains an unknown, an enigma. It is completely *illogical* to be an atheist. The negative is generally very hard to prove. Atheists make the same mistake as those who have "God in a box" and can conceive of nothing spiritual or other-dimensional save for that which fits their own definition and pre-conceived notion of what God is or should be. Atheists believe events are random and chance, yet given all we know about the vastness of the universe each of us just happens to be a thinking, intelligent, self-aware being on this tiny, blue-green ball? The atheist is his own contradiction.

Many of us would rather close our eyes and walk around in a sleep-like state than muster the willpower and courage to question our current framework of beliefs, whether it might not be random after all. A lack of proof for one proposition does not provide proof for the other.

For believers it's the opposite. Believers already don't believe their existence is random. They believe in meaning and purpose. So, is all of time, all of space, all of the rest of creation, outside of this tiny blue-green ball, just a waste of time and space - does it serve no meaning or purpose? Which is it? Is your God a God of waste or a God of meaning and purpose? Does all of the extensive space of the universe exist for us few individuals on our tiny, blue green speck and the rest is simply a waste of space and matter and energy? Does all of time exist for us to have a brief span here before eternity and the remainder exists for eons with no purpose?

Do you believe God capable of revelation, to others as well as yourself? It happened to me. I was instructed from a dream to write this book, and sorely did not wish to do so. I did not wish to be ostracized. I did not wish to be reviled. I believed there were others equally or more capable than myself to do such a work, and resisted, for years. But how does one continue to seek guidance and instruction when one has refused to do as instructed? So I wrote this book. Don't take my word for anything. But don't take anyone else's either. If you pray, meditate, look inward and seek answers, you will be lead where you are supposed to go. I was. It is my fervent hope and prayer that nothing contained herein should lead any astray but that all should find themselves closer to the way, the meaning and the purpose that Jesus sought to bestow upon us. These mysteries have a purpose, to make us question and seek. If someone else's answers are not your own, so be it. But that does not absolve any of us of the task of finding our own answers. Seek with an earnest heart and an open mind and be prepared to be surprised and amazed.

APPENDIX

THE SUPRESSION

Well over 500 years after the crucifixion the Roman Emperor, Justinian, made defining declarations, without the cooperation and agreement of the official church leader at the time, Pope Vigilius, on what was and was not to be appropriate teachings and interpretations of the scriptures (church doctrine) - essentially what was and was not to be taught and consequently believed. Much of the populace at the time was illiterate. Justinian essentially outlawed belief in reincarnation within the Christian Church *and his empire* 500 years *after* the death of Jesus. But this was not the first time Christianity had been defined by the whim of those in power. emperors and church leaders had already been twisting Jesus' teachings for hundreds of years.

The First Ecumenical Council was the Nicene Council (also Nicaean) held in Nicaea in 325 A.D. This is well known in history and documented, but the vast majority of Christians are woefully unaware of their own theological history, the history of current Christian doctrine.

For modern Christians the birth of their religious beliefs can be traced back to and through what became the Catholic Church, even if many are not currently Catholic. Protestant denominations splintered off of Catholicism after the Reformation, begun in 1517, but Catholicism was the large root from which most of Christianity (at least as it currently exists) sprang. The major doctrinal philosophies of current Christian philosophy grew out of, and at times, in opposition to, Catholic doctrinal philosophy and scriptural interpretation.

It is always astonishing to note how many "Christians" have no idea that the books of their Bible were selected, or chosen, over the course of several hundred years after the death of Jesus. At the time that the church and secular (or "state") authority selected these particular books from a multitude of options, certain beliefs held at the time about authorship of the various books influenced their choices about which books to "accept." This acceptance and selection was also being influenced by the exercise of certain choices in preferring some "doctrines" over others. It is now generally accepted and known by scholars that many of the books that became "canonized" and made a part of the commonly accepted Bible, were not written by whom they were purported to be written. It was far from settled, even hundreds of years after the death of Jesus, which books were the best sources of study. The New Testament, as it is understood to exist today, consisting of a set list of books, did not exist in that definition for hundreds of years after the death of Jesus. Prior to the establishment of a "set" New Testament Canon there were a great many books claiming to be teachings of Jesus. If some were included, clearly some were excluded. How was it dictated which teachings were "acceptable"? And by whom?

Many of the excluded books were Gnostic Christian writings which referenced an acceptance of reincarnation as truth. Where would this other group of Christians have gotten this teaching? Why would teachings of reincarnation be suppressed? Who would suppression of reincarnation serve?

Additionally, the writings of many early church leaders, such as Origen, were outlawed by later (sometimes much later) Ecumenical Councils. Because their ideas were not being favored, their writings were destroyed in order to suppress ideas, opinions and interpretations of the scripture. In addition to reincarnation, one of these ideas was Universalism, the idea that it is intended that all souls are to be saved. The Ecumenical Councils were meetings held over the course of hundreds of years after the death of Christ, which decided disputed issues. Their decisions became doctrine. These councils were generally attended by church leadership and secular authority. However, some of the councils did not enjoy the full participation of church hierarchy and their edicts were issued by the emperor and those bishops whom the emperor could control or chose to favor. Many church leaders, teachers, and their writings were anathematized, deposed, exiled, or excommunicated when they supported interpretations of the scripture that the emperor did not favor. For some, this happened even after they had lived and died in good favor with the church. For many, their writings were purged many years later, without ever having been out of favor during their lifetime and without having the opportunity to defend their ideas, beliefs, interpretations or writings. The Ecumenical Councils were largely called to settle interpretational and doctrinal disputes between church authorities with secular authority frequently taking sides, or seeking consensus. Many now well-known Christian doctrines were *born* at these councils, *not* explicitly from the scriptures themselves and not from the time of Jesus. These Councils and *not* scripture itself determined such now accepted principles as:

- The Trinity;
- The Nicene Creed;
- Jesus Christ as God (and an object of worship); and

* Everlasting damnation to Hell (vs. Universal Salvation).

These aren't concepts that were clearly articulated by the texts that followed Jesus' time or the crucifixion. Rather, religious and secular leaders have "decided" what the scriptures meant over hundreds of years later. They also "decided" what constituted "accepted" scripture in the first case. In the case of some of these councils, Church leadership did not even call the councils to settle disputes, but rather, secular political power did. Is there a problem with that? Should there be?

The Councils went around and around with the conundrum of the nature of Jesus Christ and, ultimately, the dual characterization of Jesus as human and divine.

The portions of the discussion contained herein which detail history of the Ecumenical Councils are in general summarized from, with some direct quotations taken from, *The First Seven Ecumenical Councils (325-787) Their History and Theology*, (Collegeville, Minnesota: The Liturgical Press, originally published by Michael Glazier, Inc., Wilmington, Delaware, 1983, 1990) by Leo Donald Davis. In some cases, specific quotations and citations are taken from translation of the Ecumenical Council documents themselves as shown in *Nicene and Post-Nicene Fathers*, Second Series, Volume XIV, Edited by Philip Schaff and Rev. Henry Wallace, Cosimo Classics, New York, first published in 1900, 2007. Just a cursory review of the Councils' documents themselves is enough to reveal a mind-boggling and staggering amount of politicism, and the extremely creative and antagonistic nature of the evolution of 'the Church' and 'Christian doctrine.'

THE FIRST ECUMENICAL COUNCIL

The First Ecumenical Council was held in Nicaea in 325 A.D. It was called by the Holy Roman Emperor Constantine. It was said to be attended by roughly 300 "holy Fathers," although sources vary as to the exact number in attendance. One of the larger reasons this council was called was to resolve differences in teachings in different areas. It was also deemed necessary to establish the nature of Christ. *Some Christian leaders believed Jesus was a man, some a God.* Some thought Christ's human and divine elements formed an entirely new nature. Over time, it was repeatedly deemed by some in power that different interpretations or opinions on the texts should not be allowed to exist, and that their opinion or interpretation should prevail. The fact is that different interpretations of a written document will almost always be possible. This fact alone employs many of the world's lawyers in attempts to prevent alternative interpretations to written texts. As we all well know, that has *not* led to the extinction of all lawsuits and legal actions involving disputes over written texts, contracts, and agreements.

In *The First Seven Ecumenical Councils (325-787) Their History and Theology*, (The Liturgical Press: Collegeville, Minnesota, 1990, originally published by Michael Glazier, Inc., Wilmington, Delaware, 1983), author Leo Donald Davis puts forth the varied and different opinions and approaches of groups of the day and church leaders distinguishing differing viewpoints within "the development of Pre-Nicene trinitarian speculation" (Leo, p. 50),[i.e. prior to the all-important first Ecumenical Council that drove the selection of texts in the Bible] among the "Jewish converts," the "Gentile converts," Irenaeus, Monarchians, Origen, and

Arius. All of these varying takes and opinions on the trinity are what led to the Council of Nicaea (Leo, p. 50).

Why would we think or believe the Council got it correct? Why wouldn't we suspect that a power structure might seek to impose an interpretation beneficial to itself regardless of any detriment that might come to the masses?

It is worth noting that Jesus himself never seems to impinge on anyone's free will to think, listen, consider, decide, and reconsider for himself. A common phrase attributed to Jesus is let he "who has eyes" see and he "who has ears" listen or hear.

As a result of the Council of Nicaea, it was determined, among other things that Christ's nature was *homoousios*, the word adopted to refute Arianism. Among other things, Arius "insisted that if the Father had begotten a Son, then the son began to exist; and therefore, there was a period in which He did not exist." *The First Seven,* p. 53. This insistence went against other ideas on unity of Godhead. It should be noted that Arius was not the only religious leader and teacher to be a proponent of the idea and belief that God the Father is greater than and not equal to the Son, a belief which would seem to be well based scripturally given words attributed to Jesus in John 14:28, "my Father is greater than I." Arius recognized a distinction between the Father and son and did not advocate that they were exactly the same. "Alexander the bishop called a meeting of his priests and deacons" in which Alexander "insisted on the unity of the Godhead." *Ibid.*, p 53. Even though Arius "was called upon to recant" his position, he "refused and continued to spread his teachings." *Ibid.*, p. 53. According to Davis, Alexander led the charge to have Arius condemned (*Ibid.*, p.53). The problem was there was hardly any consensus among bishops, and while not necessarily Arian, there were other bishops who felt the son was distinguishable from the Father. Arius' supporters held their own synod and Emperor Constantine discovered that he had united his domain to find it divided by religion. There were also other synods with other ideas, discussions, and descriptions on the nature of Jesus and God. The Emperor Constantine is the authority that summoned the bishops to the First Ecumenical Council of Nicaea in 325 A.D.

Davis notes that Constantine "found in the organization of the ecclesiastical synods a procedure akin to the workings of the Roman Senate itself." *Ibid*, p. 57. Constantine, the Emperor, *also took an active part in the debates*. *Ibid*, p. 57. As Constantine would write later to the bishops on the subject of Easter, "Whatever is decided in the holy councils of the bishops must be attributed to divine will." *Ibid*, p. 57. Why say that unless he is quite rightly concerned that it will be claimed that the council actually reflects his influence and the imposition of his power on the process and results.

There you have it. If we say it is so, then it must be so. *According to divine will, because we said so*. Although it is commonly and routinely reported that 318 bishops attended the First Ecumenical Council, Davis asserts that research of source material has one eyewitness who said there were 250, while another deacon and secretary to bishop Alexander of Alexandria said 300. He also asserts that modern scholars analyzing extant lists estimate only 220. Later the symbolic number of 318 was assigned. Davis states that this is the number of Abraham's armed servants in Genesis 14:14. It is also a number reading TIH in Greek, a symbol of the Cross and Jesus. No minutes were kept of the First Ecumenical Council. *The First Seven,* pp. 57-58. The Council of Nicaea becomes the foundation upon which the six subsequent general ecumenical councils lie.

In response to the disagreements as to the nature of Jesus, his humanity, and, it was argued, his divinity, as well as his relation to God, it was also determined that "believers" should adhere to a creed. Davis states that "the finished creed has been preserved in the writings of Athanasius, of the historian Socrates and of Basil of Caesarea and in the acts of the Council of Chalcedon of 451" (a later council). The creed approved by the Council reads as follows:

> "We believe in one God the Father Almighty, Maker of all things visible and invisible; and in one Lord Jesus Christ, the Son of God, begotten of the Father, only-begotten, that is, from the substance of the Father, God from God, Light from Light, True God from True God, Begotten, not made, of one substance with the Father, through Whom all things were made.
>
> Who for us men and for our salvation came down and became incarnate, and was made man, suffered and rose on the third day, and ascended into heaven, and is coming with glory to judge living and dead, and in the Holy Spirit.
>
> But those who say, there was when the Son of God was not, and before he was begotten he was not, and that he came into being from things that are not, or that he is of a different hypostasis or substance, or that he is mutable or alterable - the Catholic and Apostolic church anathematizes." *The First Seven,* p. 60.

It should be glaringly obvious that much of the specific language of this creed does not in fact exist in the scriptures given in the New Testament canon. In this creed was the reply to Arianism with the phrase "of one substance (homoousios) with the Father." According to Davis, "This phrase asserts that the son shares the same being as the Father and is therefore fully divine." *The First Seven*, p. 61. *Additionally, the phrase only begotten was inserted to refute the Arian ("two natures") argument. The outcomes of the Ecumenical Councils and their very political nature influenced the early translations of the Greek New Testament texts. Church doctrine on some of these matters was "decided" prior to the translations which occurred afterward and had to be "consistent" with the prevailing church doctrine. Furthermore, early translations wield influence over later translations which may be hesitant to use differing terms both due to the history and practice of older familiar usage, and of course, to again remain consistent with church doctrine. These translations were ordered at a time when the Church was an entity that could punish virtually anyone it liked, however it liked, in the gravest manner. He who picks the translation first, picks best; or rather, he who translates first, wins the argument.*

The point is that it was not clear, nor widely accepted, that Jesus the man was actually God, 325 years after the crucifixion, at the time of the First (Nicaean) Council. What does this mean? ***It means that for well over three hundred years there were church leaders and teachers who believed and taught something other than that***. The *Emperor convened* a council for the express purpose of squelching disharmony and he *participated* in the debate of the Council. *Ibid,* p. 58.

The Nicene Creed itself was shaped purposefully to bar Arianism, (one of the proponents of the concept that God and Jesus were not or may not be one and the same). ***A***

scriptural basis for the precise wording of the Creed was avoided because the scripture <u>could</u> very well lend itself to such an interpretation, that Jesus never declared himself to be worshiped as a God. This means not only that the scripture can be read to be supportive of the position that Jesus and God, the Father and the Son, are distinct and separate, but also that the Council purposefully enacted, chose, and elected to foreclose and circumvent the very valid scriptural position that Jesus is distinct from God. Although it was decreed by the First Ecumenical Council of Nicaea that the Father and Son are equal, Jesus himself stated that "the Father is greater than I" (John 14:28, YLT).

Since their own authority as high members of the Church organization was derived from Jesus, giving Jesus more - or rather, the ultimate - authority also had the result of bestowing greater authority upon themselves and their actions and decisions. In essence, it appears that some people sought to change Jesus' words to give him more personal authority, as God himself, to invest themselves with more authority and power.

One of the biggest problems with this is that as the organization of the church (as it then existed) and the emperors continued to wrestle with arguments and disagreements, over the course and passage of time, the Nicene Creed came to be treated as inviolate as later dignitaries strove to keep it intact, not only to lend validation to the "actions" and "decisions" of the later Ecumenical Councils, but also to bolster their own power and positions. The Nicene Creed had been a step *away* from the texts that could not be altered later without undoing all doctrinal decisions made after the Creed and which relied on it as foundation and authority. Much of the Creed is still part and parcel of the teachings and beliefs in the vast majority of Christian denominations. But today, most of us have the opportunity to read and research texts for ourselves. Why should we adhere to translations influenced by "church" doctrine in the face of direct access to older writings? Why don't we just examine the texts, as close to the original as we can get?

The Creed was opposed by some bishops *but anyone who would not sign it was threatened with exile.* This tactic and consequence occurred again and again with subsequent Councils and arguments. Those who lost the argument and still opposed a council decision or determination were given the options of either endorsing the decision or be exiled or excommunicated. This was true even if steps had been taken to assure that your side of the argument was purposefully not represented at a council or purposely underrepresented. In some cases, church fathers who had lived *and died* in good favor with the church were later excommunicated posthumously to extinguish teachings which had become unpopular or were no longer useful to those currently in power.

Davis writes of the First Ecumenical Council of Nicea, "By 327, Constantine was having second thoughts on the work of the Council." *The First Seven,* p. 75.

It is noteworthy that the earliest translations of the canonical texts which are relied on for further translation into an increasing number of languages were translated *after* these doctrinal disputes which essentially manipulated (and forced) certain meanings to be assigned to the texts.

The Holy Spirit was later added to the creed. It seems to have taken longer for the Holy Spirit to become God than it did for Jesus, the man. Division grew between bishops in the East and bishops in the West. Many did not want three Gods but dissenting bishops kept getting exiled.

They argued over how much of Jesus was man, how much not man. They argued over whether God was greater than Jesus. They desperately needed to make Jesus different from the rest of us, more than the rest of us. Jesus was the source of their authority and power, and many didn't want to limit themselves to just the text attributed to Jesus. Best to make Jesus, the man, God himself. And best to have no argument about it. In ongoing disagreements for hundreds of years blowing back and forth between opposing ideas with new twists and turns born and argued, the "authorities" conspire and insist that Jesus, who lived as a man, was quite unlike the rest of us, yet Jesus himself did not say that.

Jesus not only said "my Father is greater than I" (YLT, John 14:28), Jesus also said "I ascend unto *my* Father, and *your* Father, and to *my* God, and to *your* God (John 20:17, YLT). Jesus states his relationship to the Father and others. He gives others the same relationship to God/the Father that he gives himself.

Jesus also said that where he is going we have *known*, and the way we have *known*. "[4] And whither I go away ye have known, and the way ye have known." (John 14:4, YLT.)

As you can see, the creed seeks to establish that Jesus is equal to God. The creed itself makes an interpretation that prevents other contextual interpretation of the text. The creed has assumptions and declarations that are not present in the canonized Greek text. *The work of the Councils and the arguments they attempt to settle are, by and large, attempts to determine and decide matters not always clearly determinable from the texts themselves. Even worse, some matters were decided in contravention of the texts themselves. Given this, older practice and teachings may have more merit than later doctrinal decisions.*

THE SECOND ECUMENICAL COUNCIL

There were many councils and synods, not all of which were recognized as Ecumenical. In 381 A.D., the Second Ecumenical Council was held in Constantinople (Constantinople I). This Council was not regarded as Ecumenical until the later-held Council of Chalcedon in 451 A.D., and not as highly regarded as the Council of Nicaea and therefore not as influential.

There had continued to be schisms, arguments and disagreements in the concepts both put forward in the Nicene Creed and in the concepts which the creed was intended to squelch. According to Davis, the Second Council claimed the Nicene faith again over other concepts and ideas. One hundred fifty Eastern bishops assembled in Constantinople in 381 A.D. It appears likely that the topics of the Holy Spirit and Trinity Doctrine loomed large at this Council. *The First Seven*, pp. 120-121.

There are disagreements as to the Creed of Constantinople, but in any case Davis asserts that the present text of the Creed of Constantinople made its first appearance as an official formulary at the second session of the later Council of Chalcedon in 451 A.D., read aloud and had never been heard before by many of the fathers of Chalcedon who viewed it with "initial suspicion" but who nevertheless ratified it. *The First Seven*, p. 122.

The Council of Constantinople I (381 A.D.) went on to anathematize many opposing ideas and many "holy fathers" who did not support these ideas. According to Davis, the Council "was never intended to be an Ecumenical Council: the Bishop of Rome was not invited; only 150 Eastern

Bishops were present; only one by accident from the West...Strong doubts were later expressed about the authenticity of its creed. Its canons were rejected in the West for nine hundred years." *The First Seven*, p. 129.

THE THIRD ECUMENICAL COUNCIL

The Third Ecumenical Council was held in Ephesus in 431 A.D. It was called by the Emperor, Theodosius II. Among other things this council dealt with the express labeling of Mary, Jesus' mother, as Mary, the Mother of God, theotokos, a title having been traditionally used (in Greek) since the third century after Jesus' death. *The First Seven,* p. 140.

There was tremendous disagreement about the manner of Jesus' divinity, whether Christ the Word and Jesus the man were two separate entities, whether Jesus was born a man and became divine, whether his humanity was a different nature than the rest of humanity's, whether he had one will or two, whether he was divinity in a man, or all divinity and no man, at least no man like the rest of us, whether his elements of humanity and divinity remain distinct, or whether they combine to form a unique quality, unlike mere man. Some defended the full humanity of Jesus and argued how could a redeemer redeem that which he was not? Some argued that Christ could not be divisible, as man and God, else how to worship the God without erroneously elevating the not-God aspect?

The bishop Nestorius was condemned for his beliefs and arguments that two separate natures, human and divine, were encompassed by Jesus Christ. The profession of faith, which was drawn up, rejected Nestorius' beliefs, and instead affirmed one nature of Christ. *The First Seven*, pp. 161-162.

This profession of faith contained the phrase "God the Word became incarnate and was made man, *and from the very conception* united to himself the temple taken from her" [Mary]. *The First Seven*, pp. 161-162. This phrase clearly negates what Jesus himself asserts when he signals that his authority comes from the baptism (Mark 11:29, Luke 20:3, and Matthew 21:24). Naming Mary "mother of God" over 300 years after the crucifixion also attempts to shift Jesus' authority by birth rather than the baptism.

Cyril, patriarch of Alexandria, had proposed Twelve Anathemas against Nestorius which were not adopted but not withdrawn by him during the ensuing arguments and attempts at compromise. Nestorius was exiled and several of his supporters were deposed and "were forbidden to read or transcribe his books which were to be searched out and burnt." *The First Seven,* p. 163. But Nestorius' ideas and support were not extinguished and disagreements remained.

THE FOURTH ECUMENICAL COUNCIL

The Fourth Ecumenical Council, reconvened in 451 A.D. at Chalcedon from an earlier situs in Nicaea, was called by Emperor Marcian. At this point, church fathers were still wrestling with the various elements of a Christ figure. Divinity and humanity were tough to define in the same person and arguments continued. Mostly, the prospect of Jesus as a man, like us, was largely rejected. And still the problem existed that if Jesus was unlike us in humanity, better than us, and equivalent to God, how to say that the Word suffered, died and rose from the grave?

Emperor Theodosius II died in 450 A.D. after 42 years in power. His older sister Pulcheria seized power and married the Senator Marcian, installing them both as the new Empress and Emperor. Emperor Marcian ordered the council originally called to Nicaea to reconvene at Chalcedon and on October 8, 451 A.D., the new Council opened. Largely at issue was the position of Dioscurus of Alexandria urging "one incarnate nature of the divine Logos" and the actions of the previous Council of Ephesus and the condemnation of Flavian of Constantinople for his position of two natures of Christ after the union of the Word to the flesh. Davis asserts Dioscurus, who was put on trial at the Council of Chalcedon, affirmed that Jesus was human, like the rest of us. The First Seven, p. 183.

The Eastern bishops were not eager to condemn one of their own and the papal legates to the council were asked to decide the issue. The papal legates deprived him of his episcopal office. The Council next called for the condemnation of Eutyches, and those who did not so condemn were handed over to the patriarch of Constantinople.

The bishops were expected to produce a doctrinal statement. One had been drawn up and proposed to the council but there is no extant text. Most acclaimed the statement but some protested. The proceeding deteriorated to such a point that the papal legates asked to return to Rome. Eventually a Definition of the Council of Chalcedon was created. The Definition presented the Creed of Nicaea (from the Council of 325 A.D.) as inviolate. Then the Council accepted the Creed of Constantinople I as an "authentic interpretation of the faith of Nicaea, thus raising the Council of Constantinople to the level of what today we would term an ecumenical council." *The First Seven,* p. 185. Davis further quotes the Definition, "On account of those who impugn the Holy Spirit, it ratifies and confirms the doctrine delivered subsequently, concerning the essence of the Spirit by the 150 holy Fathers" [of Constantinople I]. *Ibid.,* p. 185. The Council further accepted the Council of Ephesus of 431 A.D. presided over by Cyril as of equivalent stature as the Councils of Nicaea and Constantinople. The Council went on to support Cyril's letters denouncing Nestorius and his ideas, Pope Leo's Tome and the Archbishop Flavian. Cyrillians later believed the Definition itself to be more Nestorian than Cyrillian and later became known as Monophysites for the proposition that Christ was of one nature, not two, after the incarnation. Davis puts forth the Definition in his work which states, in part:

> "...Wherefore, following the holy Fathers, we all with one voice confess our Lord Jesus Christ one and the same Son, the same perfect in Godhead, the same perfect in manhood, truly God and truly man...." *The First Seven,* p. 186.

"Of one voice!" With so many condemned, excommunicated, removed from their positions and sent into exile, one voice will surely be created eventually. It is a wonder so many "church fathers" were willing to argue given the dire consequences of winding up on the wrong side of the argument or on the wrong side of the emperor as the case may be.

How is one "begotten," who, it is argued and was decided, did not ever fail to exist? How to be just human enough to be "like" us, enough to "save" us, but so unlike us, so unreachable and unattainable in perfection and divinity?

Davis concludes, "The Definition ended, "it is unlawful for anyone to produce another faith, whether by writing, or composing, or holding, or teaching others," and provided suitable penalties for those who would attempt to do so." *The First Seven,* p. 187.

How can such a "faith" ever result in further revelation? This "faith" results in any revelation being stifled and rejected as spirituality is equated with religious dogma - fixed, isolated, and dead, in a way that no other part of creation is, cemented by the early (but not *that* early) church and emperors, over three hundred years after the crucifixion.

"They" squabbled and deposed and declared and all *must* follow what has been determined *and* it is all declared the work of the Holy Spirit. "They" contort the message to their satisfaction and no other meaning can be gleaned. The Holy Spirit must have been splintered and confused to yield such chaos through these repeated council proceedings. What is set forth here is just the barest sketch of the full extent of the chaos and the capriciousness with which church doctrine, ideology, and dogma were set. (By way of a minute example, in addition to many other matters regarding discipline and procedure the first official pronouncement was made at this, the Fourth Ecumenical Council held at Chalcedon *in 451 A.D.,* about *monastic celibacy.*)

After the Council, the followers of Cyril, now Monophysites, strongly opposed this Council believing it Nestorian. Conflict and disorder were prevalent. Cyril had strongly emphasized the divinity of Jesus and the popularity of his position grew.

In 491 A.D., Anastasius I became emperor. He was a staunch Monophysite. Many patriarchs were still opposed to Leo's Tome and the Definition of Chalcedon and anathematized them. There was anything but consensus and agreement. Arguments continued as to the nature of Jesus and schism remained between the East and the West. Largely at issue, and in varying degrees and theories depending upon personnel, is still the old argument regarding the nature of Jesus. One nature (monophytism) vs. two natures. Successive decrees and anathemas and still no resolution to disagreements. However, time was always on the council "winners" side. At this point in time, the Nicene Creed from 325 A.D. was viewed as virtually ironclad and unalterable and any new decrees were always deemed to fit within it. Yet the Nicene Creed from 325 A.D. had been just another prior disagreement and "decree," and time had given it greater and greater legitimacy. This became a theme that would be repeated.

In 518 A.D., after reigning for 27 years, Anastasius I died and Justin I became the new emperor. Justin I was a Chalcedonian supporter. New calls for the recognition of Chalcedon were made. Exiled Chalcedonians were recalled. Justin ordered publicly that the bishops must accept Chalcedon and all those who did not were barred from civil service as well as service in the army. There followed persecution of Monophysites.

In 527 A.D. an ill and elderly Emperor Justin had his nephew Justinian declared emperor and crowned with his wife Theodora. Justinian was orthodox, his wife a Monophysite. The empire was still Chalcedonian in the West and Monophysite in the East. "Justinian intervened in ecclesiastical matters more forcefully and systematically than any of his predecessors." *The First Seven*, p. 226. Justinian had no tolerance. He sought to wipe out the sizeable remnants of paganism and "decreed that all pagans undergo religious instruction and, under pain of confiscation of their goods, receive baptism." *Ibid.*, p.227. Those who still kept to paganism were put to death. Convert or suffer legalized theft, revert and die. A number of universities still included pagans among their professors. "Justinian tolerated the Jews but forbade them to testify against Christians or buy the lands and goods of Christian churches, and though taxed like the municipal middle class they could not share its privileges." *The First Seven*, p. 227.

Justinian was monstrous to all heretics, excluding them from civil and military office and certain professions, testifying in court and inheritance.

Justinian hoped to win over Monophysites (who believed in a Jesus of one nature) while preserving Chalcedon. To do this he attempted to hold on to the Definition of Chalcedon, but to interpret it according to Cyril who had anathematized and disavowed Nestorius and his views (a Jesus of two natures).

In 531 A.D. Origenist teachings came under attack. Requests were made to Justinian to address these teachings. In 539 A.D., the Roman legate Pelagius made another request to Justinian to oppose Origenist teachings. *Emperor Justinian finally issued a theological tract in 543 A.D. and ten anathemas against Origen.* Origen, born circa 185 A.D., was an early Christian theologian widely regarded as one of the early Church fathers. He was a Christian scholar from Alexandria and a prolific Christian writer. His works were said to number in the thousands, although most do not survive his fall from favor within the church. He had lived and died in good favor with the church. But his teachings and writings, from the second and third centuries had now become the newest bug to be squashed.

The Second Council of Constantinople, also known as the Fifth Ecumenical Council of Constantinople II, held in 553 A.D., repeated the condemnation of Origenism by Emperor Justinian (from 543 A.D.). In addition to the Fifth Council's anathematization of Origin, there are fifteen anathemas which are purported by some to be a product of the council and denounced as not part of the work of the council by some. Most interesting and pertinent to this discussion is a closer look at Emperor Justinian's undisputed ten anathemas against Origen in 543 A.D., (prior to the Fifth Ecumenical Council of 553 A.D.) shown in part as follows:

Translated as shown in *Nicene and Post-Nicene Fathers, Second Series, Volume XIV*, Edited by Philip Schaff & Rev. Henry Wallace, Cosimo Classics, New York, originally printed in 1900; reprinted 2007; p.320:

"THE ANATHEMATISMS OF THE EMPEROR JUSTINIAN AGAINST ORIGEN.[1]

(Labbe and Cossart, *Concilia*, Tom. v., col. 677.)

[Emphasis shown by underlining is added and does not appear in the original.]

I.

Whoever says or thinks that human souls pre-existed, *i.e.*, that they had previously been spirits and holy powers, but that, satiated with the vision of God, they had turned to evil, and in this way the divine love in them had died out (*ἀπψυγείσας*) and they had therefore become souls (*ψυχάς*) and had been condemned to punishment in bodies, shall be anathema.

II.

If anyone says or thinks that the soul of the Lord pre-existed and was united with God the Word before the Incarnation and Conception of the Virgin, let him be anathema.

III.

If anyone says or thinks that the body of our Lord Jesus Christ was first formed in the womb of the holy Virgin and that afterwards there was united with it God the Word and the pre-existing soul, let him be anathema.

IV.

If anyone says or thinks that the Word of God has become like to all heavenly orders, so that for the cherubim he was a cherub, for the seraphim a seraph: in short, like all the superior powers, let him be anathema.

V.

If anyone says or

thinks that, at the resurrection, human bodies will rise spherical in form and unlike our present form, let him be anathema.

VI.

If anyone says that the heaven, the sun, the moon, the stars, and the waters that are above heavens, have souls, and are reasonable beings, let him be anathema.

VII.

If anyone says or thinks that Christ the Lord in a future time will be crucified for demons as he was for men, let him be anathema.

VIII.

If anyone says or thinks that the power of God is limited, and that he created as much as he was able to encompass, let him be anathema.

IX.

If anyone says or thinks that the punishment of demons and of impious men is only temporary, and will one day have an end, and that a restoration (ἀποκατάστασις) will take place of demons and of impious men, let him be anathema.

Anathema to Origen and to that Adamantius, who set forth these opinions together with his nefarious and execrable and wicked doctrine,[2] and to whomsoever there is who thinks thus, or defends these opinions, or in any way hereafter at any time shall presume to protect them.

[1] The reader should carefully study the entire tractate of the Emperor against Origen of which these anathematisms are the conclusion. It is found in Labbe and Cossart, and in many other collections.

[2]The text is I [the Editor] think corrupt, at all events the Latin and Greek do not agree."

Nicene and Post-Nicene Fathers, pp.320. (Again, emphasis is added where underlined.)

These anathemas of the emperor, given 500 years after Jesus lived, clearly outlawed the following teachings and concepts:

- the soul of Jesus pre-existed;
- the pre-existing soul of Jesus was separate from

God the Word;

- Jesus' body was separate from his pre-existing soul and God the Word;
- the punishment of impious men is only temporary and will one day end; and
- a restoration will take place.

By this point it should be abundantly clear that one of the reasons we could have a difficult time discerning what Jesus actually attempted to teach is that as we go back in history, so much scholarship and history was purposefully, willfully destroyed and distorted for power and political gain. The records of the Ecumenical Councils, Justinian, and church officials themselves, not only record the destruction, but, in some cases, the subject matter of what was destroyed, *leaving a record of what they erased and eradicated, a window to what was believed and taught before their destruction.*

THE FIFTH ECUMENICAL COUNCIL

The Fifth Ecumenical Council of Constantinople II was called by the Emperor Justinian in Constantinople in 553 A.D. for the purpose of reconciling Chalcedon and Cyril (one nature). The emperor operated with considerable threat and consequence. Dealings with Pope Vigilius were particularly contentious as the Pope was opposed to the condemnation of certain writings that the emperor had ordered condemned. The emperor used every means available including arrest of certain of the Pope's personnel, isolation of the Pope from advisors and personal servants, and virtual house arrest of the Pope to force the Pope to condemn the writings as the emperor wished, until the Pope escaped and fled.

Justinian, still wishing to have a council and achieve his goals, eventually made conciliatory measures to have the Pope return to Constantinople for the Council. The Pope wished to have the Council in Sicily or Italy in order to effectuate the presence and participation of Western bishops, but the emperor refused. The emperor again made ready for a mostly Eastern Council. While the emperor sought to insure an Eastern council, the Pope proposed that he himself would have the authority to publish the council's decision. This the emperor refused.

The Council was convened on May 5, 553 A.D. The emperor called for condemnation of certain writings, over the protest of Pope Vigilius, referred to as the Three Chapters regarding the work of three Antiochenes. Pope Vigilius was opposed to their condemnation because they had died in communion with the orthodox church. Orthodoxy had been a steadily moving status for some time. The Council was further instructed to review writings "by which Nestorians wished to impose their views on the Church, to consider the absurd assertion that heretics might not be condemned after their death and to act with all due speed." *The First Seven*, p. 241. The Pope was not in attendance. All out doctrinal warfare between the Pope and the emperor developed, with the emperor having far more force of consequence on his side. The emperor won, not surprisingly, with his 'Eastern' council deciding most all in his favor. They broke off communion with Pope Vigilius, personally, and later declared it lawful to condemn "heretics" *after* their death. These people were not deemed heretics during their lifetime. Their "heresies" only developed as church doctrine and dogma developed.

In their Sentence following the final sessions of the Council, they bolstered and accepted the previous Councils. They denounced Theodore and Nestorius and resolved all matters to preserve Chalcedon.

See Acts 13:32-34, YLT.

> "32 'And we to you do proclaim good news—that the promise made unto the fathers, 33 God hath in full completed this *to us their children*, having raised up Jesus, as also in the second Psalm it hath been written, My Son thou art—I *to-day* have begotten thee.
>
> 34 'And that He did raise him up *out of the dead, no more to return to corruption*," (Emphasis added).

It is astounding to see the work of the Councils given that so much of the language much less the ideas urged by the Councils and the official doctrine and position of the Church are *not* found in the canonized books of the New Testament. In fact, one can readily find language and ideas generated by the Councils that are *clearly contrary* to what is found in the canonized texts. For example, the Council's Sentence proclaims Mary "the Mother of God" and always a virgin, but the texts state that Mary had other children (see Matthew 13:55–56; Mark 3:31–32; Mark 6:3; John 7:3; Acts 1:14; Galatians 1:19; 1 Corinthians 9:5).

The anathemas, arguably attributed by some scholars to the Fifth Ecumenical Council, may also be found set forth in *Nicene and Post-Nicene Fathers, Second Series, Volume XIV*, Edited by Philip Schaff & Rev. Henry Wallace, Cosimo Classics, New York, originally printed in 1900, reprinted 2007, as translated, p. 312, et seq. Although some scholars argue that the fifteen anathemas against Origen were proposed and adopted by the Fifth Ecumenical Council (the Second Constantinople Council of 553 A.D.), others state that it is not clear whether that is so. In any case, the Council did clearly condemn Origen and intended to condemn his teachings and it seems logical that Emperor Justinian's *prior* ten anathemas against Origen from 543 A.D. were endorsed and accepted by the Council's unquestioned condemnation of Origen in 553 A. D.

Almost all of the bishops in attendance at the Fifth Ecumenical Council called by Justinian were from the East.

Origen and his writings were condemned by the Fifth Ecumenical Council although he had previously lived and died in good favor with the church. He had operated a school, and was a prolific writer on the subject of Christianity. Not much remains to show what, in fact, Origin wrote. It is hard to know whether or not the following fifteen anathemas, attributed to the Fifth Council, were actually the work of the Council. Scholars line up on both sides of the argument. The fifteen anathemas of Origen, (sometimes attributed to the Fifth Ecumenical Council) are as follows.

> Translated as shown in *Nicene and Post-Nicene Fathers, Second Series, Volume XIV*, Edited by Philip Schaff& Rev. Henry Wallace, Cosimo Classics, New York, originally printed in 1900, reprinted 2007. (Emphasis shown by underlining is added and not shown in the original text).

"THE ANATHEMAS AGAINST ORIGEN

I.

If anyone asserts the fabulous pre-existence of souls, and shall assert the monstrous restoration which follows from it: let him be anathema.

II.

If anyone shall say that the creation (*τὴυ παραγωγὴν*) of all reasonable things includes only intelligences (*νόας*) without bodies and altogether immaterial, having neither number nor name, so that there is unity between them all by identity of substance, force and energy, and by their union with and knowledge of God the Word; but that no longer desiring the sight of God, they gave themselves over to worse things, each one following his own inclinations, and that they have taken bodies more or less subtile, and have received names, for among the heavenly Powers there is a difference of names as there is also a difference of bodies; and thence some became and are called Cherubims, others Seraphims, and Principalities, and Powers, and Dominations, and Thrones, and Angels, and as many other heavenly orders as there may be: let him be anathema.

III.

If anyone shall say that the sun, the moon and the stars are also reasonable beings, and that they have only become what they are because they turned towards evil: let him be anathema.

IV.

If anyone shall say that the reasonable creatures in whom the divine love had grown cold have been hidden in gross bodies such as ours, and have been called men, while those who have attained the lowest degree of wickedness have shared cold and obscure bodies and are become and called demons and evil spirits: let him be anathema.

V.

If anyone shall say that a psychic (ψυχικὴν) condition has come from an angelic or archangelic state, and moreover that a demoniac and a human condition has come from a psychic condition, and that from a human state they may become again angels and demons, and that each order of heavenly virtues is either all from those below or from those above, or from those above and below: let him be anathema.

VI.

If anyone shall say that there is a two-fold race of demons, of which the one includes the souls of men and the other the superior spirits who fell to this, and that of all the number of reasonable beings there is but one which has remained unshaken in the love and contemplation of God, and that that spirit is become Christ and the king of all reasonable beings, and that he has created[1] all the bodies which exist in heaven, on earth and between heaven and earth; and that the world which has in itself elements more ancient than itself, and which exists by themselves, viz.: dryness, damp, heat and cold, and the image (*ἰδέαν*) to which it was formed, was so formed, and that the most holy and consubstantial Trinity did not create the world, but that it was created by the working intelligence (*Νοῦς δημιουργός*) which is more ancient than the world, and which communicates to it its being: let him be anathema.

VII.

If anyone shall say that Christ, of whom it is said that he appeared in the form of God, and that he was united before all time with God the Word, and humbled himself in these last days even to humanity, had (according to their expression) pity upon the divers falls which had appeared in the spirits united in the same unity (of which he himself is part), and that to restore them he passed through divers classes, had different bodies and different names, became all to all, an Angel among Angels, a Power among Powers, has clothed himself in the different classes of reasonable beings with a form corresponding to that class, and finally has taken flesh and blood like ours and is become man for men; [if anyone says all this] and does not profess that God the Word humbled himself and became man: let him be anathema.

VIII.

If anyone shall not acknowledge that God the Word, of the same substance with the Father and the Holy Ghost, and who was made flesh and became man, one of the Trinity, is Christ in every sense of the word, but [shall affirm] that he is so only in an inaccurate manner, and of the abasement (*κενώσαντα*), as they call it, of the intelligence(*νοῦς*); <u>if anyone shall affirm that this</u>

intelligence united (*συνημμένον*) to God the Word, is the Christ in the true sense of the word, while the Logos is only called Christ because of this union with the intelligence and *e converso* that the intelligence is only called God because of the Logos: let him be anathema.

IX.

If anyone shall say that it was not the Divine Logos made man by taking an animated body with a *ψυχὴ λογικὴ* and *νοερὰ*, that he descended into hell and ascended into heaven, but shall pretend that it is the *Νοῦς* which has done this, that *Νοῦς* of which they say (in an impious fashion) he is Christ properly so called, and that he is become so by the knowledge of the Monad: let him be anathema.

X.

If anyone shall say that after the resurrection the body of the Lord was ethereal, having the form of a sphere, and that such shall be the bodies of all after the resurrection; and that after the Lord himself shall have rejected his true body and after the other who rise shall have rejected theirs, the nature of their bodies shall be annihilated: let him be anathema.

XI.

If anyone shall say that the future judgment signifies the destruction of the body and that the end of the story will be an immaterial *ψύσις*, and that thereafter there will no longer be any matter, but only spirit (*νοῦς*): let him be anathema.

XII.

If anyone shall say that the heavenly Powers and all men and the Devil and evil spirits are united with the Word of God in all respects, as the *Νοῦς* which is by them called Christ and which is in the form of God, and which humbled itself as they say; and [if anyone shall say] that the Kingdom of Christ shall have an end: let him be anathema.

XIII.

If anyone shall say that Christ [*i.e.,* the *Νοῦς*] is in no wise different from other reasonable beings, neither substantially nor by wisdom nor by his power and might over all things but that all will be placed at the right hand of God, as well as he that is called by them Christ [the *Νοῦς*] as also they were in the feigned pre-existence of all things: let him be anathema.

XIV.

If anyone shall say that all reasonable beings will one day be united in one, when the hypostases as well as the numbers and the bodies shall have disappeared, and that the knowledge of the world to come will carry with it the ruin of the worlds, and the rejection of bodies as also the abolition of [all] names, and that there shall be finally an identity of the *γνῶσις* and of the hypostasis; moreover, that in this pretended apocatastasis, spirits only will continue to exist, as it was in the feigned pre-existence: let him be anathema.

XV.

If anyone shall say that the life of the spirits (*νοῶν*) shall be like to the life which was in the beginning while as yet the spirits had not come down or fallen, so that the end and the beginning shall be alike, and that the end shall be the true measure of the beginning: let him be anathema."

Nicene and Post Nicene Fathers, pp. 318-319. *(Footnote 1 shows a translation note therein.* (Emphasis added where underlined.)

On whether these fifteen anathemas were actually the work of the council, it is noted in *Nicene and Post Nicene Fathers*, in the Excurses (at p. 316) that "Scholars of the highest repute have taken, and do take to-day, the opposite sides of the case, and each defends his own side with marked learning and ability...."

While noting that it is not clear from the call of the Council or letters in connection with it, that these anathemas were discussed, "there is a vast amount of literature subsequent in date to the council which distinctly attributes a detailed and careful examination of the teaching of Origen and a formal condemnation of him and of it to this council." Schaff, p. 316, *Nicene and Post-Nicene Fathers.*

Further, it is noted, **"even if these anathemas were adopted at the Home Synod before the meeting of the Fifth Ecumenical Council, it is clear that by including his name among those of the heretics in the XIth Canon, it practically ratified and made its own the action of that Synod."** Schaff p. 317, *Nicene and Post-Nicene Fathers.* (Emphasis added.)

This isn't really surprising given that Emperor Justinian would have been firmly in control of the Fifth Council and there is much evidence that he could and did exert considerable power and consequence to get what he wanted.

It is worth noting that the fifteen anathemas do, to some extent, follow a substantial portion of the same content and ideas as the ten anathemas by Justinian even though the fifteen are more elaborate.

As stated, some scholars believe the fifteen anathemas sometimes attributed to the Fifth Ecumenical Council are not the product of the Fifth Ecumenical Council itself but of the earlier local synod. Even if that were the case, the church has clearly demonstrated its disapproval of Origen and his writings by declaring him excommunicated/ anathematized at the Fifth Ecumenical Council. Even if the fifteen anathemas were not the work of the Fifth Ecumenical Council, but of an earlier, local synod, the Fifth Ecumenical Council clearly rang in their agreement with them with the anathematization of Origen specifically. More than a local synod was needed to completely destroy and stamp out the sheer magnitude of Origen's written works generated hundreds of years earlier while Origen was in good standing with the church. These works would have been circulated and copied within the Christian community for some time prior to Origen's being anathematized. ***Emperor Justinian's Ten Anathemas from 543 A.D. make pretty clear the Emperor Justinian's position on these beliefs and teachings.*** His power and influence over the Fifth Ecumenical Council later in 553 A.D. is also clear even if it is not possible to definitely credit the Council with their own purported (and separate) fifteen anathemas. The Fifth Council's anathematization of Origen and his works in 553 A.D. under the authority of Emperor Justinian who previously outlawed belief in reincarnation (belief in the preexistence of human souls and the eventual restoration of all souls) in 543 A.D. further ratifies and solidifies Emperor Justinian's position regarding the belief and teaching of reincarnation within Christianity.

The big question is why would any beliefs need to be outlawed unless they were in fact held at the time? Why, unless they were taught and espoused by important and influential religious leaders? Why, unless these beliefs were held by at least some religious leaders and scholars ***for over 500 years following the death of Jesus?*** Reincarnation is a belief and teaching Justinian wanted eradicated, and he is willing to use force and intimidation to get it done. Almost all of the attending bishops were from the East with the West virtually unrepresented. Justinian got his way (as did many earlier emperors) and most Christians believe the resulting adopted set of beliefs was all there ever was from the time of Jesus forward. Nothing could be further from the truth.

Consider how the teaching and acceptance of reincarnation could, and most likely did, complicate the issue of the nature of Jesus. Reincarnation reinforces the duality of spirit and flesh as distinct in all of us. It might also make it harder to distinguish Jesus from the rest of humanity, because all of humanity would have a spiritual identity with continuity severable from their transient fleshly one. That spiritual identity would transcend and last beyond one lifetime. Could this be at least some of the reason the arguments had continued to flourish? Would reincarnation make it more difficult to say that Jesus was born perfect? What about the question whether Jesus was of one nature rather than two? Was this particular eradication key to making Jesus so different from the rest of us and cementing church authority over souls? If we, like Jesus, had only to understand the objective of tempering ourselves over time, lifetimes, in fact, then could we could become like Jesus, as Jesus himself stated in John 14:12, YLT.

> "he who is believing in me, the works that I do—that one also shall do, and greater than these he shall do."

If we get the opportunity of perfecting ourselves over time, over lifetimes, then the gulf between us and Jesus isn't exactly as presented by the Church. Rather it is as Jesus states above, each of us is capable, potentially, of even greater works.

See John 10:33, YLT.

> "[33]The Jews answered him, saying, 'For a good work we do not stone thee, but for evil speaking, and because thou, being a man, dost make thyself God.' [34]Jesus answered them, 'Is it not having been written in your law: I said, ye are gods? "

It is no wonder reincarnation had to go, and with it the core of the message, the good news.

If you believe the Bible is your guidance then consider: the arguments and doctrinal decisions made by others ***are only their interpretation*** of the written texts, often contrived and imposed for a variety of reasons, many useful to themselves. The earliest translation of texts, on which the later translations are based, were commissioned by the Councils and emperors and influenced by the Councils' doctrinal determinations. ***The translations were created to be consistent with church doctrine***. The foundation translations are inherently biased with these doctrinal determinations on what the meaning of the text "should" be. Older versions of the texts, and comparison of translations, are now widely available for your own study in a way that they weren't in ancient times and even much later.

The Fifth Ecumenical Council (553 A.D.) was promulgated without, and over the protest of, the highest ranking church leader, Pope Vigilius. Furthermore, it was ordered, and in fact forced, by the political leader of the time, the Holy Roman Emperor, Justinian. Doesn't that suggest substantial opposition?

Justinian, and not church leadership, sought and demanded that belief in reincarnation be outlawed. There would be no purpose or use in this, unless there existed not only a belief in reincarnation, but a substantial historical and textual basis for that belief. If you are wondering how you could be a church goer, or student of the Bible and not have known this, you are justified. There is historical, verifiable justification for the proposition, both in the previously referenced scriptures and contained within the anathemas of Origen by Justinian and the works of the Ecumenical Councils themselves, that reincarnation was taught by Jesus himself and his followers, and that reincarnation was an early church teaching for over 500 years before it was outlawed by state political authority. The elimination of reincarnation gives more power to authorities to achieve subservience to their created doctrine. The only hope of achieving salvation in a one-shot chance, no matter what each person's individual circumstances, is to follow their church made doctrine, however they may need to twist or turn it as they proceed in order to serve their own purposes.

During the several hundred years following the life of Jesus, secular authority and church authority made of the man who lived more and more of a god and less and less of a man, separating that person from the rest of us by an ever widening, unbreachable gulf of unattainability. But is that what Jesus himself taught?

The doctrines formulated by the church, never uttered by Jesus, undermine Jesus, the man, his mission and his accomplishments as a powerful example of how to achieve salvation from the cycle of reincarnation with its veil of forgetfulness. The church wants everyone to unquestioningly view Jesus as God and as far superior to and separate from us as a result of these formulated doctrines in a way not taught by Jesus himself. The church and its doctrinal determinations and forbiddance of opposition rob all of the truth Jesus came to reveal, "the way." On a personal level, many Christians instinctively recognize and respond to Jesus' humanity, far more than the debates and decisions of supposed "authorities," of which they are largely accepting but unaware.

The further problem with the evolution of doctrines *not* explicitly contained within the canonized texts was that each new clarification and defining statement was required to be contained within all the previous "positions" taken by "authorities." Otherwise, the authority to make such determinations on doctrine would be undermined.

The result of hundreds of years of twisting and distorting is a vast reduction to much of Jesus' teachings, rendering them far less useful to humanity. According to the church, the only lesson and the only result is to believe and be saved. But many believed in God before Jesus lived. What really is the difference, if belief is all that is required? And if, although Jesus instructed 'love your neighbor as yourself,' you don't quite make that benchmark but can achieve salvation anyway, what's the point?

Jesus' teachings illustrate that giving of oneself and aiding others are more purposeful, intentional sacrifices involving the application of will in brotherly love. Wrongs are not left unanswered as each person must meet himself the circumstances he has dealt out for others.

Many have experienced spiritual support, love, and guidance, though unseen. This is what has kept belief in Jesus, and religion in a larger context, alive. Spirituality is very much a reality for many who don't need convincing. For many believers, religion aids in the realization and pursuit of spirituality, or something beyond what we are able to perceive with our normally limited senses. But that does not mean that religious belief and spirituality are the same. That does not mean that all of the concepts, definitions and limitations imposed by religious doctrine and dogma are accurate.

The pursuit of truth and understanding, and the pondering of what is beyond the limitations of our senses is not only valid, it may even be intended for us to have to seek in order to learn and grow. But shackling ourselves and our pursuits to the limitations imposed on certain selected texts which have been distorted over hundreds of years doesn't appear to be the most direct route to those goals. To the extent the texts may have a message that is helpful, it is most valid to examine them in their oldest form, the form closest to their original state, in light of the perversions of history and those in power – maybe even those in power still. To simply look inward to find the guidance of the still small voice may be the quickest and simplest route to those goals. If you are a believer, it should be easy to look to God for guidance and ask the questions that so many people think they already know the answers to but may well not. If you are not a believer, you might just be surprised – very surprised at what you are lead to and learn. Religion is a man-made institution. It should not serve poison against others or poison hearts and minds of followers.

God allows each of us the full use of free will to find and follow inspiration. He does not impose any strict constraints on us. You will reap what you sow in order to learn. But you are allowed free will to choose what you sow. Why do we seek to impose our particular set of "religious" beliefs on everyone else when God himself does not do so? Are we not violating and limiting something important needed to grow and learn and become more aware? Are we not violating something even God holds sacred when we violate one another's non-violent and non-destructive use of free will?

It is way past time that doctrinal disputes of power seekers be put aside. Older texts can be reconsidered as close to their original expression as possible. What did Jesus actually try to teach? Are any of us following that teaching today?

EPILOGUE

[7]'Ask, and it shall be given to you; seek, and ye shall find; knock, and it shall be opened to you; [8]for every one who is asking doth receive, and he who is seeking doth find, and to him who is knocking it shall be opened.

MATTHEW 7:7, YLT (ALSO FOUND AT LUKE, CHAPTER 11:9, YLT)

ADDITIONAL READING

For skeptics looking for further evidence in support of reincarnation, a review and study of the works and research of Dr. Ian Stevenson is invaluable. Dr. Stevenson has, in essence, proven, through scientific investigation, that reincarnation is a truth.

Books by Brian Weiss and his experiences with regression therapy are also enlightening. Further information on regression therapy, including regression therapy case studies to the periods between lives, can be found in books by Michael Newton.

www.ingramcontent.com/pod-product-compliance
Lightning Source LLC
LaVergne TN
LVHW010640110826
845149LV00014B/2899